Vienna, My Vienna

Endpapers: Silver wedding procession of Emperor Franz Joseph I and Empress Elisabeth passing the Opera House on Ringstrasse
Frontispiece: Self-portrait of Anton Pilgram on the pulpit in St Stephen's Cathedral

Vienna, My Vienna

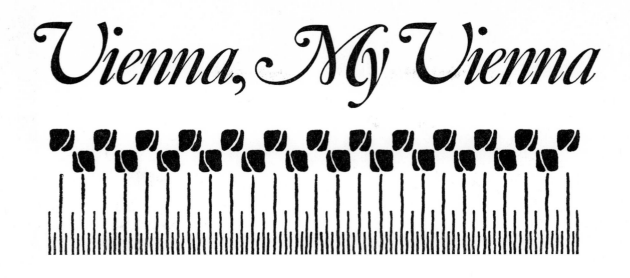

JOSEPH WECHSBERG

PHOTOGRAPHS BY

WERNER FORMAN

NOTES ON THE ILLUSTRATIONS BY MICHAEL RAEBURN

The Macmillan Company

NEW YORK

The Macmillan Company, New York

Manufactured in Switzerland

Contents

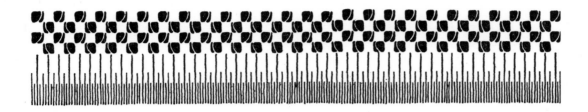

Introduction

Only after living in Vienna for a long time can one begin to understand why the Viennese are so often unable to separate reality from legend and truth from make-believe. The Viennese are essentially a baroque people. For over three hundred and fifty years, 'baroque' has been a way of life in this city. In art, the term 'baroque' was originally used by critics as an expression of disapproval, to describe works of art which failed to conform to the 'classical' standards of beauty. 'Baroque' meant something that was elaborate and theatrical, grotesque and extravagant, bizarre and flamboyant. An imperfectly shaped pearl, for instance, was classified *barroco* by Spanish jewellers. After 1600, 'baroque' came to describe a cultural epoch, the period following the Counter-Reformation. By the end of the seventeenth century, the threats of Protestantism and of Turkish aggression, which had been present for over two hundred years, were gone. Men were jubilant, yet humbly and gratefully aware of God's omnipotence. The contradiction was outwardly resolved by baroque exuberance. 'Vienna reached its cultural zenith during the baroque, and remained baroque in its strangest and finest expressions of life', wrote Egon Friedell, himself a baroque mixture of philosopher, essayist, actor and cultural historian.

Beginning, then, as an architectural style, baroque was later to influence all the other arts, and finally to become a state of mind. There was baroque music, baroque furniture, baroque weapons, baroque interiors, even baroque coffins. The Empress Maria Theresia and her consort, Franz of Lorraine, are buried in sarcophagi with beautiful baroque ornamentation. The baroque appealed to the sensuous love of the Viennese for beauty and gracefulness, and to their perennial infatuation with drama and music. Emperor Leopold I (1640-1705) remains the

3   Death wearing the Crown of the Holy Roman Empire,
from the baroque coffin of Emperor Charles VI

most popular Habsburg ruler of the baroque era because he loved music and was an able composer – ninety-seven pieces of church music, nine 'theatrical festivities', one hundred and two dances, and a requiem for his wife which was also performed during his own funeral. A legend says that when he felt death approaching, he ordered his *Hofkapelle*, the Imperial Orchestra (founded in 1496 by Emperor Maximilian, and thus the predecessor of the Vienna Philharmonic), to perform his favourite pieces in an adjoining hall, whereupon he died at peace. A great many Viennese would like to die that way.

'The whole world is a giant theatre', wrote the Hamburg critic Johann Mattheson in 1728. Life to the Viennese is nothing but a play. They will often tailor reality to fit their imagination. The playwright and critic, Hermann Bahr, a shrewd observer of the Viennese character, once said that for the Viennese life began at the theatre. They think of their city as a vast stage where everybody performs a part while watching his own and others' performances. The Viennese is a born character actor who performs with considerable skill the part that life has assigned to him. It is only foreigners who are impressed by the polite manners of the Viennese. The natives know that there is no conviction behind the charming smile. People fight too, but are soon friends again – after all, they have only played a scene. In his verse play *Paracelsus*, Arthur Schnitzler writes, 'We all act parts, and wise is he who knows it.' Schnitzler was the brilliant analyst of a decadent epoch of Vienna, who transformed this disorganised play of life into the sublime, bitter-sweet play on the stage where all the characters wore masks, playing themselves as well as their *alter ego*.

This baroque schizophrenia of the Viennese is the essence of their *Lebenskunst*, their way of life and their philosophy. In times of oppression and censorship, music and theatre – the stage – are used to express the secret and true feelings of the people. When the prisoners in Beethoven's *Fidelio* sang for the first time their exciting 'freedom' chorus, at the Theater an der Wien, on 20 November 1805, Vienna had recently been occupied by Napoleon, and French officers sat in the auditorium. Later, in the *Vormärz* (pre-March) days, prior to the 1848 revolution, the theatre, once again, became the mouthpiece for Vienna's poetic fighters for freedom. Unlike in Poland, Hungary, and Italy, it was no political leader who inspired revolutionary feelings in Vienna but the great satirical poet and playwright, Johann Nestroy, whose *Freiheit im Krähwinkel* was a typical Viennese

4 'The Victor of Aspern', Archduke Charles, who defeated Napoleon and the French army in 1809.

mixture of wit and irony, and exultation ending in disenchantment. (One character in the play says, 'human beings start from baron upwards'. This was not Nestroy's whim but an opinion often expressed by Austrian aristocrats at that time.) Again the stage was speaking the truth.

Life begins, and ends, at the theatre. The Viennese has learned to take nothing seriously – least of all himself. Since he performs only a part in a play, he experiences even disaster with a certain detachment. Nothing is really as bad as it seems; life may be hopeless but it is never serious. Many people have wondered what has made the Viennese the complex, fascinating, strange people they are. Franz Grillparzer, the great Austrian poet and playwright (and her bitter and sardonic critic) created his characters from them, with all their contradictions. More recently, Helmut Qualtinger and Carl Merz let the Viennese look at 'Herr Karl', the unprincipled rascal with the irresistible charm. The Viennese have all met Herr Karl, the fellow who does not try to fight against an absurd fate but tries instead to outwit it by absurd means. No wonder. Their city has lived through an endless chain of disasters. Having had to learn the art of survival, the Viennese now considers himself 'a born survivor'. *Biegen, nicht brechen,* 'bend but do not break', is a popular Viennese saying.

Vienna is a romantic city – one of the last romantic cities on earth. Its air vibrates with charm and sentiment, and often with mystery and a kind of despair. The Viennese poet Hugo von Hofmannsthal called Vienna 'the wonderful, inexhaustibly magical city with its mysterious, soft, light-filled air'. Here the haze is never harsh; even fog, that can be hostile and terrifying in the cold wet cities further north, is but a soft, friendly mist that seems to float along the banks of the Danube, to caress the green slopes of the hills. Climatically, Vienna may be a northern city; the heat is on in most houses for more than six months of the year. But emotionally Vienna is a southern city. Gustav Mahler sensed it instinctively when he was a young *Kapellmeister* in cool Hamburg, missing the musical and *musische* ('Muse-minded') warmth of Vienna while he waited for the call from 'the god of the southern zones'.

Vienna is a synthesis. The heroic and the *gemütlich*, the hidden and the ostentatious, the past and the present, the romantic and the modern, are blended into a harmonious whole. Somehow the cheerless, grey streets of the ugly suburbs

with their dark tenement houses, and the noble baroque palaces and Gothic churches form a perfect composition, framed by the lovely hills of the Wiener-wald. The city is surrounded by a permanent mist of clichés which obscure the outlines, but underneath the sugar coating of commercialised Vienna there is the genuine Vienna, not always so sweet to the taste. As in a well-mixed marzipan, the bitter almonds rather than the sugar dominate the quality and the taste.

Vienna's very name inspires the imagination, excites the fantasy. *Ein gewisses Etwas*, 'a certain something', seems to surround the sound of its name, creating magical associations. But this magic of Vienna is hard to define. Hofmannsthal wrote about Vienna's 'magical air': 'How beautiful is all this! How beautiful is beauty!' *(Wie schön ist Schönheit!)* It is an improbable mixture of wistful charm and veiled eroticism. Long before Schnitzler – a doctor who understood the dark secrets of body and soul – dissected Vienna's sensuality, the town was notorious for its erotic passions. Hedonists called it heaven and moralists called it hell. Vienna's charm, a highly elusive element, is one of Austria's greatest hidden assets, though it never appears in the country's balance of payments.

The illogical German language, which distinguishes three sexes, makes 'Wien' neuter (one says '*das* Wien'), but everybody who comes to Vienna feels that 'Wien' is a very feminine city, capricious, charming and utterly unreliable. It can be a dangerous city, *une ville fatale*. Detached, usually unemotional people have felt disturbing emotions as they walk down Ringstrasse on a mild evening in June. The scent of the linden trees is very strong. An attractive woman I know who is usually calm and composed admits that the scent sometimes makes her *deppert*; in such a mood one might do something very foolish and later be unable to explain what made one do it.

She is not the only one. The Viennese mixture of scents – linden and lilac, jasmin and acacias – penetrates the skin, and, according to the poets, the heart and the soul. The poets of Vienna are always searching for the 'soul' of their city. All of them feel that Vienna has a soul though they cannot agree on where it is to be found: perhaps in the narrow streets of the old town, or between the trees in the Wienerwald (which, thanks to Johann Strauss, will always be known to the English as the 'Vienna Woods'). Others find the soul of the city in the dreamy introduction to some of the great waltzes of Johann Strauss. But undoubtedly

6 The Burggarten

the soul is there, as is the Wienerwald, or the vineyards that form a tiara round the western outskirts.

The magic of Vienna catches you at unexpected moments. I once spent a summer afternoon in the Pfarrplatz (the church square) of Heiligenstadt, the western suburb where Vienna's migratory composer, Beethoven, came in 1802, and later in the summer of 1808, and then again in the spring of 1817, when he lived in the house No. 2, near the baroque statue of St John Nepomuk. That afternoon there was an al fresco symphony concert in the church square, a performance of Beethoven's Fifth Symphony and the Pastoral Symphony, the two works that Beethoven had written in Heiligenstadt, 'City of the Saints'. In the brief pause between the second and third movement of the Pastoral, while a few violinists were furtively tuning their instruments, the birds were singing. An American friend and musician who was with me, a man blessed (and cursed), with absolute pitch, exclaimed softly, 'Listen! They sing *in tune*!' He seemed flabbergasted but I was not at all surprised. For not only the birds were singing in tune; the air around us was also in tune, as was the ground on which we sat, and the façades of the old houses, and the acoustics of the square, better than in many famous concert halls.

Sometimes this magic is purely visual – as when one is among the rose gardens, in the Volksgarten. Here there are hundreds of varieties of roses, some of them very rare, all of them beautiful, each carrying a small wooden sign with the Latin name and the place of origin. In Vienna, blossom time lasts from early March until late November.

The magic is still alive in the dreamy suburban streets where the city dissolves into meadows, vineyards and woods. The street names have bucolic sounds – Sommerheidenweg, Haubenbiglstrasse, Rohrerhüttenweg – and there is an idyllic mood in the sleepy squares that Moritz von Schwind, Schubert's friend, the Romanticist among Vienna's painters, caught accurately in his Biedermeier paintings. At the beginning of the nineteenth century, Vienna was still a town of garden palaces whose baroque façades artfully blended with the landscaped gardens, such as in the Palais Trautson or Schönborn. Later, the expanding metropolis devoured most of these gardens. Only the gardens of the Schwarzenberg Palais, the Belvedere, the Palais Starhemberg-Schönburg, and the Liechtenstein Palais have survived to this day.

7 Garden façade of the Palais Starhemberg-Schönburg

Belvedere sphinx

One of the most beautiful palace gardens lies behind the Schwarzenberg Palais (and behind the tall monument of the Unknown Soviet Soldier, called 'The Unknown Rapist' by the Viennese, to remain there forever, according to an article in the Austrian State Treaty of 1955). The German poet Joseph von Eichendorff sat here one day in June 1811, 'on a concealed bench near the wall from where one looks on to the fields'. 'Everything is lonely and quiet, only a few people are nearby, reading.' The fields have become expensive building sites, but the garden is still loved by children playing their mysterious games and by old people in search of a place that is 'lonely and quiet'. For Vienna's public gardens are oases of tranquillity in the heart of the hectic inner city. They are smaller, more intimate than the spacious parks of London or the carefully laid-out pleasure grounds of Paris. As one steps from the noisy, traffic-jammed Ringstrasse into the Burggarten, one is transposed into a peaceful world where there are no screeching tyres, no exhaust fumes. Trees look down upon a small lake, and children play around the statue of Emperor Franz Joseph I. Young couples walk arm in arm in this beautiful garden. Here it is easy to fall in love.

Oskar Kokoschka once reminisced about a 'forbidden garden', separated by a high fence from the courtyard of the house where he lived as a child. The fence consisted of gilded lances with flashing bowls made of yellow, red, blue and green glass which reflected even more colours as the sun went down. 'At noon these burning reflections made our hearts sad, for the garden was forbidden territory for us children. At the beginning of autumn, the large soft lawn invited games, and the trees were heavy with fruit. But we were permitted to walk only in the courtyard, and behind the fence the garden kept its secrets, almost near enough to be grasped by our hands – making it even more attractive if that was possible.'

From late spring until autumn Vienna is a city of flowers. In front of Westbahnhof (the West Railroad Station) where most people arrive, they are welcomed by lovely flower beds. Several years ago the city of Vienna arranged a magnificent flower show, with the city gardeners transforming a former swampland area near the Danube into a sort of Klingsor's magic garden. The show has long been closed but the garden has remained and now makes life more bearable for the citizens in one of Vienna's drab and dreary suburbs.

The magic of Vienna becomes even more powerful as winter approaches, when the visitors and tourists have gone home. For a short time – which gets shorter every year – the town belongs to the Viennese. On these early winter afternoons a misty curtain screens the noble decay of the Imperial city. The old districts, around St Stephen's, Freyung and the Hofburg, are enveloped in silence and beauty, and by a sense of timelessness. Soon fresh snow will cover the scars that poverty and the passage of time have inflicted upon the grandeur of the baroque palaces.

An old friend of mine, a retired Hofrat (court councillor), lives in a modest two-room apartment in the Leopoldine wing of the Imperial Palace, just below the richly ornamented rococo rooms with their Florentine mosaics and old tapestries once inhabited by the Empress Maria Theresia and now the official residence of Austria's federal president. It was given to him, at a nominal rental, by the government, as a sort of consolation for his low pension. Other small apartments in the Hofburg were allocated to deserving opera singers, to influential bureaucrats, or to people 'who know the right people'. The Hofrat's pension just enables him to pay his bills, buy some food, ride on the streetcar and spend the afternoon at his favourite coffee-house. He had to give up his subscription to the

Philharmonic concerts but once in a while he gets a free seat at the State Opera – where he knows the right people.

On the early winter afternoons he loves to walk through the older parts of the inner city. He knows that 'the best time of the year' has come when he sees saddle of venison and other game specialities appear on the menus of the better restaurants. He loves to study the menus that are displayed in framed glass cases next to the entrance. Sometimes he is tempted to enter, but then he remembers the business of tipping and walks on. In a Viennese restaurant you tip not only the waiter who brings your food and the girl who brings your beer or wine, but also the 'pay-waiter' (head waiter) who writes your bill, the gnome called 'piccolo' who brings your bread and rolls (they will appear on the bill), the hat-check girl (usually a dignified lady in her late sixties), the cigarette girl (very pretty), the man who sells flowers, the fellow who plays on the piano (even if he is the owner), the doorman, who looks like a retired Bohemian admiral (and may well be), and the *Wagentürlaufmacher* (the-man-who-opens-the-door-of-the-car). Karl Kraus, the Viennese satirist, once said that on the day of resurrection the first thing the Viennese will see is the outstretched hand of the *Sargdeckelaufmacher*, the man-who-opens-the-coffin-lid.

The Hofrat lost his savings four times in his life, which is considered 'normal' in Vienna, but he does not think of this when he leaves for his regular afternoon walk, though the short distance from the Hofburg to the coffee-house is filled with memories. He steps from his apartment into the inner courtyard, once the scene of the colourful mounting of the guard, always watched by 'The Old Gentleman', Emperor Franz Joseph I, when he happened to be in town. The Hofrat likes to remember those good old days because what came afterwards were the bad old days. Now the guard-house is empty and the courtyard has become a vast parking lot. The Hofrat walks through the pseudo-baroque gate built in 1890 on the site of the former Burgtheater; on some evenings the entrance is beautifully illuminated, and the Hofrat pauses briefly to look back. Now he is walking past Michaelerkirche where the requiem mass was read after his wife's death, years ago, and past Josefsplatz, Vienna's loveliest baroque square, with the magnificent façade of the National Library forming the backdrop. Alas, it is now another vast parking lot.

Nearby stands the old building where the Hofrat once had his office, with the

8 Swiss Court of the Hofburg

dear and familiar sounds of the creaking wooden floorboards, the big white-tiled stoves, the musty smell of dust-covered files in the antechamber, where the 'parties' were humbly waiting for him – citizens who needed the Herr Hofrat's nod or his signature on an *Akt* (a file). The Hofrat dearly loved his files and kept them on his desk as long as possible before reluctantly affixing his signature and sending them on. He hated saying goodbye to a file; a file signed was a file lost. The Hofrat speaks about his files in the same way than other people speak about their friends; the files were more alive to him than the 'parties' whom the files concerned. The 'parties' were only human annexes to the files.

On these dark winter afternoons the local melancholy becomes as contagious as the common cold. Sometimes the street lights have to be turned on soon after midday. In Vienna the street lights are always turned on during a state funeral, and on such a winter day people would ask hopefully whether anyone important had died, seeming somewhat disappointed to learn that it was just another dark winter afternoon.

We lived for years in the Thirteenth District, in Hietzing, where many houses have façades the colour of egg yolk ('Schönbrunn-yellow'), indicating buildings that once belonged to the Imperial Household. There were old-fashioned gas lamps in our street which would take me right back to the days of my youth when we teenage boys in my hometown used to hold spitting contests. One had to spit through a narrow hole in the lower rim of the lamp to blow out the gas flame. Healthy lungs and a careful aim were essential, and afterwards one might have to make a quick escape when the furious lamplighter or a policeman suddenly emerged out of the darkness.

I did not really enjoy this cold war which we boys were waging against the lamplighter, whom I secretly admired. He would walk through the streets at dusk, a lonely fellow, carrying his long stick on his shoulder. At the end of the stick was a flaming taper. The lamplighter would reach through the narrow hole and light the lamp. There would be a soft, muted explosion as the gas caught fire, and the mantle would begin to glow with a warm, soft light. The lamplighter has remained with me, a permanent association of my youth, as has the chimney sweep in his top hat, and the chestnut roaster at the windy street corner, who would snatch the hot chestnuts from the coals with his bare, blue hands, never burning his fingers – an astonishing feat which I never tired of watching.

9   House in Sievering with an old gas lamp

Alas, the lamps in our street in Hietzing had been fitted with an automatic device which turned them on and off, and no lamplighter was needed. But on Saturday morning a municipal employee, wearing a dark-blue uniform without insignia of rank, would appear in the street, carrying a long ladder over his shoulder. He would lean the ladder against the lamp post, climb up, and carefully wipe the inside of the lamp with a clean cloth. Then he would get down again, take his ladder, and walk toward the next lamp. He was a quiet man with a Buster Keaton face, and he was surprised when I offered him an unopened bottle of wine at Christmas.

In Vienna one gives Christmas presents to many city employees. This habit, as so many others, was imported from the bakshish-minded Balkans. Nowadays, most employees do not wait for their gifts but come to the house to collect them: the municipal garbage collectors, the street cleaners, the men working down in the sewers (they appear wearing their rubber boots reaching up to their thighs so that they cannot possibly be mistaken), the man whose job it is to inquire every three months whether one has noticed 'any rats, mice or vermin' in the house. (The Viennese have remained rat-conscious since the Great Plague of 1679 that killed seventy thousand people.) Even the traffic policemen at certain intersections get beautifully wrapped wine bottles and other small gifts. The motorists know that a certain policeman is on duty at a certain intersection, and they hope he will be lenient with them when they make a wrong turn or pass through an amber light. The policeman knows that the wine bottle is a down-payment for favours to be returned later on – in fact a bribe – but he considers it an 'acceptable' bribe, and places the bottle on the small heap of gifts in the middle of the street, saluting with his right hand while he keeps directing traffic with his left. Many of Vienna's traffic policemen are would-be Karajans who love to conduct their symphony of horse power. They give a cue to every car, creating forte and piano effects, silencing a noisy Volkswagen with two fingers of the left hand, building up a black Mercedes with a very low number on its license plate (probably somebody who is 'important'), and providing stunning feats of traffic harmony. Foreigners often stand at the curb watching the policeman's performance in admiration. Some traffic conductors actually find time to greet each driver as he passes. One man, an admirer of the late Toscanini, would hold his right hand in a characteristic gesture in front of his chest, imploring the driver to drive with

10 Yellow façade of Schönbrunn Palace

more feeling. Years ago, when one of these popular traffic maestros was hit by a car and had to be taken to the hospital, his admirers made a collection and presented him with a small car. Eventually his competitors and superiors got so irked by his popularity that they exiled him to the suburbs – more or less what happened to Karajan when *he* got too popular in Vienna.

My lamp cleaner, though, was surprised when I gave him the bottle of wine. He said he did not 'rate' a gift. I did not tell him I was giving it to him because it was too late to give it to the lamplighter of my youth whom we had so infuriated. Later, the lamp cleaner would often come in for a chat. He was dedicated to his job. He did not aspire to be the mayor of Vienna or to become a millionaire, but he did want to be the finest lamp cleaner in Hietzing. He knew very well that his days were numbered. Progress was inexorable. Soon the modern lamps would be reaching our street, driving out the old gas lamps and the lamp cleaner. And one day they did.

On Christmas Eve Vienna becomes a silent city. Mariahilferstrasse, the big shopping street, remains a fairyland boulevard under its canopy of coloured lanterns, bells and emblems, but the lights in the shop windows are turned off, the cinema marquees are dark, and the side streets are deserted. In this Catholic city everything is closed on this holy night, the restaurants and cafeterias and coffee-houses. Even the 'ladies', who ply patiently up and down the Kärntnerstrasse have gone home for the evening (though one wonders what 'home' means for them), and the State Opera is closed. (It performs every night from 1 September to 30 June except for Christmas Eve and Good Friday.) Behind the windows one sees beautifully lighted trees and one thinks of the people opening their presents. And there are burning candles in many, many windows, put there by people who lost someone 'in the war', which in Vienna means the two world wars. Around midnight, the streets become alive again with people going to their favourite church for midnight Mass.

A Catholic friend from Germany feels that Vienna's churches are 'friendlier and happier' than the austere cathedrals of Germany. They are less severe than the cool churches of Italy or the dark churches of Spain where the women go to pray before breakfast for strength to see them through their working day. The Viennese step into their favourite church casually, as into their favourite pastry

11 Gothic portal of the Minoritenkirche

shop, for light spiritual refreshment. Everybody has 'his' church, and 'his' deli-katessen, and 'his' coffee-house, and 'his' hairdresser. 'Here one owns every-thing', the Viennese say.

Perhaps the only thing in Vienna that no one claims to own is St Stephen's Cathedral, though nearly everybody goes there once in a while. Vienna's oldest church is St Ruprecht's, a merry, intimate church in Romanesque style. Near-by is Sankt-Maria-am-Gestade, a fourteenth-century church with a seven-sided Gothic tower crowned by a small cupola, which was once the church of the poor fishermen and later the church of the Czech population in Vienna. My own favourite church is Minoritenkirche, which has a fine Gothic portal and is very warm and cozy with its profusion of old wood. Two nearby churches have an austere, forbidding touch – Augustinerkirche near the Hofburg, the scene of many great weddings, and Michaelerkirche, solemn and dark, with candles burning at side altars, not exactly a place for easygoing sinners. But as you step out of the gloomy church, you see the elegant five-storey building with the gold-lettered name above the entrance, flanked by three gold medals on each side: Demel's.

New Year's Eve too has its strict ritual in Vienna. The State Opera puts on a gala performance of Johann Strauss' *Die Fledermaus*. Everybody waits impatient-ly for the third act when Frosch, the jailer, makes topical jokes which are sure to bring down the house. On New Year's Eve Frosch enjoys *Narrenfreiheit*, a fool's immunity. He may, and does, attack sacrosanct institutions and sacred cows; anything goes. Last year, Austria's federal president and the cardinal-arch-bishop of Vienna, representing the country's worldly and spiritual powers, sat in opposite boxes and laughed at this impertinent jailer; during the intermission they toasted each other with a glass of champagne.

Across the Ringstrasse, meanwhile, the waltzes of Johann Strauss are played at the New Year's concert of the Vienna Philharmonic. The pleasant ritual was introduced after the last war by the late Clemens Krauss, the elegant conductor and opera director, a Viennese born-and-bred, and a former member of the Wiener Sängerknaben (the Vienna Boys' Choir). He understood the musical soul of his city, where New Year would not be New Year without Johann Strauss. The Philharmoniker play the great Strauss waltzes with warmth and sentiment,

12 Stained glass from St Stephen's Cathedral

brio and buoyancy, and always with impeccable taste. Since the death of Clemens Krauss the concert is conducted by Willi Boskovsky, the orchestra's first concert master, also a true Viennese, who mounts the conductor's platform, with fiddle and bow in his hand, wearing the striped pants, patterned waistcoat and morning coat worn at the time of Johann Strauss. Boskovsky conducts with his bow, but occasionally he will put his violin to his chin and play a beautiful solo melody. Everybody smiles happily, the old ladies behind their tears; their mothers had known Johann Strauss and had told them about the great Hofballmusikdirektor, the genius who wrote some of his finest waltzes in the morning, rehearsed them in the afternoon, and premiered them at night. And *dear* Willi Boskovsky looks and acts *exactly* like Strauss, swaying with the rhythm, holding the fiddle high up and closing his eyes, as he loses himself in one of the immortal melodies. 'How beautiful is beauty!'

I doubt whether Johann Strauss and his musicians played the music as beautifully as Boskovsky and the Philharmoniker perform the waltzes in this age of musical precision – with subtle ritardandi and sudden changes of mood, with that ever-so-slight accent, after an inaudible pause on the second beat, which distinguish a real Viennese waltz player from his imitator. Some horseplay is added, when the third percussion player dresses up in the mask of Johann Strauss to present Boskovsky with a golden wreath, or puts on a hunter's hat and fires off a couple of shots during the 'Hunt Polka'. The concert always ends with encores, and the encores are followed by the encore's encore, the 'Blue Danube' waltz. By this time some people are quietly crying. Others seem to be on the verge of jumping up and dancing in the aisles.

Like politicians shaking hands again in front of the camera for the benefit of reporters and readers, the Philharmoniker nowadays play the *Neujahrskonzert* twice – on New Year's Eve for the Viennese, and the following morning for the largest television audience in the history of Eurovision (western Europe) and Intervision (eastern Europe). Last year it was planned to transmit the concert 'live' via Telstar to America but the time element made this impossible. Still, an estimated four hundred million viewers saw Strauss-Boskovsky and watched the Vienna State Opera ballet. Somehow the elaborate showmanship did not kill the spirit of Johann Strauss. Perhaps it cannot be killed.

All Viennese music has haunting undertones of sadness and sorrow. Even Haydn, the most optimistic of Vienna's great composers, had his melancholy moments. 'For quite some time now I have had days of depression without really knowing why . . .', he wrote in 1791 to Mme Luigia Polzelli, his great friend. The sounds of sorrow are audible in almost every major Mozart opus; the tears and the smile are there in his great G minor String Quintet (which he wrote after the death of his father), and in his G minor Symphony. The G minor key expresses Vienna's everpresent mixture of gaiety and sadness, euphoria and gloom, cheerfulness and resignation: Vienna is a city in G minor.

The most Viennese of all composers, Schubert and Johann Strauss, always blend lightheartedness and melancholy. Some of Schubert's finest songs are also his saddest; his 'Heidenröslein' (after Goethe's *Sah ein Knab' ein Röslein steh'n*), is so moving and beautiful that it has become an 'anonymous' folk-song. Johann Strauss begins some of his most exhilarating waltzes with a dreamy introduction and ends with a plaintive, wistful echo in the *coda*. Strauss well understood that the Viennese are not happy because something nice has happened to them – but in spite of it. For centuries, Vienna's favourite communal pastime has been

14 Franz Xaver Messerschmidt, *An Archvillain*
15 (*overleaf left*) Stove-tile with the Imperial arms, from the Cathedral sacristy
16 (*overleaf right*) Statue of Emperor Charles IV, from the Cathedral

Raunzen – a cheerful, paradoxical form of complaining that is often misunderstood by non-Viennese. In 1906 Hermann Bahr wrote, 'The Viennese is unhappy about himself, hates his fellow Viennese but cannot live without them. He has no respect for himself and is often moved by himself. He gripes all the time but wants to be praised all the time. He is unhappy – and happy to be unhappy.'

The Viennese does gripe about Vienna but he loves his city dearly. He finds everything wrong with it, yet he would never live elsewhere. He remains a loyal member of the family; though he himself is very critical of the family, he can get very angry with any outsider who expresses criticism. Any attempt to change the Viennese way of life is met with outright hostility. Robert Musil, the great Austrian novelist, whose gift for universality has been compared to Proust and Joyce, writes in his brilliant satirical novel, *The Man without Qualities*:

> For it was not only dislike of one's fellow-citizens that was intensified into a strong sense of community; even mistrust of oneself and of one's destiny here assumed the character of profound self-certainty. In this country one acted – sometimes indeed to the extreme limits of passion and its consequences – differently from the way one thought, and one thought differently from the way one acted. Uninformed observers have mistaken this for charm, or even for a weakness in what they thought was the Austrian character...

What makes the Viennese the complex, contradictory people they are? The question has puzzled Vienna's satirists and moralists, writers and poets for over three hundred years, ever since an eighteen-year-old Augustinian friar from Swabia, Abraham a Sancta Clara, came to Vienna in 1662 to become the city's conscience and its greatest Catholic preacher. Like many 'imported' Viennese, he became more Viennese than the natives; he knew them well and wondered about them. In his rough rhymes and robust homilies he preached against their sensuous enjoyment of pleasure, their distrust for authority, their tendency toward muddling through, their occasional displays of courage and frequent displays of fickleness, their aversion to facing cold facts. Looking for the truth, Abraham a Sancta Clara found

> false talk, false writing, false coins, false wines, false gold, false silver, false flowers, false jewelry, false hair, false faces, false friends – yes, the whole world is false.... The portal of the church looks as if it were made of the finest Salzburg marble but it is only plaster made to look like marble.... The women are as beautiful as a bride but nothing is genuine about them – neither their hair, nor their pearls, nor their clothes, nor their teeth, not even their undershirt....

17   Head of St John, from A Crucifixion group

The outbreak of the great plague in 1679 had been preceded by 'ringing trumpets and music resounding everywhere, making a noise as though a hole had opened in the sky', as Pater Abraham writes in *Mercks Wien* ('Take Notice, Vienna!'). But when the plague was over and the dead were buried, the sound of music was heard again 'in noblemen's houses and courtyards'. The same happened after the Turkish Siege of 1683. The funerals ended, and the fun began again.

But underneath this Viennese myth of waltz and wine, operetta and whipped cream there is what Nestroy called 'threadbare *Gemütlichkeit*', what Ilsa Barea calls 'the legend of the Heart of Gold of the Viennese'.

All winter long the Viennese – at least a considerable number of them – spend their weekends in the Wienerwald with their skis and sledges. There are ski trails within a short streetcar ride from many people's houses; it is only twenty minutes by car from the Opera to the snow-covered hills. (All distances in Vienna are measured by the time it takes to get to or from the Opera.) Even people who do not ski go to the Wienerwald for a walk in the snow; the paths are cleared and beautifully marked. Spending the day in the snow and sunshine is considered a healthy therapy after too much dancing and merry-making. In many families the older people skate while the youngsters go skiing. There are over fifty ice skating rinks in the city, among them some artificial ones of high quality. The Stadthalle's artificial ice skating rink is used for the performances of the 'Wiener Eisrevue', a world-famous ice-show; the Eislaufverein's ice skating rink was the largest in Europe until part of it was sold to an American-owned hotel. Advanced skiers drive out to the Semmering, Vienna's 'Hausberg' (private mountain), the Schneeberg or the Raxalpe. On Monday morning the newspapers publish frightening tales of sporting accidents and broken bones. Everybody is shocked about so many accidents, and the next weekend they all go out again to be 'in the snow'.

Vienna's aristocratic palaces still dominate the image of the inner city. Many palaces, and many people who once lived in them, have seen better days. Both are slightly run down but keep up an elegant front. In Vienna the upper middle classes always imitated the *Lebensform* – the way of life – of the aristocratic class. It was important for a man to be a 'Kavalier' (as the Baron Ochs von Lerchenau,

18 Grand staircase in the Town Palace of Prince Eugene

Palaces and
houses
in the Graben in
eighteenth-
century Vienna

who does not always behave like a 'Kavalier' in the opera *Der Rosenkavalier*, likes
to emphasise).

Most of the palaces were given up by the descendants of the former owners,
who now live in bourgeois circumstances, or prefer the conveniences of a modern,
centrally heated apartment. Some of these palaces have the most magnificent
baroque staircases – but there are few bathrooms and the plumbing in the
palaces is totally inadequate. There was a time when the feudal owners of these
palaces were exempted from taxes, civic duties and military service, had their
own seals and held patrimonial courts – the privileges of a feudal aristocracy.
During the liberal era, towards the end of the last century, the Habsburgs and
the landed gentry, not more than eighty families, were the ruling elite, with
inherited rights and definite prerogatives that could not be taken away. When
a young aristocrat failed to pass his examination at the law faculty of Vienna's
university, the professor said, 'Count, I can't prevent your appointment to be
governor of Lower Austria, but I can at least postpone it for a year.'

These privileges no longer exist. In the republic of Austria, aristocratic titles
are not legally admitted though they are actually used and generally respected.
Of this erstwhile glory only the big houses remain, silent witnesses of a great era.
They are houses of true breeding which have survived the ravages of time and
war with more dignity than the less exalted bourgeois buildings around them.
Some palaces have become schools, and others – Palais Starhemberg, Mollard-
Clary, Modena, Prince Eugene – have become ministries. Only a few families

still keep their palaces, among them the Harrachs who have some beautiful Breughels and Rembrandts in their private art gallery, and the Liechtensteins who rule over the sixty-two-square-mile principality in the Alps between Austria and Switzerland.

The oldest palaces were built after the victory over the Turks, towards the end of the seventeenth century; a second group was put up in the middle of the eighteenth century – the Palais Questenberg, Schönburg, Schönborn, Daun-Kinsky. At the time of the Congress of Vienna some wealthy foreigners, such as the Rasumofskys, built their palatial town houses in Vienna. Almost all these palaces are in the inner city; in Freyung (Palais Kinsky, Montenuovo, Harrach), in Minoritenplatz (Starhemberg, Liechtenstein), Herrengasse (Wilczek, Modena, Trautmannsdorff). There was little space in the narrow streets; the old files often contain requests for permission 'to build into the street'; and there was no room for elaborate balconies. But the entrance gate was always monumental with the coat-of-arms in stone relief.

Many of these old palaces are hardly noticed by the passers-by in the narrow, dark streets. At night they disappear between the bright neon signs and the coloured lights of the brash upstart buildings on both sides. The old palaces are reticent; they always were reluctant to give away their secrets. The thick, discreet walls never did reveal much of the fascinating life that went on behind them.

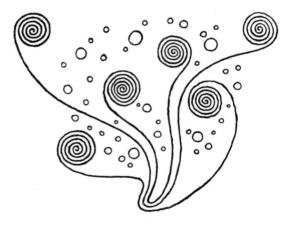

I

Scenes from History

VINDOBONA AND MEDIEVAL VIENNA

Vienna was built in the centre of a thirty-mile broad basin where the Danube flows between central Europe's two major mountain ranges, the Alps and the Carpathians. Here people have lived since before the dawn of history. The oldest relic known, the tiny stone figure of a woman, perhaps a fertility symbol, 'Venus of Willendorf', was found near the Danube, north-west of Vienna. It is believed to date from the Old Stone Age, around 20,000 BC. The Celts were living here at least three hundred years before the Roman legions came north through the Alps in about 100 BC. The Romans founded the settlement of Carnuntum, in Pannonia, twenty-nine miles east of Vienna, on the highway now leading to Bratislava, Slovakia. In the second century AD, Carnuntum had an amphitheatre with thirteen thousand seats, and was the provincial capital and residence of the Roman emperors who then ruled over an empire stretching from Egypt to Britannia and comprising fourteen per cent of the area of the known world. The emperors liked to cure their gout in the hot springs of nearby Baden – where later Beethoven wrote his Ninth Symphony. (Today Baden is best known for its gambling casino.) The Roman province of Noricum was largely formed out of what is now Austrian territory. In nearby Vindobona the Romans set up the garrison of the Thirteenth Legion, which was later replaced by the more famous Tenth Legion. The name of Vindobona comes from the Celtic *Vindo* (white) and *bona* (field).

Little love is now lost between the politicians in Vienna and Rome who wrangle about the South Tyrol, but the Viennese owe much to the Roman legionaries who built roads and towns, transplanted vines and southern fruit,

21   The oldest house in Vienna incorporating a tower
from the ancient city wall

47

and established Roman law. The descendants of the former Danube savages could say '*civis Romanus sum*'. By 300 AD Christianity was beginning to spread. One hundred years later the Roman provinces were overrun, by the Vandals, the Markomans, the West-Goths, the Huns under Attila. In AD 487 the Roman legions were ordered to return home. New tribes came and went across the Danube: the Langobards, the Avars, the nomadising Teutons, the Slavs, the Franks and Bajuvars, predecessors of today's Bavarians, and the Magyars. All intruders left something: customs, traditions, folk-songs, melodies. Charlemagne definitely established Christianity and in 800 was crowned as the first 'Roman Emperor of the German Nation', then only a symbolic title.

The name of Vindobona appears in old records until the end of the fifth century. Then there are five hundred years of silence until 'Wiennis' (Wien) is mentioned in the Niederaltaich Annals of 1030. It seems that for several centuries after the fall of Vindobona no town existed on the site of present-day Vienna. Exactly when Vienna was built for the second time is not known, but it was probably during the reign of Margrave Adalbert (1018-55). A document with the birth certificate of the *civitas* exists from the year 1137, shortly before the Babenbergs moved to Vienna. Most Viennese originally were of German-Austrian origin, from lower and upper Austria, Bavaria, Franconia; later came Czechs, Poles, Croats, Hungarians and Italians. Under the greatest Babenberg, Heinrich Jasomirgott, Vienna became the rulers' residence and the country was made a duchy. Vienna was then an important trading centre; there the Crusaders could buy their provisions and equipment (until Venice took over that lucrative business). Merchants and burghers prospered, nobility and Church became rich.

The last Babenberg ruler, Duke Friedrich II, died in the 'Hungarian' Battle (1246) against King Bela IV of Hungary. During the following interregnum King Przemysl Ottokar II of Bohemia occupied Vienna, then in chaos, and immediately tried to make himself popular with the Viennese by giving extravagant festivities. At the banquet, after his second marriage, to the niece of the Hungarian king, 'the tables were so long that you could walk between them for hours'. When one tenth of the city burned down in 1262, King Ottokar rebuilt churches and convents at his own expense, and donated 'a whole forest of timber' for new houses for the citizens. Vienna even then was a place for good living, and many nobles 'stayed much longer than their affairs demanded'.

22 Roman head found in a Döbling vineyard

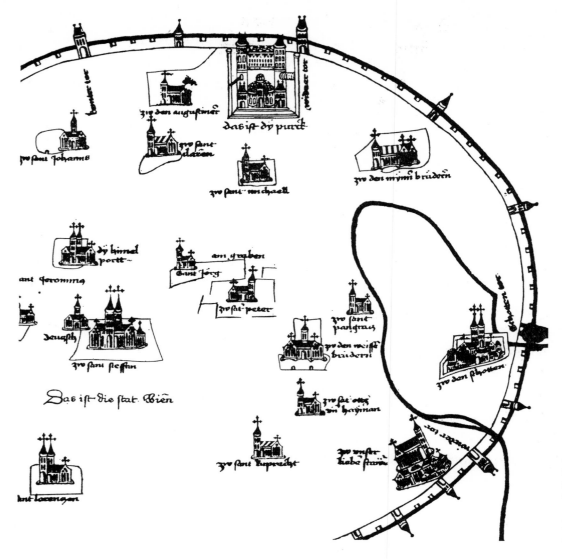

Part of the city of Vienna in the fifteenth century, with St Stephen's (left) and the Hofburg Palace (top)

King Ottokar lost land and life on the Marchfeld in 1278 to an impoverished nobleman from Aargau, Switzerland, whose name, taken from the old Habsburg Castle there, was often ridiculed as *Habenichtsburg*, 'Have-not-Castle'. The following century brought to Vienna an almost improbable chain of disasters. In 1327, a large part of the town burned down; in 1338, locusts destroyed the harvest; in 1348, there were floods and an earthquake (for which the Jews were blamed); and in 1349, the Asiatic cholera killed 'tens of thousands' of people.

But the survivors made merry. In the month of May a special public holiday greeted 'the first violet'. Under Duke Otto the Merry – one wonders how merry

23   Tomb of Emperor Friedrich III in St Stephen's Cathedral

he must have been to deserve that surname! – the aristocracy wore cloaks coloured in accordance with their coats of arms and edged with small silver bells, 'as was the custom of former clowns'. Even Justice joined in the spirit of general merriment. Criminals were compelled to sit in a large dog-kennel, exposed to public ridicule and dishonest bakers were put into a cage which was then lowered into the Danube, 'amidst widespread hilarity'.

LET OTHERS WAGE WARS!

The expansionist policy of the House of Habsburg was well summed up by King Matthias Corvinus of Hungary who said, '*Bella gerant alii ; tu, felix Austria – nube !*' (Let others wage wars; you, lucky Austria, marry!) Lucky Austria grew fast by appropriate marriages. Maximilian I married Maria of Burgundy in 1477. His son Philip 'the Handsome' in 1496 married Joanna (the 'Madwoman') of Castile and Aragon. These marriages brought Burgundy and Flanders into the Habsburg Empire. Philip's son, Charles I of Spain, became Charles V of the Holy Roman Empire. Now the Habsburgs were in Big International Politics. (Charles V was the first ruler, though not the last, to speak of his empire as one 'on which the sun never sets'.) By 1519 he controlled Spain, Flanders, Austria and Germany. In 1521 he divided his possessions with his brother Ferdinand who had married Anna of Hungary and Bohemia, which made lucky Austria even luckier. There now existed two branches of the Habsburg family, one in Spain and one in Austria.

In 1526 Archduke Ferdinand (later Ferdinand I) left Spain to take possession of his Austrian dominions. He had been brought up in the strict absolutist traditions of the Spanish court, and Vienna, then predominantly a Protestant town, did not like him. The dislike erupted into a rebellion among the burghers and lower nobility. Ferdinand did not even bother to go to Vienna. Instead he set up his residence in the nearby, fortified town of Wiener-Neustadt, and from there crushed the mutiny. The leaders were executed (Ferdinand himself was presiding judge of the tribunal) and others were exiled. Vienna's autonomy was rescinded, and the formerly elected city fathers were from now on appointed civil servants. This was the beginning of the still powerful Austrian bureaucracy.

But peace was not to prevail for long. In 1529 the sultan of Turkey, Suliman II,

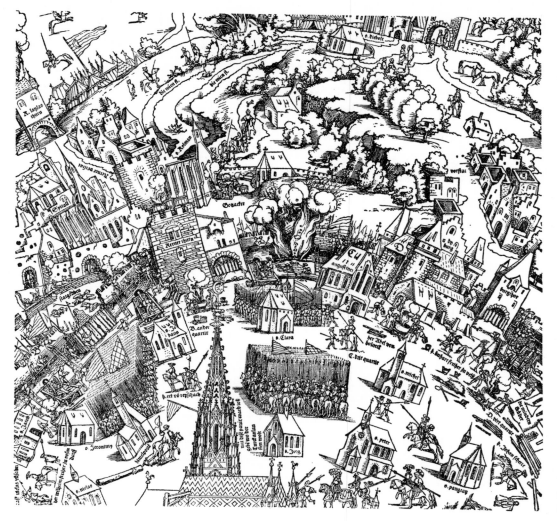

Vienna during
the Turkish Siege
of 1529

arrived at the gates of Vienna with an army of 280,000 men. This First Turkish Siege was broken by Niklas Count Salm and his eighteen thousand defenders, but the danger was only postponed. During the following seven years the Turks remained in neighbouring Hungary, from where they made over two hundred minor invasions into Austria.

Despite his inauspicious debut in Vienna, Ferdinand was no Spanish-style despot. To fight Protestantism he called the Jesuits to Vienna, but these masters of psychological warfare did not use the methods of the Spanish Inquisition – not in Vienna. Instead they built theatres where they performed plays with a liturgical message, combining religion with entertainment. They knew that the shortest way to the hearts and minds of the Viennese was not the stake, but the stage. (That was a hundred years before Abraham a Sancta Clara used the same method, combining fun with preaching, jokes with his message.) In Vienna the battle against Protestantism lasted a long time. Occasionally there would be an execution, by way of setting an example. Booksellers were punished for selling 'heretical' literature. The Protestants fought back. Catholic chroniclers report that Protestant noblemen 'rode on their horses through St Stephen's during the service', that Catholic priests were beaten up and prevented from saying Mass (quite a few archdukes, noblemen and even a Habsburg ruler, Maximilian II, were believed to be secretly Lutheran). The Battle on the White Mountain in 1620 signified the end of Protestantism in Vienna. Three years later a decree stated that non-Catholics could not be made citizens. Many Protestant families emigrated. Others, among them the Khevenhüllers and Starhembergs, recanted.

THE SECOND TURKISH SIEGE

It was a member of the Starhemberg family, Count Ernst Rüdiger, who was commander of the Vienna garrison and who became the hero of the Second Turkish Siege in 1683 – the most glorious event in Vienna's entire history. In July 1683, a Turkish army comprising 230,000 men and large supply forces (the Turks even brought along their own herds of cattle) arrived near Vienna from Adrianople. On the way they picked up some irregular forces of Magyar and Tartar tribesmen. Eleven months earlier, in August 1682, Sultan Mohammed IV, after consulting with his chief minister Kara Mustafa and other high advisers, had decided to disregard the peace treaty that Turkey had with Emperor Leopold I of Austria, and to launch another military campaign against Austria, before the treaty expired in 1684. The Turks were gambling on the dissension among the German princes, the confusing jealousies among Austria's allies, and the hostility between Leopold I and Louis XIV of France.

The arrival of the Turks created a panic in Vienna. Emperor Leopold, judged by various historians as being anything from 'pious and judicious' to 'weak and undecided', led the flight from the city, followed by most of his grandees and court officials, and by sixty thousand Viennese. Leopold went first to Krems and

24   Pulpit outside St Stephen's from which the Viennese had been roused against the Turks since the fifteenth century

later to Linz. Despite much diplomatic activity, it was impossible to reach an agreement with the allies to dispatch troops to Vienna. The Imperial forces under Charles v, Duke of Lorraine, were too weak to stop the Turks. Vienna would have to depend temporarily on its own garrison. Once more, as during the earlier siege of 1529, the suburbs were razed to shorten the line of defence.

On 14 July the Turks had completely surrounded the city. Kara Mustafa asked the defenders inside the walls to surrender. 'Accept Islam, and live in peace under the sultan! Or deliver the fortress, and live in peace under the sultan as Christians . . . But if you resist, death and spoliation and slavery shall be the fate of all!'

Count Starhemberg dismissed the messenger and ordered the city gates to be walled up. His garrison consisted of sixteen thousand men: regular troops, and a militia made up of burghers, students, merchants and a few court officials who had chosen to stay in Vienna. He had three hundred guns inside the walls of Vienna. Kara Mustafa's forward base was within gunshot, less than 450 paces, from the city walls. The main Turkish forces faced the Burg bastion and the Löwel bastion (today's Volksgarten near the Ringstrasse). Starhemberg moved most of his artillery to near the Hofburg.

The Turks were optimistic, and there was much talk of 'final victory' in Kara Mustafa's elegant headquarters tent, but it soon appeared that this talk was somewhat premature. The Turks needed three weeks to occupy the *Glacis* and to reach the edge of the counterscarp which the Viennese engineers had strongly reinforced with iron spikes. On 6 August the fight for the inner city began. Paradoxically, there was no panic now inside the walls. The schools had been closed, but the churches remained open. There were ample food stocks, and prices remained steady. When the first incendiary bombs began to fall, the fire brigade went efficiently into action. All householders were ordered to keep buckets of water ready and to dismantle any roofs made of shingles. Paving stones were dug up. They were needed on the fortifications. Also, it had been noticed that shots falling on the soft earth caused less damage.

But there were serious problems. One had to find space to bury the dead, to get rid of the garbage, to get enough water when the Turks cut the conduits of fresh water that led into the city. An epidemic of dysentery spread quickly through the city. The situation was bad, but outside the city walls it was even

The fortifications
of Vienna during
the Second
Turkish Siege

worse, where the irregular forces – the Tartars and Magyars over which Kara Mustafa had no control – were burning, looting and killing.

By the middle of August, Count Starhemberg had established contact with the outside world through a number of messengers. The most famous of them was a man called Franz Kolschitzki (or Franz Georg Kulczycki), an extremely gifted double agent with a flair for publicity; he later published an account of his adventures which created 'enthusiasm mingled with scepticism'. Kolschitzki disguised himself as a Turk, managed to leave the city and eventually reached the headquarters of the Duke of Lorraine to give the allied commander authentic information about the situation inside Vienna.

All round Vienna the Turks were closing in. At 2 p.m. on 4 September a violent explosion shook the Burg bastion; a Turkish mine had torn a large hole in the wall. Turkish troops and Janissaries shouting 'Allah! Allah!' and carrying flags and standards, poured in through the breach. For over one hundred

26 Sankt-Maria-am-Gestade

minutes the fate of Vienna – and of Western civilisation – hung in the balance. Then the attackers were beaten back. Starhemberg lost over two hundred men, the enemy many more.

By now the situation was getting desperate. The death rate, due to dysentery and other fevers, was going up. There was by now so little food that 'older men and women quietly died off'. People ate donkey and cat meat. There was very little bread, despite the municipality's instructions to the bakers to arrange for a fair distribution. From the top of the tower of St Stephen's observers kept constant watch over the area, particularly towards the hills of the Wienerwald. Would the relieving armies arrive before it was too late?

Starhemberg knew there was little time left. Defeatism and illness were spreading in the city. During the night of 8 September flares had been seen rising from the Kahlenberg, on the Vienna side of the Danube, but the following morning they could not see any troop movements. Actually, the signs had been given, somewhat prematurely, by advance patrols; only on the night of 10-11 September did the troops of the Duke of Lorraine occupy the heights of the Kahlenberg and Leopoldsberg. Once again flares went up to tell the people in Vienna, five miles away, that help was coming at last.

Kara Mustafa had made a fatal mistake: intent on breaking the resistance of the defenders of besieged Vienna he had brought all his troops forward, neglecting to occupy and keep under control the heights of the Wienerwald. Now he was caught between two fronts – the defenders of the city who were preparing to attack, and the relieving armies on the hills. Kara Mustafa left thirty thousand troops near the city walls, and threw one hundred and seventy thousand men against the Duke of Lorraine's forces. The decisive battle began at dawn, on 12 September. According to all reports it was not a co-ordinated action but a series of confusing minor encounters. One general said later, 'We fought from ridge to valley and from valley to ridge.' It must have been a bewildering sight for the desperate defenders in Vienna, watching from the tower of St Stephen's. It was impossible to tell how the battle was going though gradually the allies seemed to be approaching Vienna. The Duke of Lorraine had begun the attack by driving into the right wing of the Turks. Ibrahim Pasha, Kara Mustafa's deputy (and the sultan's brother-in-law) realised the danger and ordered the partial withdrawal of the troops on the Turkish right flank, for regrouping and

27   Tower of Michaelerkirche, one of the chief landmarks of the city during the Siege

12 September:
the armies
engaged

counter-attack. This was probably the correct decision, but it cost Ibrahim Pasha his head; he was later decapitated, by order of his brother-in-law.

Around noon there was a pause in the fighting. The Duke of Lorraine held a short meeting; all his commanders wanted to press forward. The Saxon general Goltz said, 'I am an old man and I want comfortable quarters in Vienna to-night.' Count Waldeck agreed, and so did Sobieski. By now the advance units of the allied armies were only two miles away from the walls of Vienna.

The final attack began at twenty minutes past three, 'in the fierce heat of the afternoon'. The Imperial troops, the Saxons and various empire units pushed forward. The Poles made a southward sweep with their cavalry which the Turks resisted for some time. Then the Poles broke through, reaching the encampment of the grand vizier. Acting on the spur of the moment, the Duke of Lorraine now swung to the right, pushing the Turks toward the centre of the front, where the Saxons attacked, also swinging to the right by way of the suburbs of Döbling and Währing. Kara Mustafa saw that he was in danger of being cut off from

28   Entrance hall of the Upper Belvedere, the ceiling supported by Prince Eugene's Turkish captives

his line of retreat into Hungary. He threw twenty thousand Turkish riders against the Poles, between the suburbs of Hernals and Breitensee. It was too little and too late; the Polish cavalry, aided by the Imperial troops, beat back this last counter-attack. By 4 p.m. the Turks were in full flight. Meanwhile the defenders of Vienna had attacked and driven the Turkish Janissaries out of their positions. The Turks who had remained in their trenches and galleries facing the Hofburg turned and fled. Finally, Kara Mustafa himself had to retreat in rather undignified haste.

At 5.30 p.m. trumpets at Vienna's Schottentor announced the arrival of the first units of the relieving army – two regiments of dragoons under Hermann, Margrave of Baden. Vienna was saved. But the aftermath of the siege was less glorious than its final phase. Almost at once the 'harmonious' commanders (as the papal legate had referred to them) began to wrangle among themselves for precedence at the victory celebrations and over the partition of the booty.

In Vienna, the post-siege situation was described as 'desperate but not serious'. Taxes remained unpaid, the rights of the guilds were abolished. Some promotions were given to men who had behaved well during the siege; gratuities in cash were promised, and in some cases even paid. The Vienna municipality gave presents to the commanders of the relieving forces. They were named 'paladins of the Church', and Count Starhemberg was praised as 'the saviour of the Holy Roman Empire and of Europe'. But Emperor Leopold I issued a decree that contained more reprimands than praise. He exhorted the Viennese to fight against vice, 'to practise virtue, honesty and the fear of God', and forbade 'hatred, envy, fancy dresses, gossip, also the many dissensions inside the Church, and immorality, all of which have been widely practised'. In vain did the burghers ask for measures to limit the import of Hungarian wines, tax exemptions and 'tolerance money' (which had been formerly paid to them by the Jews, many of whom had been driven out). The burghers also asked for the guns that the Turks had left behind. The Imperial bureaucrats granted none of these requests; only a few old guns were handed over. It was quite an anti-climax. Double agent Kolschitzki obtained a tax-free house from the city fathers and opened his first coffee-house near St Stephen's. After a while, everything was forgotten, and the people of Vienna returned to their pleasures. Once again (as Abraham a Sancta Clara said), music resounded 'from noblemen's houses and courtyards'.

29 Franziskanerplatz: the Franciscans' cloister was used
as a hospital during the Second Turkish Siege

THE PLAGUE

Between 1349 and 1713 there were at least fourteen major epidemics of plague in Vienna, creating disasters of baroque dimension. The epidemic of 1679 killed 'half the population', according to some chroniclers. Figures vary between 12,000 and 140,000 victims; probably over 35,000 people died. Everybody who could afford it left town – the emperor, his court, the nobility, the court officials, the rich burghers. Chroniclers write that pompous state processions were stopped on intersections 'by carriages with piles of dead bodies ... a truly apocalyptic contrast'. Among the dead bodies were people who were dying or merely sick. Some were only dead-drunk. According to a well-loved Viennese legend, a certain popular folk singer and piper by the name of Augustin Marx had a wild theory that wine killed off the plague. Naturally, he regularly got himself dead-drunk during an outbreak. P. Fuhrmann, a local chronicler, writes that one day Augustin passed out, was carted off with the dead, and thrown into the 'plague pit', 'but they did not cover him completely with earth and the said man, after sleeping it off all night long, woke up in the morning, and tried to get out, but the ditch was too deep. He tried to get up, stepping on the dead, and finally was rescued by the *Ziehknechte*, who after dawn appeared with other dead bodies and helped him out. ...'

Alas, Augustin Marx and the alcoholic therapy seems to be only another Viennese legend, that was debunked not long ago by the Viennese historian, Gustav Gugitz. He writes that drunks were often carted off with the dead by mistake – not only in Vienna, but also in Erfurt, Danzig and Memmingen. Pater Abraham a Sancta Clara reports that 'a drunk named Augustin' was thrown into a plague pit and survived, but no other proof exists that Augustin Marx really lived in Vienna. Gugitz says that the famous song, *O, du lieber Augustin, alles ist hin* ('Oh, my dear Augustin, everything is lost') that symbolises the cheerful Viennese pessimism was not created in Vienna but imported from Saxony where people first sang it when King Augustus the Strong was dethroned. It reached Vienna much later, around 1800.

A report of the famous physician Paul de Sorbait (who later became rector of the university of Vienna) about the plague of 1679 describes the criminal ignorance of the official authorities and the incredible sanitary conditions in Vienna where 'dead dogs, cats and fowl were thrown into the street', and 'goats

30 *Pestsäule* (Plague Memorial) in the Graben
31 (*overleaf*) View to Vienna from Leopoldsberg, with the church of St Leopold, rebuilt to commemorate the victory over the Turks at the Battle of the Kahlenberg

were kept in living rooms because their smell is said to suck up the germs of the plague'. Sorbait tried to persuade the emperor's 'consilium sanitatis' to do something about the epidemic and suggested the ringing of church bells 'because this will clean the air and move the winds that have been locked in ... Yes, the bells will drive out the evil spirits that float through the air.' But Dr Sorbait did not have much confidence in his therapy for he and almost all other doctors disappeared when things got really bad. In the end there were no people left to bury the dead and the prisoners had to be released from jail to do the job. Later Leopold I had the *Pestsäule* built of white Salzburg marble, and all was well.

1848

Flippancy and a tendency towards fickleness were apparant in the aftermath to the great events of 1683 and even during the great plagues. These qualities in the Viennese character were to reveal themselves again during the heroic period in Vienna's history now remembered as the revolution of 1848.

The 1848 revolution had been preceded by the eerie *Vormärz* atmosphere, when many sensitive people felt that 'something was going to happen'. The only people who pretended to notice nothing were those against whom the revolution was to be directed. In 1845, a committee of writers and intellectuals had presented to Metternich a petition against censorship. (Metternich disdainfully remarked that he did not understand what a 'committee' signified.) Among the petitioners was Franz Grillparzer who called himself 'a poor foreigner in his own fatherland'. Writing in verse, taking advantage of a poet's prerogative, he called Metternich's system 'prehistoric', and commenting on Metternich's plan of an 'Academy' said, 'It is – may God forgive me – as though the devil were to build a church.' Grillparzer realised that Metternich's system was disintegrating and going to end in chaos. He was worried about his beloved fatherland but did not know what to do. Since the Burgtheater failure, in 1838, of his comedy, *Weh dem, der lügt* (Woe to Him Who Lies), a brilliant, very Viennese play about the many-sided problem of truth, he had withdrawn into morose silence, an eccentric misanthrope deeply worried about the future.

Neither Grillparzer nor other *Vormärz* reformers were against the monarchy (the feeble-minded and weak Emperor Ferdinand I was actually called 'the

Benevolent'), but the people wanted to get rid of Metternich. The students whose fraternities were forbidden became the cadres of revolutionary thought; they were joined by liberal members of the Legal-Political Reading Society, the Association of Booksellers (who had been badly hit by the censorship patent), liberal members of the *Bürgerschaft*, and finally by working men who had lost their jobs or had been unable to make enough money. The workers laboured fourteen hours a day and still were unable to earn a living wage. Mechanisation of the factories had created mass unemployment and there were hunger demonstrations. In 1847, the Aid Society (*Hilfsverein*) in Vienna distributed 264,000 portions of 'relief soup'. Vienna was a powder keg, but in Ballhausplatz they consoled themselves with the words of the Emperor Franz, 'Let the Viennese gripe – as long they gripe, they'll leave you alone', and refused to worry. When they began to worry, it was too late.

The 1848 revolution lasted seven and a half months, from the middle of March until the end of October. It began with a rather harmless demonstration in the morning of 13 March, in Vienna's Herrengasse, where students, burghers (wearing frock-coat and top hat) and workers met in front of the Landhaus. They demanded the resignation of Metternich, freedom of the press and a municipal charter. At 1 p.m., soldiers fired the first shots into the crowd, and the demonstration became a revolt. Thirty men died that day – students, artisans, workers. Late that night Metternich resigned and went abroad. Grillparzer later called it 'the gayest revolution imaginable ... the whole population filled the streets all day long'.

A new press law was promulgated; armed citizens were permitted to form a national guard. A second revolt occurred in May. A democratic constitution was proclaimed. (A Viennese newspaper published a bad poem, 'Greetings from Saxony', written by a fellow revolutionary, one Richard Wagner, *Kapellmeister* in Dresden.) From Vienna, the revolution spread to other countries: to Poland, where it was suppressed; to Hungary where the peoples (Croats, Banatians, Serbs, Slovaks, Rumanians) resisted centralist tendencies; to Bohemia, Moravia and Silesia where the Czechs tried, unsuccessfully, to form a sovereign kingdom. The final stage of the revolution brought chaos to Vienna. On 6 October the revolutionaries occupied the railroad station from where Austrian grenadiers were to be sent from Vienna to Hungary. The soldiers and grenadiers mutinied

33 Landhaus (House of the Lower Austrian Estates), starting point of the March Revolution

and joined the revolutionaries. They stormed the war ministry and the war minister, Count Latour, was lynched. Emperor Ferdinand and his court fled to Olomouc, Moravia, and over a hundred thousand Viennese left the city. Field Marshal Prince Alfred Windischgrätz was named supreme commander and he marched against Vienna.

The revolutionaries' last hope was the insurgent Hungarian army, which was reported near and coming to their help. A state of siege was proclaimed. Once again the city walls and bastions were turned into barricades, while the forces of Windischgrätz – nearly fifty thousand men – began to shell the isolated city. Windischgrätz demanded unconditional surrender; the siege continued; on the fourth day the Hungarians were said to be near, but they were defeated. By now the situation was hopeless; during the last days the worst street fighting occurred near the gates of the Imperial Palace – exactly where the climax of the Turkish siege in 1683 had taken place.

On 31 October Windischgrätz and his army entered Vienna. Military dictatorship was proclaimed. The day of reckoning was near. Emperor Ferdinand abdicated, and his eighteen-year-old nephew became Emperor Franz Joseph I. In November 1848 nine people were executed and more executions were to follow. According to the Austrian historian, Alexander Bach, 2,375 people were arrested, but no one knows exactly how many people died during and after the revolution, which ended on a typically Viennese note, in recrimination and scepticism. The dust had not yet settled before the Viennese were asking themselves, flippantly, with characteristic self-irony, 'Why did we have to start the whole damn business?' Nothing had been achieved. (In *Freiheit im Krähwinkel*, the finest play to come out of the 1848 revolution, and actually performed during the revolution, Johann Nestroy predicted that everything would be just as it had been before.) In Europe, the Viennese revolution was overshadowed by the national liberation wars in Hungary and Italy where great revolutionaries, such as Kossuth and Mazzini, captivated people's imagination, while in Vienna the resistance of the workers and students 'was viewed with scepticism by the better-off sections of the population' (Heinrich Friedjung).

Freedom of the press was rescinded; there would be no more public trials. In 1850, the twenty-year-old Emperor Franz Joseph I wrote to his mother, 'On Sunday there was a great church parade on the *Glacis*, to show our dear Viennese

34 Civic Arsenal, headquarters of the students' National Guard in 1848

that troops and guns still exist ...'. That year absolute monarchy was re-intro-
duced, and a proclamation of the emperor said, '... disturbing are the effects not
of freedom, but of the misuse of freedom. To stop this misuse, and to end the
revolution, is Our duty and Our will ...'. Only in 1854 did the emperor eventually rescind the state of siege which had now lasted for eight years.

FRANZ JOSEPH I

Youth has long been somewhat suspect in Vienna; it is synonymous with rashness
and rebellion, inexperience and outright danger. Youth cannot be trusted; old
age implies wisdom. This attitude stems from a mentality which became widespread toward the end of the monarchy. '*The* emperor' – Franz Joseph I – is still
called 'the old gentleman' by the old gentlemen in Vienna who remember him.
In 1900, when they were young, he was already seventy years old. Nowadays the
emperor reappears occasionally on the stage in some Viennese operetta as a
charming and well-loved character. He is always portrayed as '*alter Herr*', be-
whiskered and benevolent; many Viennese believe that the Good Lord in heaven must look like 'the old gentleman'. During the performance of one of these
operettas the audience has been known to get up from their seats, cheering and
applauding, as the actor playing the part of the emperor appeared on the stage;
in fact as though he *were* the emperor. Foreigners were baffled by what they
thought was a monarchist demonstration. Actually it was only the baroque Viennese, with their passion for confusing the stage with life. Even staunch anti-
monarchists in Vienna who have no use for Otto von Habsburg, the present head
of the family, love Franz Joseph I (or rather, the legend of 'the old gentleman').
When the emperor was portrayed recently as a remote, tired old man in a realistic television version of Joseph Roth's *Radetzkymarsch*, hundreds of enraged
viewers wrote letters of protest against this demolition of a legend. Vienna's
socialist administration has placed the emperor's monument in an inconspicuous
place, near the children's playground in Burggarten, but there are often fresh
flowers laid before it. In the unlikely event of a plebiscite being held, the Austrians would not vote for a return of the Habsburgs but they cherish the memory
of Franz Joseph I.

   For a long time the emperor's image was blurred, oscillating between that of

35 Monument to Franz Joseph I in the Burggarten

the heroic ruler unable to prevent the break-up of his empire and a senile old man terminating his public appearances with the phrase, '*Es war sehr schön, es hat mich sehr gefreut*' (It has been very nice, I've been very pleased). But now the picture is coming into focus. There is much evidence in Franz Joseph's letters, to his wife, to his daughter, and to the actress, Katharina Schratt, that he was quite different from the legend created by the operettas and illustrated weekly papers, and from the anti-legend created by critical politicians, writers and historians. Franz Joseph I was an unhappy, lonely man. Hermann Broch calls him 'the abstract monarch ... the epitome of majesty ... not because he carried a burden of personal misfortune almost as excessive as in a Greek tragedy ... but because he had come to be, perhaps through his very weaknesses, capable of taking upon himself the awe-inspiring dignity of absolute loneliness ... Being the opposite of a people's emperor he yet was "the" emperor in the eyes of the people.'

THE 'MAYERLING DRAMA'

The unhappy emperor had warmth for the few people close to him and devotion to his inherited duty (which he hated). He had courage, integrity and a strong sense of austerity (not exactly widespread Austrian characteristics). His working day began at five in the morning. He lived in super-splendid isolation, seeing only his ministers and the archdukes and archduchesses of the Imperial family, but rarely 'ordinary' aristocrats. His only relaxation was stalking chamois and stag in the Alps. His personal life was tragic. In the early morning hours of 30 January 1889, the emperor was told that during the night his only son, Crown Prince Rudolph, had shot first Mary Vetsera, a seventeen-year-old girl from a rich, socially ambitious Viennese family, and then had shot himself, in the bedroom of his small hunting lodge in Mayerling, in the Wienerwald. There is little 'mystery' left about this 'Mayerling drama' which has fascinated generations of Viennese. In 1955 the records of Baron Krauss, at that time Vienna's chief of police, were published in facsimile. The basic facts of the drama are all confirmed, and so are some of Baron Krauss' dubious activities. (As soon as the tragedy was discovered, Baron Krauss ordered the body of Mary Vetsera to be taken away, propped up with a stick in the back and made to look as though she were sitting upright and alive between her two uncles, the brothers Baltazzi.

36 Votivkirche, commemorating Franz Joseph I's escape from assassination in 1853

That night the poor girl was furtively buried in the secluded Cistercian Abbey of Heiligenkreuz, but the reporters later discovered the grisly details when they talked to Mary Vetsera's mother.)

The first, hastily published reports of Rudolph's 'heart attack' were later denied. Against the wishes of nearly all his court advisers, the emperor decided to tell the people the truth, or at least the basic facts. Rudolph was said to have taken his life in a moment of depression, 'while the balance of his mind was disturbed'.

There was no official Church opposition to his being buried, with sombre pomp, in the Habsburg vault below the Capuchin church. The court ceremonial ordered 'one month of deepest mourning, one month of deep mourning, one month of minor mourning' for the crown prince. (No one mourned, officially, for the young girl he had shot.) It is only the motive of the tragedy that has never been clearly established. It might have been political: against the wish of the emperor, Rudolph was getting involved with Hungarian politics and a clique of Viennese 'progressives', and it was no secret that there was a rift between the 'conservative' father and his 'liberal' son. Others have found a motive in Rudolph's emotional and physical make-up; he was given to bouts of heavy drinking, suffered from sudden, violent spells of depression and often spoke of suicide. He was often involved with women, society women and *demi-mondaines*; his marriage was a failure; and he was said to owe over three hundred thousand florins. Two years before his death he had been treated for what may have been syphilis.

Yet Crown Prince Rudolph remains a romantic legend in Vienna, a dashing, elegant army officer who always did his duty and managed to conceal his personal problems. Only a lowly Viennese *Fiaker* (the driver of a two-horse coach) with the unlikely name of Bratfisch was really close to him and knew about most of his affairs.

EMPRESS ELISABETH AND DIE SCHRATT

Nine years after the death of his son, Franz Joseph I went through agony again. In Territet, near Geneva, one day in 1898, an anarchist, Luigi Lucheni, fatally stabbed the Empress Elisabeth. Elisabeth, whom the Viennese affectionately

37 Main staircase of the Burgtheater

called 'Sissy', is now, because of her beauty and her unhappy marriage, very much a romantic legend in her own right. (The young Austrian emperor had been engaged to her older sister, saw the pretty Elisabeth and fell in love with her at first sight.) Elisabeth was very popular in Vienna when she first came there. She was young and lovely, and on very bad terms with her widely disliked, formidable mother-in-law, the domineering Archduchess Sophie of Bavaria who was also Elisabeth's aunt. Archduchess Sophie, a product of rigid court ceremonial, would have frightened a stronger person than Elisabeth. Everybody sympathised with her, but gradually she antagonised the Viennese by her attitude toward the emperor ('she should have made him happy' they said), and because of her mysterious 'double life'. She was often away from the capital, travelling in Hungary and in Greece, fox-hunting in England, and her absences created gossip.

Elisabeth certainly manifested a sense of feminine realism – and of 'nobility', according to the legend – when she arranged for her husband to meet Frau Katharina Schratt, the Burgtheater actress whom he admired. The story of Katharina Schratt is, of course, *the* favourite Viennese legend. How the emperor would slip out through a narrow door in the Schönbrunn Palace garden wall, at seven in the morning, to have an early breakfast with Frau Schratt in her small villa in Gloriette-Gasse. The 'Schratt villa' is still there, on a charming street corner, not far from the house where Johann Strauss, Vienna's musical poet of the era, wrote *Die Fledermaus*.

The evidence today debunks the romantic notion of a passionate love affair between the emperor and Frau Schratt. Franz Joseph needed companionship and 'die Schratt' (when someone gets famous in Vienna, the first name is dropped and substituted by 'the', *die* or *der*) was gay, understanding, talked well and was a good listener. She gave him peace of mind.

Die Schratt was thirty-three when the emperor, then over fifty, met her. He must have been very much in love with her. She was a pretty woman, handsome-looking in a healthy way, a good though not a great actress, and she entertained the Austrian emperor with Burgtheater backstage gossip. She had been married and was separated from her husband, a Hungarian nobleman. She was (almost) on friendly terms with Franz Joseph's wife; sometimes the Empress Elisabeth and Frau Schratt would diet together, watching their progress on the scales;

Elisabeth loved to diet. After her tragic death, die Schratt withdrew from the emperor. In his last years he was lonelier than ever, cheered up only occasionally by his small grandchildren.

BUREAUCRATIC CONSERVATISM

Around the old emperor there were old men: old ministers, old advisers, old generals, old court councillors. The old bureaucrat who serves patiently and inconspicuously until he reaches the climax of his career and retires with a pension has long been the ideal of the *Wienertum*, the Viennese of all classes. The emperor would sign the important papers, the ministers would counter-sign them, but it was a *k.k. (kaiserlich-königlicher) Hofrat*, court councillor, who had written the important first draft ('... it was *kaiserlich-königlich*, Imperial-Royal, and it was *kaiserlich und königlich*, Imperial and Royal', writes Robert Musil. 'One of the two abbreviations, *k.k.* or *k. & k.*, applied to every thing and person, but esoteric lore was nevertheless required in order to be sure of distinguishing which institutions and persons were to be referred to as *k.k.* and which as *k. & k.* This country's ... bureaucracy could be accused of only one defect', continues Musil. 'It could not help regarding genius and enterprise in private persons, unless privileged by high birth or state appointment, as ostentation, indeed presumption.') The bureaucrats still speak their own idiom, a Viennese dialect interspersed with many French-Italian-Latin expressions (Hofmannsthal uses it in *Rosenkavalier*). They are masters of what Musil's translators, Eithne Wilkins and George Kaiser, define as 'a system of beautifully balanced compromises in every sphere, which the Austrians call "*fortwursteln*" and the English call "muddling through" '. Virtuosos of ambiguity, masters of the dilatory phrase, all sentences begin with 'Possibly', 'Perhaps', 'Most probably'. Perhaps the only thing they would not want to be ambiguous about is their titles.

The Viennese infatuation with bureaucratic and other titles goes back to the reign of Charles VI. The burghers had lost their privileges, the middle class was getting an inferior position; money was made and lost; but a title was something permanent; it gave a certain status. The baroque era had created the notion of people's 'God-given' rank. Each person had his rank and had to represent it. Emperor Leopold I, in a special 'police decree', divided his subjects into five categories, giving exact details as to what each person was permitted to have by way of clothes, jewellery, servants. Even the number of wigs was regulated, the number of guests a person was permitted to invite to a wedding, and the number of candles to be used at a funeral. Class I was made up of Imperial officials (the predecessors of the later court bureaucrats), and of secretaries, lawyers, physicians, and conductors and assistant conductors of Leopold's beloved *Hofkapelle*, the Imperial Orchestra. 'Ordinary musicians' were placed in Class II, together with accountants, mayors, judges. Class III was made up of lackeys, cellar masters, well-to-do burghers, painters, sculptors and engravers. Cooks, sacristans, doormen and hunters were in Class IV. Workers, *das gemeine Volk* (the common people) and other non-persons were way down in Class V. In this God-given, baroque society one was born into one's class; few people managed to climb into a higher class. (Just as today. 'Everybody knows his own place', writes Hilde Spiel. 'After fifty years of a republican state, people respect differences in rank, and revere titles and inherited position.')

Under Emperor Charles VI, and later under Empress Maria Theresia and Emperor Joseph II, the enlightened absolutist monarch, a sort of 'minor nobility' was granted to deserving officials. Members of the minor nobility expected to be addressed by the fraternal '*du*' (thou) when they met members of the 'real' (born) nobility. This created problems for it was not always certain whether a person belonged to the real or the minor nobility. Today the Viennese are as conscious of titles as ever, using them quite subtly, expressing respect or disapproval in the title which they give to a man. There are inherited titles, academic titles, and titles which are awarded by the population and require neither ancestors nor degrees. As a result, nearly everybody has a title in Vienna. There are men who do not own a 'good, dark suit' but they have a title which does more for their ego than the dark suit. It is not polite to address a man by his name; one has to call him by his title, either his actual title or, if one wants to be *really* nice, by the title he would like to have, always one notch above his present title. Thus the *Herr Buchhalter* (bookkeeper) is respectfully addressed by his employees as '*Herr Oberbuchhalter*' ('head-bookkeeper'), a simple waiter ('*Kellner*') becomes head-waiter ('*Oberkellner*', or just '*Herr Ober*', for short) and a vice-president must be addressed '*Herr Präsident*', unless you want to offend him. Often the prefix '*Haupt*', as in *Hauptmann*, is used. There are people titled

'*Amtsrat*' (councillor) and others who are addressed '*Wirklicher Amtsrat*', real councillor, which creates the rather baroque notion that the ordinary *Amtsrat* may not be real at all. The lower a man's position, the longer his title: *Herr Ministerialsekretär, Herr Kanzleiunteroffizial.* Consequently monosyllabic titles have become very elegant.

A title is a valuable substitute for money. It is less expensive to give a man a prefix to his title than to raise his salary or buy him a gold watch. (The prefix is certainly more valuable than a gold-plated watch.) Nowadays many people can afford to buy a good watch but how many are chosen to become *Ministeria[i]oberkommissar* or *Amtsoberrevident*? Women and widows are often addressed after their husbands' titles. The wife of a doctor becomes '*Frau Doktor*', the wife of a general manager '*Frau Generaldirektor*'. If the deceased husband was only a *Rentner* (pensioner), his widow may still be addressed '*Frau Rentnerswitwe*'. The owner of a house is 'Mr Landlord', if he is nothing else. If he has a factory, he is '*Herr Fabrikant*', an arch-capitalist.

Certain titles are subtle insults. Nearly every person wearing glasses automatically becomes a '*Doktor*', and a bald-headed, heavy-set man is often addressed as '*Herr Direktor*'. Waiters, porters and taxi-drivers call their customers '*Herr Baron*', generally considered a somewhat vulgar expression, or perhaps '*Exzellenz*', if they expect a really good tip. (Other people titled '*Exzellenz*' are members of the diplomatic corps, even below the rank of ambassador, or owners of large American automobiles, though the final instalment may still be unpaid.)

Viennese aristocrats with old, inherited titles sometimes honour their more plebeian friends by adding 'von' to the commoner's name. That means that the commoner is 'accepted', even though he does not actually 'belong'. At certain Viennese balls (the invitations say 'white-tie and decorations') one is almost certain to meet a gentleman with a non-existent title, a rented dress suit and an impressive row of decorations bought at a local store.

There exist baroque titles in Vienna. The captain of a Danube River steamer calls himself *Donaudampfschiffahrtsgesellschaftskapitän* (Captain-of-the-Danube-Steamship-Company). Among the Schema-1 employees of the Vienna City Administration there is a *Feldbahnfeuerlokomotivführer* (engineer-of-a-field-railway-fire-engine), a *Niederdruckheizer* (fireman-of-a-low-pressure-boiler), a *Naphthalinaufbereiter* (naphthalene dresser, whatever *he* may do). Some church

39 Imperial arms surmounting the Wing of the Imperial Chancellery in the Hofburg, centre of baroque court officialdom

titles have bizarre abbreviations – such as 'Pfrmprv.' for '*Pfarrmitprovisor*', or 'Pfrexprv.' for '*Pfarrexurandoprovisor*'. The title 'Professor' is usually awarded by the populace as a token of genuine respect. At the Vienna State Opera, the old ushers call their long-time habitués who have shown loyalty and stamina during long nights of *Siegfried* and *Palestrina* simply '*Herr Professor*'. And if a man happens to have several titles – suppose he is *Doktor, Direktor, Kommerzialrat* and President of the Chamber of Commerce, one uses his most distinguished title, '*Herr Präsident*'.

Prince Metternich who came from an old, aristocratic Rhineland family and set up a police bureaucracy in Austria, used to say, 'Austria is not ruled, it is being administered'. To belong to those who administer the country is the wish of many inhabitants. In Vienna, not only members of the bureaucracy are public officials but also railwaymen, postmen, gendarmes, the ushers at the state theatres, streetcar conductors, the riders of the Lippizaner horses at the Spanish Riding School, and the members of the Vienna Philharmonic. All of them are *unkündbar* after a certain time of service (they cannot be fired), and will eventually receive a pension amounting to 80 per cent of their last salary. One fifth of the country's working population are public officials; one third of the country's entire budget is spent on them. Many people dream of being pensioners; and when their dream comes true at last, the pensioners say, 'It isn't much but at least we've *got* it.' A little security is highly valued in a traditionally insecure city. A young official starts out with the equivalent of twenty pounds a month; three out of four civil servants earn forty pounds a month or less.

At the higher bureaucratic levels the various councillors – *Herr Amtsrat, Herr Regierungsrat, Herr Hofrat, Herr Oberbergrat* – dominate the bureaucratic society. They have spent many years of faithful though undistinguished service to become what they are, and they are deeply conscious of their position and title. They do not believe in short cuts to success. Young officials who want to make a career in public service are expected 'to behave and be patient'. It will take years before they may *hope* for a promotion and even more years before their promotion comes through. Young people are supposed to do only what they are permitted to do. When Emperor Ferdinand I was told, on 13 March 1848, that the students of Vienna were demonstrating in the streets he asked, in genuine wonder, 'But who gave them permission?'

40 Grillparzer's living-room, a typical apartment of a middle-class government official

Ever since, Austria's schools have moulded ambitious young men into pliable, prematurely old men who are taught the Austrian art of compromise and are constantly warned not to show any initiative or enterprise. During the monarchy, the young men studied the technique of the meaningless smile and the facility of the conventional phrase. They were told to greet their elders with the phrase 'I have the honour', and to kiss the hand of a lady. 'The schools of Old Austria educated at the Theresianum and in Kalksburg [a famous Jesuit college near Vienna] the best specimens of characterless youth', wrote Max Graf, the noted critic. And Robert Musil writes in *The Man without Qualities:*

> Ever since [the world] has existed, most people have in their youth been in favour of turning things upside down. They have always felt that their elders were ridiculous in being so attached to the established order of things and in thinking with their heart – a mere lump of flesh – instead of with their brains. These younger people have always noticed that the moral stupidity of their elders is just as much a lack of any capacity to form new combinations as is ordinary intellectual stupidity.... Nevertheless, by the time they reach years of fulfilment they have forgotten all about it and are far from wishing to be reminded of it....

In Vienna today, bureaucratic conservatism still dominates public thinking. The Viennese ideal was always a certain mediocrity – the bland, faceless, polite nonentity who came 'from the right family' and had 'good manners'. Talent was – and is – suspect, and genius dangerous.

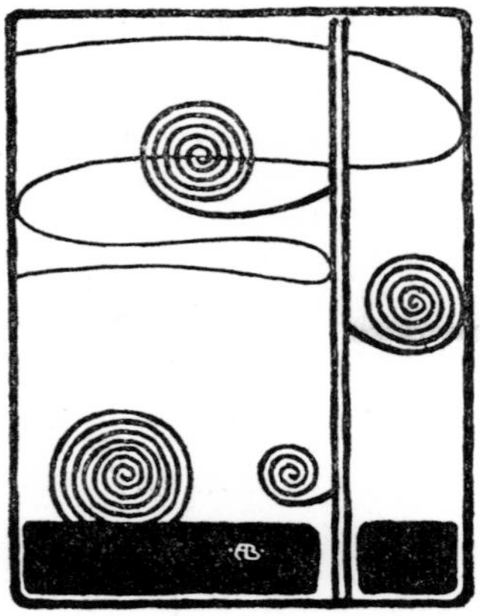

2

The City of Vienna

A MIXTURE OF STYLES

The Viennese know much about music but relatively little about the second most important among their creative arts. They are rather vague about the meaning of 'baroque' in architecture and give this name to any building with no recognisable style. Many Viennese who have never studied music can tell the difference between a late Haydn and an early Mozart symphony (not always easy to recognise, even for a trained musician), and know too that Beethoven was 'a composer of symphonies', that Schubert wrote mostly *lieder*, that Richard Strauss and Oskar Straus, the operetta composer, were no relatives of the 'waltz kings'. But about their architecture they know little, because they do not really care. Otto Wagner, a prominent architect around the turn of the century, and one of the original members of the 'Secession' movement in 1897, once said that the Votive Church, an elegant structure in French (neo)-Gothic, meant a lot to the Viennese 'because they can easily see it is Gothic'.

The Votivkirche was built on the site of the attempted assassination of the young emperor Franz Joseph I in 1853. (A popular folksong later castigated the fumbling would-be assassin for his failure.) At night, during the tourist season, the Votive Church is beautifully illuminated by projectors hidden inside. It is a fairy-tale sight, looking as if it had been made out of marzipan by the famous Viennese guild of pastry cooks and sugarmakers. In 1883, Heinrich Ferstel, the architect who designed the Votivkirche and the new university, wrote to the famous Danish architect Theophil Hansen, who had been summoned to Vienna to build the Parliament and other important buildings, that before 1848, 'architecture was in a state of deepest degradation; architectural art was nothing but

42 Towers of Vienna at sunset

an expression of the bureaucratic system which dominated the state and the life of the people alike'.

Purists often criticise the mixture of styles that forms Vienna, but the city reflects two thousand years of Roman-German history and could hardly be different. Vienna's catacombs below St Stephen's date from the days of the Romans; the Roman element is also apparent in the crypt of the Michaelerkirche. The city has been called 'a collection of architectural treasures' but no great builder of the past thought of giving the collection a frame. Until the second half of the nineteenth century, architecture was considered something of a luxury in Vienna; the 'architectural treasures' were put up by rulers and rich noblemen and by the Church, 'those who can afford it'.

Few buildings in Vienna are 'easy to look at' for students of architecture. Examples of pure style are relatively rare – one is the pure Gothic of the fourteenth-century church, Sankt-Maria-am-Gestade, once the church of the fishermen, hidden in an inconspicuous part of the old city. A lovely cupola crowns its seven-sided tower. Nearby too is Vienna's oldest church, St Ruprecht, a fine example of pure Romanesque style. Other 'unspoiled' churches are the austere, early-Gothic Augustinerkirche near the Imperial Palace, and the lovely Minoritenkirche with its fine French-Gothic portal.

ST STEPHEN'S CATHEDRAL

But Vienna's most famous church, symbol, and city landmark, is St Stephen's Cathedral, a dear member of the family to most Viennese who are fond of their 'Steffl', even though they may never go inside. The pyramidal form of its powerful, elegant, tall southern tower, reaching from the fundament to the summit, is more pronounced than in the towers of Strasbourg, Cologne or Regensburg. These other great Gothic towers show the form of a pyramid only in their uppermost parts. The northern tower of St Stephen's has remained a torso. It was begun in Gothic style but the church ran out of money, and meanwhile the Gothic era came to an end. A green patina lid was put on top of the truncated tower; perhaps the church authorities considered that two tall, symmetric towers would be too overpowering for the nave with which there exists only a loose connection, and today the unfinished northern tower is as much part of

43 The dome of St Peter's and the roof and towers of St Stephen's

Vienna as Schubert's *Unfinished Symphony*. To finish the tower would be considered as sacrilegious as to attempt to 'finish' the symphony.

In 1137 Reginbert, the bishop of Passau, Bavaria, 'received' St Stephen's in Vienna, and in return was given a vineyard outside the walls of the town. In 1144, Oktavian Falkner began to build the parish church of St Stephen's, on the site of the present cathedral, which was then outside the walls of Vienna. It was dedicated in 1147 by the bishop of Passau, but burnt down in 1258, and again in 1276. Meanwhile the Babenberg dynasty had come to an end in Austria, and during the interregnum, 'the years of terror', Przemysl Ottokar II, king of Bohemia, ruled in Vienna, until his defeat on the Marchfeld in 1278 decided the future of the 'Holy Roman Empire of the German Nation'. Vienna, not Prague, was going to be its capital, and the residence of the Habsburg dynasty for seven centuries.

In 1290, the rebuilding of St Stephen's began. Everybody agreed that the capital would have to have a great cathedral worthy of Vienna's position in the Christian world. The early history of St Stephen's clearly expresses this ambition. Originally built in Romanesque style, it was expanded in Gothic style, and later the various styles were harmoniously and gracefully blended by Vienna's ubiquitous baroque. The ancient Romanesque west front – now the main entrance facing St Stephen's square – had been begun in 1259 under King Ottokar. Two Habsburg dukes, Albrecht I and Albrecht II, continued the expansion. What happened after that is a fascinating source of conjecture to students of architecture who (theoretically) knock off the roof between the two Romanesque towers, block up the Gothic window which was put into the wall in 1422, remove the Gothic balustrade below the roof, eventually to arrive at the 'original' Romanesque west front. Gothic additions, the nave and the choir, were not added until 1446, and ever since there have been changes and additions. The sounds of hammering have rarely stopped in and around the great church.

Spiritually, however, St Stephen's (which became a cathedral church only in 1469) is definitely Gothic – dark, sombre and austere. ('I went in and became suddenly pious', writes Leopold von Ranke in 1827. 'The darkness, the lights, the people praying, coming and going, created a strange magic; the trouble is that one's piety lasts only as long as one remains inside.') In the subterranean catacombs of St Stephen's thousands of skeletons lie buried. In the Prince's Vault

44 Detail from the Romanesque west porch of St Stephen's

the internal organs of the Habsburgs (except the hearts) were kept, while their embalmed bodies were buried in the Capuchin Church in Neuer Markt. After 1738, no more burials took place in St Stephen's. It is an overpowering, dark, mystical cathedral. People often instinctively escape out of the Gothic dimness toward one of the side altars with their gay, triumphant baroque.

FISCHER VON ERLACH: PALACES AND CHURCHES

Vienna's baroque is different from the original, Italian baroque (for instance the Gesù Church in Rome, finished in 1584). Its earliest sponsors were not the economically minded Habsburg rulers but the wealthy aristocrats ('I'm glad to see a country where the subjects have more elegant palaces than the ruler', wrote Montesquieu). After the Turkish Siege, when so many fine houses and palaces had been destroyed, new buildings were needed. The rich people had plenty of money and wanted to show their exalted position in the world. Austria's economic structure was rather unsound and, compared to France and England, quite reactionary. The wealthy people had no confidence in the financial policies of the Habsburg court and there was widespread fear that sooner or later the state would go bankrupt. It was safer to put up beautiful buildings than to invest one's money in more speculative ventures. The Viennese baroque, the biggest building boom in central-European history, was caused by what today would be called the flight of capital.

Vienna became 'a city of palaces', and the rich noblemen became dilettante architects and amateur builders. In his guidebook, Prince Liechtenstein admitted, 'One builds to leave beautiful monuments for eternal memory'. Building became a fad and a passion among the rich aristocrats. 'A devilish passion,' wrote Kurfürst Schönborn, 'but once you have started, you cannot stop.' And he asked, 'What would happen to artists and artisans whom God created if He did not also create fools to support them?' The golden era of Austria's baroque was financed almost completely by these rich noblemen who had caught the building craze – the Liechtensteins, Schwarzenbergs, Schönborns, Harrachs, Dietrichsteins, Althans, Starhembergs, and others. Luckily for them, there also existed at that time a wealth of great architects, gifted builders and, in general, fine artistic talents.

45 Staircase in Schönbrunn Palace
46 (*overleaf*) Wrought-iron gates of the Upper Belvedere

'We are fortunate,' said Pope Urban VIII after his enthronement, 'that Cavaliere Lorenzo Bernini lives at the time of our Pontificate.' The Viennese aristocrats did not have Cavaliere Bernini but they did have Johann Bernhard Fischer (later ennobled and called Fischer von Erlach). Fischer was born in Graz, Styria, and spent sixteen years in Rome as a pupil of Bernini, before coming to Vienna in 1678, to become the greatest builder of the Austrian baroque. With Lucas von Hildebrandt (his chief competitor) he ennobled the urban façade of Vienna. He died in 1723 and was buried, like Mozart, in an unmarked grave. Unlike Mozart though, Fischer von Erlach died a rich man, but his coffin was taken to St Stephen's at night, and the exact spot where he is buried remains unknown. The baroque cult of funerals had not yet begun.

It must have been a lucky day when a rich Viennese grandee, Johann Michael II Count Althan, discovered young Fischer, 'the fellow who was with Bernini'. The young man was living, rather impecuniously, with a sculptor in an old house in Vienna. Fischer von Erlach's career is given impressive outward form through the magnificent monuments he left 'for eternal memory'. He began with rather modest assignments, renovating and 'Italianising' the houses of noblemen living in the suburbs, but gradually took on more and more ambitious projects. At the same time Lucas von Hildebrandt, the protégé of Count Schönborn, was building small palaces, more Viennese in style then Fischer's projects. 'The great baroque architects,' writes Karl Scheffler, 'served the worldly glorification of their patrons. They were like actors – actors with a touch of genius.' Like actors and stage designers, the architects too created make-believe.

'The baroque builders worked fast', writes Wilhelm Hausenstein. 'There was no time to use marble, which was too heavy anyway for the needed dimensions. They needed flexible material – a mixture of plaster, lime and sand. Stucco could be easily formed and made everything possible. The material deceives the eye.' By 1720 there already existed two hundred palaces and summer villas in the gardens around Vienna. The inner city was terribly overcrowded but the rich could afford to build palaces outside the town walls, where they enjoyed themselves hunting and making their own wine in their vineyards. In the city many houses had elegant façades. Poverty was carefully kept out of sight.

In 1716 Lady Mary Wortley Montague, born Lady Mary Pierrepoint, the daughter of the fifth earl of Kingston, came to Vienna with her husband.

47 Court façade of the Starhemberg-Schönburg Palais by Lucas von Hildebrandt

Mr Montague, British ambassador to the Ottoman Porte, had been given the thankless assignment of mediating between Austria and Turkey. Lady Mary's impressions of Vienna, in her *Embassy Letters*, published after her death, give us an amusing, sometimes biased, always interesting view of baroque Vienna, which to her seemed so small and crowded. She writes,

> The town, which has the honour of being the emperor's seat, did not at all answer my idea of it, being much less than I expected to find it: the streets very close, and so narrow, one cannot observe the fine fronts of the palaces, though many of them very well deserve observation, being truly magnificent, all built of white stone....

What Lady Mary thought to be 'white stone' were really brick walls covered with white stucco. Apparently baroque Vienna was a 'white' or light-grey town, though today the city is almost as black as London. Lady Mary was puzzled, as so many people before and after her, by the contradiction between the elegant façades and the inconvenient interiors.

> The apartments of the greatest ladies, and even of ministers of state, are divided but by a partition from that of a tailor or shoemaker; and I know nobody that has above two floors in any house, one for their own use, and one high up for their servants. Those that have houses of their own let out the rest to whoever will take them; thus the great stairs (which are all of stone) are as common and dirty as the street.

But after entering the apartments, she was fascinated by the beauty and the luxury, the panelled walls, doors and windows,

> richly carved and gilt, and the furniture such as is seldom seen in the palaces of sovereign princes in other countries – the hangings are the finest tapestry of Brussels, prodigious large looking-glasses in silver frames, fine Japan tables, beds, chairs, canopies, and window curtains of the richest Genoa damask or velvet, almost covered with gold lace and embroidery....

Fischer von Erlach worked for the rich families in Vienna and Prague but his influence reached further – to Dresden, Warsaw, Salzburg, even to Berlin. His ambition was to build for the Habsburgs a summer palace which would make Versailles seem small, but the Habsburgs were less flamboyant than Louis XIV and Fischer was told to revise his costly project. When Schönbrunn was eventually built, after Fischer's death, it emerged as a much more modest palace than Fischer's original blueprint.

Fischer (and all baroque builders) was as concerned about the site of a building as about the building itself. Schönbrunn was his conception of what students

48 Rococo screen in the Dominican church

of architecture now call the 'exterior room'. Approaching the castle by way of Hütteldorferstrasse and arriving at the top of Schloss-Allee, one sees the straight axis that leads through the geometrical centre of the main gallery of the palace and up again to the exact centre of the Gloriette on top of a hill behind the palace. Unfortunately many people nowadays approach Schönbrunn by car and are more concerned with survival than with Fischer's great conception. The automobile has become the enemy of Vienna's baroque beauty.

Fischer also made the plans, and some of the sculptures, for the *Pestsäule* (Plague Memorial) that stands in Graben, commissioned by the pious Leopold I during the great plague of 1679. It is an exuberant baroque fantasy of figures, clouds, delicate reliefs and beautifully executed statuary, 'Faith Triumphant over Pestilence'. It is also a perfect test for people on their first encounter, in the middle of the crowded street, with Vienna's baroque. Puritans have been shocked by it. It is certainly theatrical, but it is also beautiful.

Fischer von Erlach's masterpiece in Vienna, the magnificent Karlskirche, is the result of another Habsburg's vow during an outbreak of plague.

In 1713, when the plague was at its height, Emperor Charles VI vowed to build a church to his patron saint, St Charles Borromeo, and asked his prominent architects to submit their plans. Fischer von Erlach won the competition against Hildebrandt and the successful theatrical designer, Galli-Bibbiena.

Karlskirche stands on a slight elevation above the large square called after St Charles. Several streets lead up to it in elegantly rounded curves which make the church look larger and higher than it actually is. It is a great expression of the high baroque – strange, bizarre, impressive and beautiful. The entrance is flanked by two free-standing 'Trajanesque' columns with spiral bas-reliefs depicting the life of St Charles. The columns have been compared to the Pillars of Hercules. Others interpret them as Fischer's vision of St Peter's in Rome, over Trajan's Column, seen from the top of the Pincio Gardens. With baroque exuberance, Fischer von Erlach built two columns instead of one, which probably pleased the emperor, as this was 'one up' on Rome. Inside the church, the faithful are overwhelmed by Rottmayr's large frescos, the gilt-stucco altar, the pomp and flamboyance; the immense cupola seems to reach straight towards heaven. St Charles' has been called a 'theatrical' church, and people sometimes find it difficult to pray there. It is certainly somewhat of a contrast to the dim, austere grandeur of St Stephen's. Fischer von Erlach never saw the church as it is now; he died in 1723, three years before Karlskirche was completed.

Baroque Vienna was an important centre for gifted architects, sculptors, stucco-workers, painters and carpenters who came from as far as Italy. Behind the noble palaces in Herrengasse, a distinguished street, the artisans lived in small houses. Anton Maulpertsch, Daniel Gran, Andrea Pozzo, Martin Altomonte and Gregorio Guglielmi painted the frescos in the churches and palaces built by Fischer and Hildebrandt. The building craze had certainly spread. In 1726, a chronicler reports that there was 'the smell of wet mortar all over town'.

LUCAS VON HILDEBRANDT: THE BELVEDERE

While Fischer von Erlach was working on Karlskirche, Hildebrandt was building *his* masterpiece for the man who expanded the empire of Charles VI and became the greatest military genius of his time. At the age of twenty, Prince Eugene of Savoy had been turned down by Louis XIV. The 'Sun King' loved beauty and Prince Eugene (according to the Duchess Liselotte von der Pfalz) was 'small and ugly ... a dirty little boy who does not seem to give hope for anything ...'. So the small and ugly prince went to Passau to offer his services to the small and ugly Emperor Leopold I. He received his baptism of fire during the great battle which ended the Turkish siege of Vienna, on 12 September 1683. Later Prince Eugene defeated the Turks so decisively that they never attempted a comeback. After the peace treaty of Passarowitz in 1718, the Habsburgs began to extend their power toward the Orient.

Prince Eugene, who never bothered to learn German and signed his name trilingually, 'Eugenio von Savoye', became Austria's 'secret emperor' and greatest art patron. He had a winter palace in Himmelpfortgasse (which has been for the last hundred and fifty years Austria's ministry of finance) and commissioned Lucas von Hildebrandt to build his summer palace on the most beautiful site in Vienna, on a slope overlooking the city and St Stephen's, with the silhouette of Kahlenberg in the rear. (Canaletto's nephew, Bernardo Bellotto, also called Canaletto in Vienna, has painted this magnificent view.) At the foot of the gently ascending slope Hildebrandt built the Lower Belvedere (which the Viennese pronounce in the French manner, 'Belve*dèr*-e', not as in Italian, 'Bel-*ve*dere'), a

50 The Upper Belvedere
51 (*overleaf left*) Frescoed garden room in the Upper Belvedere
52 (*overleaf right*) *Apotheosis of Prince Eugene*, by Balthasar
Permoser, commissioned by the prince for his Summer Palace

low, deceivingly simple-looking palace where the prince lived in beautiful rooms decorated with marble, gold and stucco. A terraced formal garden leads up to the top of the slope where Hildebrandt built the Upper Belvedere for Prince Eugene's great receptions. Here the rooms are even more magnificently decorated with marble and gold. In these rooms the general would receive the delegations from the Orient, using Imperial ceremonial as he represented the emperor. In these rooms were housed his collections of books, paintings and art treasures. Here he talked with his friends and their friends – Leibniz, Voltaire and Jean Baptiste Rousseau, his 'court poet', who said of the prince that he had 'a critical mind, cool, free from all vain ambition'. (Even so, it is reported that he kept on his hat when he received foreign dignitaries, thus assuming the emperor's prerogative.) The prince once remarked, 'With ten thousand florins a year I could finish my days. I have enough good books and I would not get bored.' He was no longer a Frenchman but not yet quite Austrian; he had become a European. He is still a legend in Vienna, hero of the folk song, '*Prinz Eugen, der edle Ritter*'.

It was from the Belvedere that Archduke Franz Ferdinand and his wife started out on their unhappy journey to Sarajevo in July 1914, from which they did not return alive. On 15 May 1955 the state treaty, which gave back to Austria its sovereignty and made it a permanently neutral state, was signed in the Hall of Marble in the Upper Belvedere by Messrs Dulles, Macmillan, Molotov, Pinay and Leopold Figl, Austria's late, courageous foreign minister, at the end of the occupation. Today the Belvedere is used as a magnificent gallery for exhibitions of paintings and sculptures (over 140,000 people came to look at the great van Gogh show in 1958, which surprised the music-minded Viennese), and as an almost perfect setting for Son et Lumière. Few visitors who come to see this spectacle on a warm summer night know that Anton Bruckner, whose artistic life began at the great baroque monastery of St Florian in Upper Austria, wrote his last symphony in the modest custodian's lodge attached to this glorious baroque palace. And it was there that he died one day in 1893.

RINGSTRASSE STYLE

Towards the end of the eighteenth century the inner city became increasingly a business district. It was still fashionable to live there but many people began

53   Figures from a garden pavilion in the Upper Belvedere

moving out into the suburbs where they had more space and air, more trees and gardens. It was a gradual development, which helped to create Vienna's present-day structure. Today the city's layout resembles a star; many of the main streets follow covered brooks. The inner city, formerly the medieval Vienna, is still the first *Bezirk* (district), which is surrounded by the Ringstrasse. Beyond the Ringstrasse are the *Vorstädte*, the inner suburbs, now the districts numbered from 2 to 10, into which the medieval town had expanded. The inner suburbs are, in turn, surrounded by a second concentric ring, called 'Innerer Gürtel' (inner belt). Around it are the *Vororte* (outer suburbs), the districts numbered from 11 to 23, the areas into which today's metropolis expanded from the Imperial city.

The earliest large buildings in these suburbs were the baroque *palais* of the aristocrats. (In Viennese parlance, a 'palace' has primarily representative functions while a *palais* is a sufficiently grandiose-looking mansion inhabited by the owners.) In the post-baroque era, the prosperous burghers and social climbers began to build their houses there. In the large lots between the houses workshops and small buildings tended to spring up. Since the baroque era the Viennese have always had a *horror vacui*; the baroque loves to fill every available space with ornamental detail, nothing most remain empty. In the districts of Mariahilf and Neubau the petit bourgeois and the Biedermeier nouveaux riches began to build small enclaves; there were new churches and even shopping districts. The character of the suburbs became steadily more confused.

When the eighteen-year-old Emperor Franz Joseph I ascended to the throne after the revolution in 1848 the Imperial city was surrounded by an outdated system of defences. The walls, moats and bastions which had held back the Turks had not held back Napoleon's armies. The *Glacis* had become a curiosity, a promenade for strollers who loved to walk there. Inner Vienna needed more space: it was high time to link the city with the suburbs. Late in December 1857, the official *Wiener Zeitung* published an Imperial Letter-Patent to Prime Minister Bach, dated 20 December. The emperor ordered the razing of the fortifications and the filling of the moats. Old Vienna was to lose its medieval face and to become a modern capital, New Vienna. The top of the wall bastion would be made into a wide boulevard, the Ringstrasse, surrounding the inner city in the shape of a horseshoe, its arms resting on the bank of a new Danube Canal. Its middle stretch would curve elegantly round the Imperial Palace.

54 Inner courtyard of a baroque house in the Neubau *Vorstadt*
55 (*overleaf*) Ringstrasse curving past the Burgtheater and Hofburg gardens, seen from the tower of the City Hall

There was unanimous agreement that 'the Ring' was to become 'the visible signal of the dignity, power and wealth of the empire'. Artists and architects were summoned from Austria and abroad. Projects were invited for January 1858, prizes were awarded to the winning blueprints, and in September 1859 the final decisions were made. Along the Danube Canal (the regulated southernmost arm of the Danube) a new 'Quai' was built. The ramparts were razed; only two sections of the old earth-work defences remain today – the Schottenbastei which had been a prominent target during the Turkish siege in 1683, and the beautiful Mölkerbastei, which was spared not for historical reasons but because there was not enough money to have it pulled down. On 1 May 1865 the Ringstrasse was opened when the emperor and the empress drove down among the cheers of Vienna's population.

Gradually, great buildings emerged on various key points. In between there would be palatial apartment houses on extremely expensive building sites. Unlike the baroque building boom of the eighteenth century, which had been financed by the Church and the noble families of the Habsburg court, the Ringstrasse building boom of the 1860s was created by the newly-rich bankers and industrialists. They alone could afford to pay the vast sums of money into the communal fund set up to pay for the new roads, parks and squares; and when the boom came to an end after the market crash in 1873, the fund also paid for the completion of several unfinished buildings. The most elegant apartment house was the Heinrichshof across from the future site of the Opera. It had been finished in 1863 and was soon fully occupied in spite of the high rentals. All the buildings, both public and private, had a common idea: they must 'represent'. There were to be various 'decorative' styles, called euphemistically by some optimists 'historical styles', with magnificent façades, big dimensions, pompous detail. It was not a slow, organic development, but a collective conception of able planners.

The first great building completed was, not surprisingly, the new Court Opera, which occupied the most valuable site, on the inner side of the Ring where the *via triumphalis* crosses Kärntnerstrasse, the city's most elegant shopping street. The opera house was built by Eduard van der Nüll and August von Siccardsburg in a romanticised neo-Renaissance style. The architects must have loved music, seeming to have conceived the house in terms of a symphony. The staircase and the foyer (the only parts to survive destruction during the last war) are decorated with statuary and paintings which seem to radiate the sound of music. Moritz von Schwind, a close friend of the late Franz Schubert, decorated the lunettes of the loggias with poetic reproductions from *The Magic Flute*. The ceiling of the auditorium had allegorical paintings by Carl Rahl, Christian Grienperkerl and Eduard Bitterlich. Purists may be amused by the confusion of mock-styles but the 'Oper' has always been close to the hearts of all Viennese – or nearly always. Before the filling in of the city moat it was confidently expected that the new opera house would be a tall, commanding structure. When the building was being erected, however, it seemed somewhat low and sunken, and it was bitterly criticised as 'an architectural Königgrätz', an allusion to a recent Austrian defeat. The emperor was said to be displeased. One of the architects, the oversensitive van der Nüll, became so depressed that in April 1868 he committed suicide. His friend Siccardsburg died two months later 'of a broken heart'. Neither of them saw the completed house.

The opera house opened on 25 May 1869, with *Don Giovanni*. The evening before a dress rehearsal was given, free of charge, for the artists' relatives and friends of the house, who were asked to come in street clothes. (The same pre-première happened in November 1955, when the rebuilt State Opera was opened; when the Viennese cannot have one première, they have two.) For the gala opening people paid one hundred florins for a box and twenty-five florins for a stall. (In 1955, top price for a stall was two hundred dollars.) The earlier opening must have been very spectacular, being attended by the emperor and the king of Hanover. The Empress Elisabeth was not there. She came a week later, accompanied by the emperor and the viceroy of Egypt, to hear Auber's *La Muette de Portici*. The newspapers reported that she wore 'a jewel-studded gown of light satin with a dark tulle wrap, in her luxuriant hair a golden clasp ablaze with precious stones'. There were many beautiful women in the audience but by general agreement she was the fairest of all.

After the Opera, the next two public buildings to be finished along the Ring were the two court museums. The Museum for the History of Art would house the great Habsburg art treasures – paintings, Greek and Roman antiquities, ivories, Renaissance bronzes, tapestries. The paintings comprise a fine fifteenth-century Flemish collection (Jan van Eyck, Roger van der Weyden, Hans Memling); German sixteenth-century masterpieces (Dürer, Holbein, Lukas Cranach); a

57 Museum for the History of Art and Maria Theresia monument
58 (*overleaf left*) Archduke Leopold William in his picture gallery; his Italian paintings formed the nucleus of the Habsburg collection
59 (*overleaf right*) Stallburg, where the collection was first housed

fine Venetian Renaissance collection (great Bellinis, Giorgiones, Lottos, Palmas, Titians, Tintorettos) ; magnificent paintings by Rembrandt, Velasquez, Rubens, and probably the world's finest Pieter Breughel collection, about half of all the surviving paintings.

(During the second world war, many paintings and art treasures from Vienna were brought to the salt mines deep in the mountains of the lovely Salzkammergut which offered natural storage rooms, bomb-proof, with ideal temperatures of 54 degrees Fahrenheit, and a steady humidity of 65 per cent. Most paintings from Vienna were brought to the Laufen salt mines, near Bad Ischl, while Goering and other Nazi 'collectors' had their stolen treasures stored in the mines of Altaussee. The largest paintings from Vienna were taken to the monastery in nearby Klosterneuburg and stored in its deepest cellars; some were kept in the low vaults of the Post Office Savings Bank in Vienna. The Austrian authorities had considered all eventualities except the destruction of the art treasures by a madman. Yet this is what almost happened. During the final weeks of the war, Ausseerland, the countryside around Altaussee, in Styria, became Hitler's 'Alpine fortress'. The local Gauleiter, an SS-Führer named Eigruber, planned to 'camouflage' the art treasures; many had been looted from museums in France, Italy, Belgium, Denmark, Holland. The Nazis had found several dud bombs which had been dropped by US Air Force planes. The bombs were disassembled, repacked as fuse bombs with explosives and concealed in crates which were then placed alongside the paintings. Eigruber was prepared to explode the bombs before the Americans arrived there so that later, American shell fragments would be found near the destroyed paintings, proving 'wanton destruction by the Americans'. Fortunately members of the Austrian Resistance got there in time and guarded the paintings until the Americans arrived and US experts removed the fuses.)

Across from the Museum for the History of Art, the next public building to be finished was the Museum for Natural History, a twin structure with neo-Renaissance façade and cupola. Between the two museums is a formal garden with a large statue of the Empress Maria Theresia, surrounded by her marshals. Gottfried Semper, the famous German architect, had proposed to turn the whole site into an 'Imperial Forum' which would dwarf anything built since the days of the Romans. Semper wanted to link the two museums by a pair of triumphal

60   Fünfhaus church by Friedrich Schmidt, architect of
the new Town Hall

arches across Ringstrasse with two new wings of the Imperial Palace. The grandiose project remained unfinished. Only one new wing of the Imperial Palace was built; the other space became a beautiful garden, not open to the public until the Austrian republic in 1918 opened all feudal preserves to the people.

Nearby the Danish architect Theophil Hansen built the white Parliament, in neo-Hellenistic style with functionally successful interiors. Hansen was also the architect of the neo-Renaissance Musikverein, opened in 1869, with its large, gilt-pilastered concert hall, considered by many musicians to be the finest in the world, because of its acoustics and the sense it gives of both size and intimacy, as though it were an enormous music room, where music is 'made', not just performed.

In 1883, the neo-Gothic Town Hall was inaugurated, a dark, powerful building to inspire civic pride, faintly reminiscent of the Gothic town halls in Belgium which had influenced Friedrich Schmidt, the architect. Across from the Town Hall, on the inner side of the Ring, stands the new Burgtheater, representing to German-speaking Europeans what the Comédie-Française in Paris is to the French. After fourteen years of building, the Burgtheater was a bitter disappointment. The entrances into the auditorium were too small, from thirty-two boxes one could not see the stage, the acoustics were bad, and there was no space backstage for storing the sets. In 1897 the theatre was completely rebuilt and emerged in today's form; it was still criticised for its pretentious mock-Renaissance style. However the Burgtheater does convey the message common to all the Ringstrasse buildings: it 'represents'.

Most critics of the new Ringstrasse were influenced in their criticisms by the medieval character and genuine styles of the old city; they disliked the pretentious mixture of 'decorative' pseudo-styles. The critics were younger people, not inspired by the pride and enthusiasm of the earlier generation of Ringstrasse architects who honestly believed that they had created 'the visible symbol of the dignity, power and wealth of the empire'. Architecturally the Ringstrasse remains a doubtful mixture; but it is definitely a masterpiece of landscaping. Its planners, men of vision, made use of large parks and green spaces – such as the Burggarten, the Volksgarten, and the Heldenplatz between them – to blend the somewhat preposterous jumble of 'historical' styles into a beautiful and harmonious synthesis. As one stands in Heldenplatz one has a panoramic view of the

61   Villa in the 'cottage' style in Rodaun (23rd District)

two museums, the Parliament, the Town Hall, the neo-Renaissance University, the Burgtheater and the Imperial Palace. In between are gardens and parks; there are the rows of trees on the Ringstrasse, with the baroquely rounded, bluish silhouette of Kahlenberg in the rear. Suddenly, one is no longer bothered by the eclecticism of the Ringstrasse buildings. Mysteriously, an orderly design seems to grow out of the jumble of mock styles, and what before seemed without style now becomes a harmonious whole. One is reminded of the confluence of musical classicism and romanticism which occurred right here, of the sounds of Biedermeier blending with the first sounds of the strange new music which was eventually to extend the horizon of music and create a new musical universe. Somehow, the Ringstrasse *does* emerge in a style of its own, and one can understand why the proud monarchists and pretentious nouveaux riches of the 1890s talked of 'the new Ringstrasse style'.

The Ringstrasse had its finest hour in 1879, when Emperor Franz Joseph 1 and Empress Elisabeth celebrated their silver wedding. Hans Makart, the painter whose name became synonymous with sensuous decadence and decorative extravaganza, and later with a pompous style of living, was the producer of the supershow, a late-baroque spectacle to delight the baroque ancestors of the Viennese. (Makart, a Salzburger who had studied in Venice, filled the dining rooms of his rich patrons with 'allegory upon allegory ... in the style of the old Venetians', as his biographer, Emil Pirchan, describes it. A good showman, Makart gave sensational parties in his bric-à-brac study in Gusshausstrasse which scandalised Viennese society – except those who were invited. He fascinated the gossipmongers with his love affairs. It was a favourite parlour game in the 1880s to guess the identity of the allegorical nudes in his paintings.) For the silver wedding he 'composed' an enormous pageant, designing every single costume, every float of the long procession. It moved from Praterstern by way of the Ringstrasse to the Imperial Palace. The emperor and empress watched from an official tent as the floats, riders, heralds, flags, bands, guilds, corporations, citizens – more than ten thousand people in all – filed past. It was the most colourful, most brilliant pageant in the pageant-rich history of Vienna. Makart himself, wearing a Rubens-like costume (he was a great admirer of Rubens *and* of Rubens' nudes) mounted a white charger and led the whole show. The horse almost threw him; quite a few people regretted that it did not.

62   Old tea-boxes in a Vienna grocery

ADOLF LOOS: THE HOUSE WITHOUT EYEBROWS

In 1898 an unknown young architect, Adolf Loos, was assigned by the leading Viennese newspaper, *Neue Freie Presse*, to write a series of critical articles. In one of them he called Vienna 'Die Potemkinsche Stadt', Potemkin's city, an allusion to Potemkin's cardboard-façade villages which the Russian general had put up in the Ukraine to impress Catherine the Great. Loos, then a twenty-eight-year-old firebrand, mercilessly attacked the pretentiousness of the Ringstrasse style, the false fronts 'stuck on with nails', the ornamental stucco details made to look like stone, the whole orgy of imitation. He called the Ringstrasse architecture 'an era of parvenus'. He exhorted the Viennese to accept what they were and told them that they must stop trying to live in stage-decoration-like houses with their fake styles, 'hoping that no one else will notice they are fake'.

There was no contemporary style in Vienna in 1898. Separating true from false, art from imitation, Loos did for architecture what the great satirist and moralist Karl Kraus was then doing for literature. The titles of the collected writings of Loos, *Ins Leere gesprochen* (Beating the air), and *Trotzdem* (Nevertheless) indicate his sense of frustration. In 1910 Loos built the first functional apartment house in Michaeler Square, soon to be called 'the house without eyebrows' because it had neither ornaments nor window-frames. But many of his projects remained on the drawing board. 'Later generations will understand why he had inscribed on his tombstone, "Adolf Loos who relieved mankind from unnecessary labour",' Oskar Kokoschka said in 1933.

THE SECESSIONISTS: THE LIVING STYLE OF A DYING CITY

In 1898, when Loos was writing his critical essays, a group of young Austrian artists who had the previous year 'seceded' from the Künstlerhaus, the Viennese Art Establishment, to protest against the society's conservative policies, had founded the 'Secessionists' ('Union of Austrian Artists') and moved into a modern building in Getreidemarkt built by Joseph Olbrich, from where they published an avant-garde magazine, *Ver Sacrum*. Their ideals of a 'Sacred Spring' were to fight against the eclectic, the epigonal, the pretentious. They wanted to rejuvenate 'the living style of a dying city'. 'That old *Musikstadt* Vienna could be made to feel excited about problems of the formative arts, is the greatest

63 Secession building by Joseph Olbrich
64 (*overleaf*)   Old and new Vienna, from the north tower St Stephen's

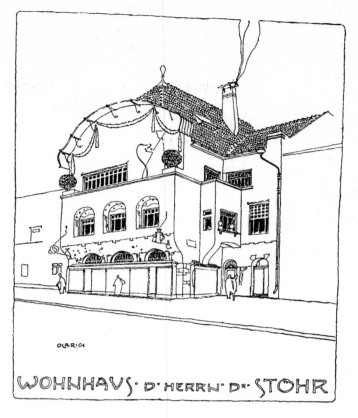

WOHNHAVS · D·HERRN· D·· STOHR

success of the Secessionists', wrote Ludwig Hevesi, one of its spokesmen. 'Only
the battle and victory of the Wagnerians, in Vienna and elsewhere, can be compared to it.' For a while Vienna became a spring board for what later became
known as the phenomenon of modern art. Among members of the movement
were the architect Otto Wagner, who designed the Vienna Underground Railway and built his own functional house in Vienna in 1904 ('Only modern life
can be the starting point of our artistic effort – everything else is archeology');
the painter Gustav Klimt, who developed his own style and became a predecessor of the Expressionists; Egon Schiele, a gifted painter who pictured the ugly
side of life 'with painful intensity' and died in 1918, at the age of twenty-eight;
Richard Gerstl, another early Expressionist, whose hectic motives and 'dead'
landscapes were not understood by his contemporaries, a very Viennese painter
with his combination of sensuousness and a strong death-wish, who committed
suicide in 1908; and the architect Joseph Hoffmann, creator of *Wiener Werk-
stätte* (Vienna Workshop), whose idea was to combine 'clarity of function and
structure with gracefulness and elegance'.

As a group, the Secessionists did not last long but they proved to Vienna, and

Joseph Hoffman
and Koloman
Moser

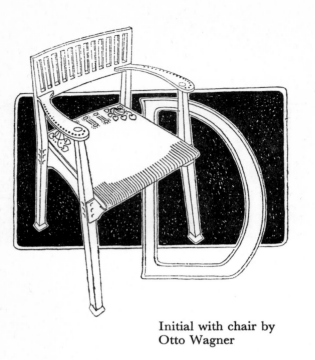

Initial with chair by
Otto Wagner

Corner of a living-room;
design by Joseph
Hoffmann

to the art world at large, that Vienna was not yet completely buried beneath the
clichés of imitation. In 1900 – the year Sigmund Freud published his *Interpretation of Dreams* in Vienna – Gustav Klimt submitted his draft sketches for allegorical paintings to be done for the Vienna university. The shocked members of
the faculties rejected them as 'obscene'. Had Klimt painted the projected
sketches, they would in all probability be in vivid contrast with the present provincial amosphere at the university, caused by the successive purges of 1933
(when the Dollfuss regime fired all National-Socialist and Marxist professors),
of 1938 (when the Nazis threw out all Jews and Catholics), and of 1945 (when
the new government dismissed Nazis and Nazi-sympathisers). In the end, only
the faceless second-raters have remained, making the once great university a
breeding ground of academic mediocrity.

66 *My Room,* by Egon Schiele

TODAY'S HOUSING PROBLEM

Today, the character of the city remains architecturally confused. In the inner city, modern structures have been put up next to baroque façades, and old palaces are flanked by bare, steel and concrete walls. Along Graben the occasional old house looks like an island from some past era, stranded in today's soulless sea. Capuchin Church, with its tombs of the Habsburg emperors, is flanked by food stores and Hoher Markt, Vienna's oldest square, looks like a stage where the stagehands have forgotten to remove some of the props. Only in the quiet, narrow side-streets has the character of the old town been preserved, and there remains a dim, timeless nobility. In Herrengasse, a distinguished street, the mysterious *genius loci* seems to hold together baroque *palais*, Empire palaces and modern buildings such as the Hochhaus ('skyscraper'). And in Schottengasse and Freyung the architects have somehow succeeded in blending the high baroque with Josefinian neo-classicism, and Empire with the early baroque. Seen from ground level Vienna often looks like a baroque city; but seen from the Hochhaus it might also be a Gothic city, or even a modern city.

Some of the western and north-western suburbs – districts particularly loved by the baroque Vienna – have preserved their village-like character: Grinzing, Heiligenstadt, Neustadt am Walde. There are dreamy squares and streets with poetic names: Eroicagasse, Rosenweg, Weinberggasse. Green meadows and vineyards create a lovely no-man's-land between baroque 'pleasure' *palais*, 'cottage' districts from the *Gründerzeit*, and apartment houses with singularly unattractive façades; but how long will it last?

Vienna's housing problem began after the first Turkish siege (1529) when some of the suburbs were razed. Under Maria Theresia and her son, the Emperor Joseph II, the problem was met by building vast tenements, which created depressing lower-middle-class enclaves in various districts. The old houses offered neither air nor light nor space, and hardly any sanitary installations. Almost half the houses in today's inner city were built prior to 1880. At the end of the first world war, tens of thousands of typically Viennese apartments consisted of one room and a tiny kitchen with a window looking out on to a corridor. In the workers' districts, one fourth of such apartments were used by six or more people. In the corridor, there is still the '*bassena*' (cold-water faucet) for half a dozen families, and a communal toilet; there is no hot water. In the summer of 1966,

67 *Bassena* in an old house in Griechengasse

half of Vienna's working families had television sets but less than twenty per cent of *all* apartments in Vienna had their own bathroom.

Even some of the *Gemeindehäuser*, large municipal housing projects built after the first world war by the Social-Democratic city administration, and much admired as models of modern city building (together with kindergartens, playgrounds, hospitals for TB patients) have now acquired a shabby look. There are no outright slums in Vienna but the building standards are lower than in neighbouring Germany and Switzerland, or in the Scandinavian countries. In the past ten years the municipality has put up sixty-five thousand modern apartments in municipal housing projects that are surrounded by light and lawns; at least five thousand new apartments are now built every year. The tenants in the old houses are protected by special *Mieterschutz* laws against higher rents, while tenants in many new apartments are victims of a liberal *laissez-faire* policy that creates what is almost a black market in apartments. A tenant in a 'protected' apartment may pay as little as a pound a month; a tenant in an unprotected apartment may have to pay one hundred times that amount. The owners of many of the old houses who get only a nominal rent are unable to repair their buildings and whole streets in Vienna seem to be falling into decay. Thousands of young couples are unable to marry because they cannot get a small place to stay (and the automobile which often replaces a baby does not replace an apartment); while in some archaic-looking villas lonely old ladies live out their lonely lives in half a dozen large rooms which in wintertime they cannot afford to heat.

3

The Golden Age of Music

THE SOUNDS OF VIENNA

Vienna is a city of sounds. (By dialling 1509, one can hear an A, at the correct frequency of 440 Hz, an invaluable help for amateur chamber music players, though many like to tune their private A a little sharper.) Vienna's architecture has been called 'music in stone'. Its melodies will survive its buildings. The music of Gluck, Haydn, Mozart, Beethoven, Schubert, Johann Strauss, Brahms, Mahler, Bruckner, Schönberg, Berg, Webern will live on after Vienna's palaces have become a noble monument to the past, or a pile of rubble. All post-war events to touch the consciousness of the Viennese have somehow been connected with sound: the signing of the proclamation on the re-establishment of the Austrian republic by the provisional government of Austria, on 27 April 1945, was celebrated by a concert given by the Vienna Philharmonic under Clemens Krauss, while fighting was still going on in many parts of the country; there was the re-opening of the rebuilt Vienna Opera on 5 November 1955; and earlier, the installation of the re-cast 'Pummerin' bell ('Regina Austriae') at St Stephen's, on 25 April 1952. The 'Pummerin', a twenty-ton bell originally cast from captured Turkish guns in 1711, rung by eight people on Sundays and national holidays, was destroyed when St Stephen's Cathedral was gutted during the Battle of Vienna in April 1945. The bell was re-cast by a famous foundry in Upper Austria and brought back in a triumphal procession. At Vienna's city limits the big bell was greeted by the canon of St Stephen's. After a procession, which caused enormous enthusiasm, through the streets of Vienna, Bruckner's 'Te Deum' was performed at the cathedral. And now, at midnight on New Year's Eve, the deep powerful sounds of the 'Pummerin' are broadcast by the Austrian radio to usher in the New Year, immediately followed by Johann Strauss' 'Blue Danube' waltz, not Austria's national anthem, but its spiritual and secular theme song, the people's anthem.

The sight-seeing tours of Vienna convey an incomplete impression of the city; there ought to be sound-hearing tours. Many squares and streets and houses have melodies associated with them. At the Höldrichsmühle in suburban Hinterbrühl the linden-tree – more exactly, the trunk, which is all that remains – still stands, the tree which is said to have inspired Schubert to compose his cycle of lieder, *Die schöne Müllerin*. 'In summertime he always loved to go into the Wienerwald, and on a nice evening he would forget that he had been invited to an elegant town-house, and then there would be trouble, which did not worry him much', writes Josef Spaun. Brahms, who often went there, once said, 'A good thing that Schubert research has not yet been able to establish it. How many memorial tablets would have to be set up in Vienna! With every step we are treading on classical soil!'

Many sights in Vienna are associated with melody, and the melody, in turn, has created an image often different from the actual sight. The Prater, park and garden and amusement ground, near the Danube, will remain forever associated with blossom-time and love, with June and a full moon, since Robert Stolz wrote, *Im Prater blüh'n wieder die Bäume* ('It's blossom time again in the Prater'). But perhaps Vienna's greatest sound asset is its name. The monosyllabic 'Wien' (pronounced 'Veen'), is often used in sentimental three-quarter-time songs, filling a whole bar, accompanied by the saccharine vibrato of fiddles. Few composers of popular songs could resist building their tunes around 'Wien' ('*Wien, Wien, nur du allein*') or the equally useful *Wein* (wine),

> '*Ich möcht wieder einmal in Grinzing sein,*
> *Beim Wein, beim Wein, beim Wein ...*'
> ('I'd like to be back in Grinzing again,
> with wine, wine, wine ...')

It is, then, an indisputable fact that the Viennese landscape is 'redolent with music, light and colour', as Karl Kobald writes. Many musicians are instinctively aware of it when they come to Vienna. Contemporary composers, conductors and instrumentalists admit that they can hear the sounds of music all around

them; it may be a perception not shared by other people, but musicians have often remarked on it. Vienna's contribution to the history of music is not that it 'created' classicism in music – classical elements appear in the late phase of the earlier Mannheim school and elsewhere in Germany. But Vienna did for music what Weimar did for German literature; it fused the past with the present, local traditions with international influences.

Vienna was geographically and ethnologically destined to become the centre of classical music. The musical melting pot of nations and races – Austrians, south Germans, Czechs, Moravians, Poles, Slovaks, Slovenes, Croatians, Hungarians, Italians – all of whom brought their peasant melodies and folk songs; the international character of Vienna's culture in the eighteenth century accepted many influences – Flemish and Spanish Church music, French comic opera, Italian baroque opera – and blended these influences to create something of its own. Johann Joseph Fux (1660-1741), the great master of counterpoint, helped to prepare the great classical school. The Habsburgs were passionate music lovers, who kept the musical traditions alive and made no compromise with munificence where music and opera were concerned. The Emperor Leopold I composed; Charles VI was an able conductor. Whole operas were performed by members of the Habsburg family and the nobility. Austrian artists were preferred but *castrati* were imported until, after 1700, the names of the first 'cantatrices' appeared on the payroll. This baroque sumptuousness ended with the death of Charles VI in 1740. But by that time the classical Viennese school was well on its way.

The golden age of classicism began with the performance of Christoph Willibald Gluck's *Orfeo* at the old Burgtheater on 5 October 1762. *Orfeo*, one of the oldest operatic libretti, is the first music drama in the 'modern' sense of the word. Vienna's classical school is now mainly associated with the names of Gluck, Haydn, Mozart and Beethoven. Actually some very able composers were gathered round the giants – Johann Georg Reutter, Georg Matthias Monn, Matthäus Schlöger, Georg Christoph Wagenseil, Leopold Hoffmann, Johann Georg Albrechtsberger, Ignaz Joseph Pleyel, Carl Czerny and others. From Bohemia and Moravia came Bohuslav Czernohorsky, Franz Tuma, Johann Zach, Joseph Seeger, Joseph Mysliweczek, Franz Benda, Georg Benda, Franz Xaver Richter, Johann Stamitz, Johann Anton Koželuch, Dionys Weber, Franz Anton Rössler,

71 Stone support of the old organ in St Stephen's, with a self-portrait of the sculptor Anton Pilgram

Johann Baptist Wanhall (who played the cello in string quartets with Haydn, first violin, and Mozart, viola. Carl Ditters von Dittersdorf played second fiddle).

A wealth of talent was attracted to Vienna by the musical-minded court and aristocratic amateurs. Leopold Mozart from Augsburg, Beethoven from the Rhineland, and Antonio Salieri from Venice – all soon became acclimatised to the musical atmosphere of the city, which trained and exported composers as it later exported pastry and waltzes. Zelenka and Jiránek went to Dresden; Mysliweczek to Rome; Johann Zach to Mainz; Johann Stamitz, Franz Xaver Richter and Anton Filtz to Mannheim; the Benda brothers to Berlin and Gotha. All of them sensed the stimulating effect of Vienna's musical mood though few were able to analyse what the Viennese call the *genius loci*. Among the first who sensed it was the twelfth-century minnesinger, Walther von der Vogelweide, who sang of Austria 'where I learned to sing and compose ... *am wünniclichen Hof ze Wiene*' (at the wonderful court of Vienna).

NO DISH FOR THE TEETH OF MY VIENNESE

Paradoxically, most composers who lived and created in Vienna were misunderstood during their lifetime. When the Emperor Joseph II asked the second-rate Dittersdorf, Haydn's friend, whether Haydn (whom the *Wiener Zeitung* in 1766 called 'the darling of our nation, whose gentle character is apparent in each of his compositions'), was not 'dallying' too much, he expressed the doubts that many Viennese had about Haydn. They did not know – and how could they? – that behind the seeming 'naïveté' was a genius tortured by emotions and passions. Haydn, unlike Beethoven, was able to control his feelings, but their sound is unmistakable in his late quartets and symphonies and the great oratorios. The image of 'Papa Haydn' is as silly as it is untrue.

Mozart as a child prodigy was spoiled and as a mature genius was ignored. *Le Nozze di Figaro* could be performed only after the Emperor Joseph II had ordered it, and was soon forgotten when *Cosa Rara* by the Italianised Spaniard Vicente Martin y Solar was enthusiastically received. (In the last act of *Don Giovanni*, the Don makes an ironical allusion to *Cosa Rara*, which, but for this reference, would have long been forgotten.) *Don Giovanni*, a smash hit in Prague, did badly in Vienna and the emperor said that the opera was 'no dish for the teeth of my Viennese'. Beethoven too felt completely misunderstood in his adopted city. His only popular success in Vienna was his symphony 'Wellington's Victory' with its realistic battlefield sounds, which he wrote in 1813 and later called 'nonsense'. When Rossini came to Vienna in 1822, after the world-wide success of his *Barber of Seville*, the much greater local composers Beethoven and Schubert were completely ignored. The Viennese never understood genius; in Vienna, genius was appreciated only by a fellow-genius. Haydn first recognised the young Mozart as 'the greatest composer I know'. Mozart said, 'No one can do everything as well as Haydn ... and move one so deeply'. In 1787, Mozart, aged thirty-one, said about the seventeen-year-old Beethoven, 'Some day the world will take notice of him'. Schubert, too shy to speak to the admired Beethoven when he met him in the street, confided in his diary, 'Who can still try to attempt *anything* after Beethoven?' Arthur Schnitzler once told Siegfried Trebitsch, the writer, 'I would rather do without Goethe than without Beethoven.' And in 1878 Brahms wrote, 'That people in general do not understand and do not respect the greatest things, such as Mozart's concertos, helps our kind to live and require renown.'

Great composers were misunderstood and maligned in Vienna – if they were lucky. The unlucky ones were just ignored. Non-Viennese composers were never fully accepted in Vienna. They came there during the second half of the nineteenth century and stayed on. They were exhilarated to be 'treading on classical soil', as Brahms had said, or were stimulated by Vienna's *Stimmung* in which they were able to create. Such divergent composers as Schumann, Brahms, Wagner, Hugo Wolf and Bruckner were exhilarated by the city, in which, however, they always remained paying guests. Wagner was both violently disliked and ardently admired. A small avant-garde group fought for him. Most Viennese would chuckle over Eduard Hanslick's satirical remarks in the *Neue Freie Presse* in the morning, but at night others would cheer Wagner's works at the Kärntnertor Theater. After the first performance of *Lohengrin*, Wagner remembers 'the incredible unanimity of the whole audience: it was a long paean of joy like a thousand trumpets that went on and on, till I began to be afraid that the enthusiasm might literally bring down the house.'

Gustav Mahler was widely admired as a director and conductor at the Opera but detested as a composer at the Musikverein Hall, three blocks away. People would listen in breathless silence – Mahler expected complete dedication on the part of the audience – when he was conducting great performances of Mozart, Beethoven's *Fidelio*, or Wagner, but when Mahler's Fourth Symphony had its first Viennese performance in 1902, Bruno Walter noticed such hostility between a small group of admirers and the majority of the audience that he feared there was going to be a fight. In the still-glittering but already crumbling society of Vienna Mahler was the prophetic voice of doom and people did not want to listen. It was the same in 1916 at the Bösendorfer Hall after the first performance of Arnold Schönberg's F sharp major Quartet. People booed and hissed, while Maria Gutheil-Schoder kept on singing, the tears streaming down her face. The Viennese are emotional rather than analytical listeners.

Schubert, too, that most Viennese of all composers and one of the few who was a 'genuine' Viennese – he was born in one district, died in another, and hardly ever left the city – was no success in his home town and would have starved to death without his few devoted friends. He is often portrayed by his biographers as the happy-go-lucky bohemian, the merry composer of Merry Old Vienna. The image has been created by the operetta legend of the *Dreimäderlhaus* ('Blossom Time') and perhaps by a water-colour done by Schubert's friend, the painter Moritz von Schwind, thirty-five years after the scene it depicts. Franz Schubert, the conductor Franz Lachner and the playwright Eduard von Bauernfeld are portrayed sitting in a *Heuriger* wine garden in Grinzing. In the background there is the church of Grinzing, the hills of Kahlenberg and Leopoldsberg, and the setting sun. On the table there are wineglasses, from somewhere – one can well imagine – comes the sound of music. It is very, very *gemütlich*. Prints of this romantic water-colour hang in many Viennese homes; what a wonderful time it must have been, people sigh. This may be so. But Schubert spent many years of his life in extremely hard circumstances. He was always struggling, and was almost always in debt. He had no wealthy aristocratic friends as the admired Beethoven had; he was 'only' a composer of songs.

For Schubert preferred the company of congenial friends and simple people. He gave only one concert in Vienna, on 26 March 1828. He loved the *Würstelbälle* (balls named after the *Würstel*, or Frankfurters, which were served with the wine) and the *Schubertiaden* – evenings devoted to Schubert's music, drinking, dancing and talking, followed by more of Schubert's music. His friend,

72 The 'Dreimäderlhaus'

Fritz von Hartmann, writes in April 1827, 'Vogl [Johann Michael Vogl, who was a great singer and enthusiastic apostle of Schubert's songs] sang the latest lieder by Schubert ... After the music, there was food and wine, and a lot of merry-making, probably caused by alcoholic drinks. ... We stayed together until half past eleven: then Schober, Schwind, Schubert, Mayrhofer, Enk, Hönig, Franz and I went into the Café Bogner where, each for himself, repeated what we had seen and heard. After one in the morning we went to bed ...'. A few weeks later, there was a *Würstelball* in Schober's house. 'Most of the ladies were beautiful which made a nice picture', writes Hartmann. 'The music was wonderful, mostly Schubert waltzes, played by the composer. ... We stayed there until two in the morning.'

Schubert perfectly expresses the soul of Vienna. 'All the depth and insight, the warmth and grace of his feelings, his easy-goingness and sometimes his shallowness [*Flachheit*] are in his lieder', the critic Ludwig Speidel wrote in 1884. Schubert's melancholy is heard in his D minor Quartet ('Death and the Maiden'), which he finished in 1826, one year after his sickness which, according to his biographer, Professor O. E. Deutsch, 'no doubt ... was venereal, probably syphilis'. He had not much time left; but he wrote the song cycle, *Die Winterreise*, three piano sonatas, the marvellous String Quartet in C major, and the Symphony in C major of which Schumann said, 'He who is not acquainted with the C major Symphony knows very little about Schubert'. He died in November 1828, twenty months after the death of Beethoven. With him died the golden age of music in Vienna. He was only thirty-two.

He was given a 'second-class' funeral; the family paid his debts. Grillparzer correctly appraised Schubert's greatness when he wrote the epitaph, 'Music has here entombed a rich treasure but much fairer hopes'. (Our musical Viennese never did for their impoverished, great composers what the Finns, not regarded in Vienna as especially musical people, later did for twenty-seven-year-old Jean Sibelius. They granted him a government pension so that he could compose without worrying about money.)

Today the 'Viennese Schubert landscape', as many writers call it, includes the countryside surrounding the Kahlenberg, and the small Gothic church in Grinzing with the ornamental baroque tower, which Moritz von Schwind painted in the Lachner Scroll. Not far from the little wine garden where Schubert

73 Old wine-house in Sievering

and his friends were shown sitting that happy afternoon, Beethoven used to walk a certain path up towards Kahlenberg, which is now known to all Viennese as Beethoven Weg. According to his friend Anton Schindler, Beethoven said, one day in 1823, 'Here I composed *Szene am Bach* and up above, the yellow-hammers, the quails and the cuckoos composed with me.' 'Scene by the Brook' is in the Pastoral Symphony, whose movements are prefaced by Beethoven's inscriptions, as 'cheerful impressions received on arriving in the country' or 'happy and grateful feelings after the storm'. *He* certainly sensed the *genius loci*. Schindler, incidentally, reports that Beethoven on his deathbed read some songs by Schubert and said, 'Truly he has the divine spark'. Beethoven, a genius, knew that Schubert was a genius.

THE MOST MUSICAL NOBILITY EVER

Whether Vienna's golden musical age, the classical era, began and ended on certain days is debatable, but not the fact that this period of about sixty-five years can be compared with the greatest epochs in Western civilisation, perhaps only with Athens at the time of Pericles and Phidias, and with Renaissance Florence, when Leonardo da Vinci, Raphael and Michelangelo lived there.

Politically, the end of the eighteenth century was a time of chaos. Europe was overrun by the armies of Napoleon and Vienna went through several occupations and liberations before the Congress of Vienna set up a New Europe. But during these short decades, Vienna collected and distributed more musical wealth than any other city at any other epoch in history. Gluck, Haydn, Mozart, Beethoven and Schubert were living and working there, almost at the same time. The only other period in musical history is Vienna toward the end of the nineteenth century when Brahms, Bruckner, Mahler, Johann Strauss and Hugo Wolf were at the climax of their creative powers, and three young men lived there – Schönberg, Berg and Webern – who were to create an entirely new kind of music.

Vienna's classic era would not have happened without the sponsorship of the Habsburg court and the city's musical aristocracy. 'The court performed music with enthusiasm, and the nobility was the most musical ever', wrote J.F. Reichardt, the Prussian Court-Kapellmeister, in 1783. The Emperor Joseph II,

74 Porch of the former Fries Palais; the spendthrift banker Count Moritz von Fries was a patron of Haydn, Beethoven and Schubert

a pupil of the composers Florian Leopold Gassmann and Antonio Salieri, always spent 'one hour after his meal' with music. Three times a week there were intimate concerts at the Imperial Palace: the emperor played piano and cello, and his brother, Archduke Maximilian, also participated. Maximilian frequently conducted in Schönbrunn park. Sometimes Emperor Franz played first violin in orchestral concerts at Laxenburg, conducted by Mozart's enemy, Salieri.

Later, Emperor Franz played first fiddle in his Imperial string quartet, at Castle Persenbeug, which consisted of him, Count Wrbna, Field-Marshal Kutschera and Kapellmeister Eybler ... 'on quiet evenings the boatmen down on the Danube would listen to the music'. (No details exist about the musical proficiency of the viola-playing Viennese field-marshal.) In Vienna musical soirées were given in Castle Laxenburg, at the Rittersaal of the Hofburg, at the Court Theatre in Schönbrunn, and at the Old Favorita. Members of the 'musical nobility', the Schwarzenberg, Liechtenstein, Esterházy, Lobkowitz, Thun, Kinsky and other families had their own orchestras. The private orchestra of Field-Marshal Josef Friedrich, prince of Sachsen-Hildburghausen, gave regular weekly 'academies' at the Auersperg Palais, conducted by Gluck and Dittersdorf. Also famous were the Sunday-morning matinées arranged by Gottfried van Swieten (whose father had been the physician of the Empress Maria Theresia) at his apartment in Renngasse, next to the Hotel 'Zu den drei Hacken'. Mozart was often there. Swieten sponsored the performance of Handel's oratorios at the festival hall of Fischer von Erlach's National Court Library. The first performances of Haydn's *Creation* and *Seasons* were privately arranged at the Schwarzenberg Palais (now demolished) in Mehlmarkt.

Court-Kapellmeister Reichardt writes happily about the private opera performances given at the Lobkowitz Palais, where Beethoven was often present and where 'you could rehearse all the time, often several rehearsals taking place simultaneously in various halls'. He remembered a performance of his opera *Bradamente*, now totally forgotten, when 'all the archdukes, the members of high nobility, and the best connoisseurs and dilettantes from Vienna ... were present. I had the pleasure to see among my listeners Salieri, Beethoven, Weigl, Clementi, Kozeluh, Girowetz, Umlauf and almost everybody else among Kapellmeisters and composers who just happen to be here.'

Karl Kobald reports that Beethoven's Third Symphony, the *Eroica*, was first

performed at the Palais Lobkowitz in 1804, in the presence of Prince Louis
Ferdinand of Prussia; according to Eduard Hanslick, Vienna's most famous
music critic (and leading anti-Wagnerian), the *Eroica* was first played in the
private home of the banker Würth before invited guests. The orchestra consisted
of amateurs, and Beethoven conducted. Prince Lobkowitz who later bought the
score, allowed non-aristocratic music lovers from the upper-middle classes to
attend. Music was beginning to bring the various social strata together. The rich
banking families, many of whom were Jewish, began to imitate the musical ways
of the nobility; all of them loved music. Soon the musical soirées at the houses of
Arnstein, Pereira, Henikstein, Fellner were much talked about in Vienna. And
gradually the upper bureaucracy, well-to-do dilettantes, the new rich bourgeoisie, and finally the middle classes began to participate in Vienna's rich
musical atmosphere.

Vienna's musical chroniclers have compiled exact lists of the aristocratic and
bourgeois houses where the great composers regularly went. Mozart was often
seen at the Countess Thun, where they made music almost every evening. 'There
was amusing conversation, one played the piano, one sang in German or Italian,
and sometimes people dance', Mozart writes. Joseph II often came for the evening. Haydn too had been there, and it was Countess Thun who had introduced
the English musicologist, Charles Burney, and Court-Kapellmeister Reichardt
to Gluck. One of her daughters later became Countess Rasumofsky and one of
Beethoven's great friends.

Mozart and Haydn often spent the evening at the home of Court-Councillor
Greiner. His daughter, Karoline Pichler, remembers that 'many professors,
actors, musicians and composers, among them Paesiello and Cimarosa, came to
our house'. Mozart loved to go to the musical house of Nikolaus von Jacquin, the
famous botanist; Jacquin's son, Gottfried, became Mozart's pupil and companion. (Gottfried wrote in Mozart's album: 'Neither reason nor imagination –
love, love, love is the soul of genius.') Mozart wrote to him from Prague in 1787,
'I must admit that although . . . Prague is a beautiful and very pleasant town I am
a little homesick for Vienna, and the main reason is your home . . .'.

A very musical house was kept by Geheimer Rat Franz Bernhard von Keess,
who sponsored the Augarten dilettante concerts and had Haydn's symphonies
performed in his home. Adalbert Gyrowetz, the classicist composer, remembers

76 Rasumofsky Palais, residence of Andreas Rasumofsky,
Russian ambassador and patron of Beethoven

that Mozart had promised to come one evening and bring along a new song for his hostess. When Mozart was late, several servants were sent to fetch him. They found him at a nearby *Gasthaus* (tavern) enjoying himself. He had completely forgotten to compose the song. He asked for some note paper, wrote the song, came to the Keess house, and sat down at the piano. 'Frau von Keess sang the song with a trembling voice but it was enthusiastically received', says Gyrowetz. Other popular homes of music were the house of Martinez in Kohlmarkt (across from where Demel's is now), where the court poet, Pietro Metastasio lived (and where young Haydn had rented a tiny room below the attic); the Trattnerhof that belonged to Therese von Trattner, a pupil of Mozart to whom he dedicated his piano sonata in C minor; the house of Dr Leopold von Genzinger, the personal physician of Prince Nikolaus Esterházy who on Sundays would always invite Joseph Haydn and his brother Michael, Mozart, Dittersdorf and J. G. Albrechtsberger, Beethoven's teacher, when they would make music and then sit down to a wonderful dinner. It seems as though music was being made in almost every 'good Viennese house'.

I DON'T WRITE FOR THE GALLERIES!

Vienna's public musical life took place in the two court theatres (the Theatre Près de la Cour and the Kärntnertor Theater) and in the Redoutensaal of the Hofburg. At the old Burgtheater Mozart's *Le Nozze di Figaro* was first performed on 1 May 1786. Emperor Joseph II who had commanded the performance attended the dress rehearsal. The Irish tenor, Michael Kelly, a friend of the composer, who sang the part of Basilio, reports that Mozart himself stood in the middle of the stage, 'wearing a red coat, a *Tressenhut* on his head, and gave the right tempi. Benucci sang Figaro's aria "Non più andrai" with his powerful voice. I stood next to Mozart who exclaimed sotto voce "Bravo, Benucci!"' After the aria, there was a terrific ovation, with everybody shouting, 'Bravo, maestro! Viva! Viva grande Mozart!', and the violinists beating their bows against their stands. 'The little man bowed repeatedly.' Yet the public and the reviewers did not like Mozart's masterpiece, and Joseph II thought it was 'lacking in finesse'.

Poor Mozart had even less success with *Don Giovanni* (1788), *Così Fan Tutte*

77 Griechengasse and the 'Griechenbeisl', a favourite
tavern of Schubert's

(1790), and *Die Zauberflöte* (1791, at Schikaneder's Theater auf der Wieden). This time Mozart conducted from the piano, and his pupil, Franz Xaver Süssmayr (who after Mozart's death completed his *Requiem*) turned the pages. Schikaneder sang the part of Papageno and Mozart's sister-in-law, Josefa Hofer, was Queen of the Night. Johann Schenck, composer of *Dorfbarbier* and a teacher of Beethoven, writes in his autobiography that 'after the overture I went into raptures, crawled through the orchestra to the conductor's chair, and kissed Mozart's left hand. He kept conducting with his right, looked at me in a friendly way and stroked my cheek.' The public, however, did not share Schenck's enthusiasm. After the first act Mozart appeared on the stage 'pale and dismayed' and Schikaneder had to console him.

At the new Theater an der Wien a few years later, in 1805, Beethoven was also 'pale and dismayed' when his *Fidelio* was a resounding flop. The following year, a second version, with the Leonora Overture No. 3, was given, but the audience was lukewarm, and Beethoven went to complain to Baron Braun, one of his patrons. According to a contemporary, Josef August Röckel, the baron said that he hoped the box office would do better during the following performances. This time only the better seats had been sold, later perhaps the galleries would also be filled.

'I don't write for the galleries !' Beethoven exclaimed.

The baron then made the mistake of remarking that 'even Mozart did not scorn to write for the galleries'. That finished it. 'I don't want the opera to be performed again', said Beethoven. 'I want the score back.' Baron Braun pulled the bell cord, gave orders that the score be returned to the composer, and the opera passed into oblivion. It was resurrected, in a third version, at the Hoftheater, on 23 May 1814, and was a success.

While Beethoven lived at the Theater an der Wien, he would often leave his rooms and go down to the orchestra, especially when a work by Cherubini or Méhul was given. Kapellmeister von Seyfried writes that 'Beethoven stood behind the orchestra barrier and, if he liked the opera, remained there silently until the last draw of the bow. If he did not, he turned round after the first act and left.'

Beethoven's friend, Wegeler, writes about Beethoven's first appearance as piano virtuoso and composer, at the Burgtheater, on 29 March 1795. The

78 Theater an der Wien: the 'Papageno porch'
79 (*overleaf left*) Organ in the church of the Merciful Brethren, where Haydn was organist
80 (*overleaf right*) Beethoven's Hammerklavier

concert was a benefit for the widows of the Tonkünstler Society, under the baton of Salieri. Beethoven performed his Piano Concerto in B flat major, opus 19. 'He wrote the Rondo only on the afternoon preceding the concert', writes Wegeler. 'He suffered from a colic and I helped him as well as I could. Four copyists sat in the antechamber, and he handed them each page as he completed it.'

Beethoven's last appearance as conductor was on 7 May 1824 when he conducted a monster programme at the Kärntnertor Theater: the overture 'Weihe des Hauses', three great hymns from *Missa Solemnis* (Kyrie, Credo, Agnus Dei), and the Ninth Symphony. Hanslick writes that the performers had secretly agreed to watch the movements of the concert-master, Schuppanzigh, and the chorus-master, Umlauf, and to ignore Beethoven who conducted. 'He was completely deaf and could hear neither the orchestra nor the applause.' About Beethoven, the Swedish poet Atterbohm writes in his memoirs, 'Beethoven stood as on a deserted island and conducted his demonic harmonies with strange movements. For instance, he would indicate a pianissimo by quietly kneeling down and stretching his arms toward the floor. At the fortissimo he would jump up like an elastic bow and extend both arms; between these two extremes he was always gliding up and down.'

At the Redoutensaal (where the State Opera company now performs occasionally) Beethoven performed, on 18 December 1795, 'a concerto' on the pianoforte, followed by 'three big symphonies, not yet heard in Vienna, which the Herr Kapellmeister [Haydn] had completed during his last sojourn in London'. At the Rittersaal of the Hofburg Beethoven participated in a court concert on 25 January 1815, during the Congress of Vienna, on the Empress of Russia's birthday. Before an audience of 'emperors and empresses, kings and queens, ministers and their cortèges', Beethoven accompanied the quartet from *Fidelio*, 'Mir ist so wunderbar', and *Adelaide*.

THE DILETTANTES

As the dilettantes began to take part in Vienna's musical life, the 'academies' arranged by non-professional musicians became very popular. The *Jahrbuch der Tonkunst* (Almanac of Music) regularly listed the dilettantes with the instruments which they played and the degree of their proficiency (not unlike today's

81 Festival hall of the Landhaus, one of old Vienna's concert halls

Directory of Amateur Chamber-Music Players in New York City). In 1799 the Viennese directory begins with:

> Bartenstein, Freiherr von, Reichshofrath, plays the violin well;
> Beck, Herr von, member of the postal administration, very musical and plays very well on the basset oboe;
> Claus, a young medic, plays the flute rather well.

The dilettantes and amateurs gave their concerts at the 'Mehlgrube' Hall (later Hotel Munsch), and at the old hall of the university. Concerts were also given at the Augarten which was called 'Vienna's Tuileries', opened by Joseph II in 1775. Mozart writes to his father about a certain Martin who received permission from the emperor to arrange twelve concerts at the Augarten and four *Nachtmusiken* in the most beautiful squares in town. At the first concert, Mozart performed with his pupil, Fräulein von Aurnhammer, a duet concerto in E flat major. 'It went well. Archduke Maximilian was present, the Countess Thun, Wallenstein, Baron van Swieten and many other amateurs.'

The *Allgemeine Musik-Zeitung* reports that Ignaz Schuppanzigh, Beethoven's friend and famous violinist, 'gave twelve to sixteen concerts at the Augarten during the nice season, which begin at seven in the morning (!) and last two hours. With the exception of the wind instruments and the double basses all parts are performed by dilettantes, and the precision should be an example for all amateur concerts and Musikdirektoren. One hears the most difficult symphonies of Haydn and Mozart performed with an accuracy that expresses each beautiful detail which the composers wrote for each of their instruments.' On 1 May of every year, 'everybody in Vienna' went in a new, elegant spring robe to the morning concert at the Augarten, 'to promenade and listen to the music'.

Not less famous were the so-called 'Kavalierskonzerte' at the old festival hall of the university, conducted by Herr von Herring, a banker, and later by a local violin virtuoso by the name of Clement. Beethoven conducted there twice. The most famous 'Kavalierskonzert' was given on 28 March 1808, when Salieri conducted Haydn's *Creation*. Albert Dies writes that Haydn, who was then eighty-six, had been officially invited.

The good weather permitted Haydn to attend the performance. Prince Esterházy sent his own coach to Haydn's apartment. As the composer got out of the coach, he was received by members of the High Aristocracy. Among the people who received Haydn at

82 Head of the River March, from G.R. Donner's Neuer Markt fountain

the gate was also Beethoven. There was such a commotion that the military guards had to establish order. Haydn sat down in an arm-chair which was carried into the Hall at the sound of trumpets and drums. People exclaimed 'Long live Haydn!' He was seated next to Prince Esterházy; on his other side was Fräulein von Kurzbeck. The highest members of the local and foreign nobility had taken their seats next to Haydn. There was much fear that the fragile old gentleman might catch cold, and he was asked to keep on his hat. Count Andreossy, the French ambassador, noticed with pleasure that Haydn wore the gold medal which he had received from the Concerts des Amateurs in Paris, and said, 'Not only this medal – you should receive all the medals that France can give.' Haydn seemed to be bothered by a cold draft. Princess Esterházy took her scarf and placed it around him. Several other ladies did as she did and in a few moments Haydn was covered with scarfs.... Haydn was deeply moved and had to drink a little wine to refresh himself but after the first part he had to leave. People cried as he was carried back to the coach.

A few months later Haydn was dead.

A CELEBRATED MAN AND DEAREST FRIEND

Musicologists and musicians are still fascinated by the influence that the great composers of the classical era in Vienna received from, and gave to, each other. Haydn, who had developed the string quartet and the modern symphony, had been deeply influenced by Mozart, his friend and pupil. In the subscription invitation to his opus 33 quartets Haydn remarked that they were composed 'in an entirely new and particular manner'. Four years later, Mozart dedicated to the 'celebrated man and my dearest friend', his 'six sons', the magnificent six String Quartets K. 387, 421, 428, 458, 464, 465.

Haydn once told Mozart's father Leopold that he considered Wolfgang Amadeus 'the greatest composer known to me either in person or by name'. At that time Haydn was Europe's most distinguished musician, and Mozart's father wrote about it to his daughter with pardonable pride. Two years later, during the trouble in Vienna over *Don Giovanni*, Haydn wrote to the Prague theatre official, Roth:

For if I could convince every music lover – and especially those in high positions – of the inimitable works of Mozart; if they would judge them, as I do, seriously and with musical understanding; if they would let his music touch their souls as it does my own – why, then the nations would compete with one another for possession of such a jewel within their borders... I am furious that this unique Mozart has not yet been taken into the service of an imperial or royal court. Forgive me if I lose my temper; I hold the man too dear.

83   Inner court of the Esterházy Palais, town house of Haydn's patrons

Haydn gave much encouragement to Mozart throughout his difficult years in Vienna.

Beethoven came to Vienna in 1792. He had hoped to study with Mozart and when his hope was shattered by Mozart's death, he approached Haydn. On 29 October 1792, Count Ferdinand Waldstein, one of Beethoven's patrons, wrote in Beethoven's album: 'Mozart's genius still mourns and bewails the death of its pupil. It has found refuge with the inexhaustible Haydn, but not employment; through him it desires once again to be united with another. Through constant industry you shall receive Mozart's spirit from Haydn's hands.' This remarkable appreciation of the relationship between Haydn, Mozart and Beethoven proves the deep musical understanding of Vienna's aristocratic dilettantes. For Mozart had spent the last ten years of his life in growing isolation in Vienna: rather than be exposed to criticism, he had retired into solitude and devoted himself to writing great music. Of all his works, only 'The Abduction from the Seraglio' was widely performed in Vienna. Few of his instrumental works were published in his lifetime. It seems incredible now, but lesser composers such as Dittersdorf, Koželuch, Wanhall and Clementi were more famous than Mozart in Vienna. The poet Jean Paul admired Haydn more than Mozart. C.F. Zelter, musician and a friend of Goethe once wrote to him: 'Mozart to Bach is as the Netherland masters are to the Greek and Italian artists, and only since I steadily perceive this fact more and more clearly do I hold both in the highest esteem, not demanding from one what is accomplished by the other.'

Haydn and the young Beethoven did not get along. To Haydn teaching did not come easily, and Beethoven was unsuited temperamentally to the role of pupil; he forever antagonised the older man. But Haydn was too big a man to let his feelings interfere with his judgement. In a letter to Maximilian Franz, the Elector of Cologne, he wrote, on 23 November 1793:

I humbly take the liberty of sending Your Serene Electoral Highness some musical works... compositions of my dear pupil Beethoven, with whose care I have been graciously entrusted. I flatter myself that these pieces, which I may recommend as evidence of his assiduity over and above his actual studies, may be graciously accepted by Your Serene Electoral Highness. Connoisseurs and non-connoisseurs must candidly admit, from these present pieces, that Beethoven will in time fill the position of one of Europe's greatest composers, and I shall be proud to be able to speak of him as his teacher; I only wish that he might remain with me a little while longer....

84   House in Kohlmarkt where the young Haydn lived in an attic room
85   (*overleaf left*)   Statues in the festival hall of the old university, where the 'Kavalierskonzerte' took place

86   (*overleaf right*)   Pulpit in the Jesuit Church

BRING ME WHAT YOU LIKE AND DON'T BOTHER ME

Though the three great masters had much spiritual influence on each other, their artistic development could not be more different during their years in Vienna. Haydn systematically progressed from his first, naive works to become the inventor of the string quartet as we know it and the creator of the modern symphony; there are almost no interruptions in this constant development. Beethoven started in the classical tradition but in his final string quartets and piano sonatas becomes a genius whose style is so intensely personal and lonely that no one would have dared imitate it. Mozart is the most difficult to assess for he began almost as a mature genius and developed only in the way that everything he did later on seemed to gain in simplicity and clarity; today we know that his simplicity is often unfathomable and his refinement the highest expression of art. Haydn was very popular toward the end of his life; Beethoven, who was deaf and eccentric was not popular at all; and Mozart was also not popular because his time had not yet come.

Mozart's 'light' melodies are the supreme expression of his genius. In 1918 Richard Strauss, himself a master of melody, said to the critic Max Marschalk:

The most perfect melodic shapes are found in Mozart; he has the lightness of touch which is the true objective. With Beethoven the melodies are heavier; one is clearly conscious of the labour. Listen to the remarkable expansion of a Mozart melody, to Cherubino's 'Voi che sapete', for instance. You think it is coming to an end, but it goes further, ever further.

When Richard Strauss was a young musician, Brahms advised him to study Schubert's dances for their melodic structure. 'To construct the melodic shape is a question of talent', said Brahms. 'But here we are also concerned with one of the most difficult of technical problems ... A melody which seems to have been born in a moment is almost always the result of intense labour.' Mozart and Schubert were the great masters of melody; their lightness is proof of their genius. Mozart's sister-in-law, Sophie Haibl, once reports that Mozart used to walk about his room, deeply meditating, when he was at work; no one can tell how much meditation preceded the actual writing down of the 'light' melody.

Beethoven is still remembered in Vienna as the eccentric, striding through the rain in Heiligenstadt, his arms bent behind his back, never looking to right or left. Grillparzer reports that his family once spent the summer in Heiligenstadt;

87 'The Austrian', figure in a mechanical orchestra from the Prater

Beethoven walking
'auf der Bastei'

they had the rooms looking out on to the garden, while the rooms facing the street were rented by Beethoven.

My brothers and I paid little attention to the strange man – who had become heavier and was dressed in a slovenly way, even uncleanly – when he raced past us; but my mother, a passionate friend of music, would occasionally step out into the corridor to listen devoutly when she heard him play the piano. That may have happened a few times, when suddenly Beethoven's door was opened, he stepped out, saw my mother, rushed back into his room, and immediately, with his hat on his head, ran down the stairway. From this moment on he never touched his piano again. In vain my mother sent him messages that no one would listen any more, and that we would no longer use the common corridor but would walk out into the garden: Beethoven remained unmollified and never touched his piano until we returned to town late in the autumn.

Bettina von Arnim saw Beethoven in Vienna and wrote to Goethe in 1810 how nice he was to her; she was surprised for she had heard that he avoided people and talked to no one. People were afraid to take her there, and she had to look

88 Old inn 'The Flower Pot' in Ballgasse, where Beethoven lived in 1819-20
89 (*overleaf*) View to the city from the Upper Belvedere

him up which was not easy, for Beethoven had three different apartments, in which he was alternately hiding; one in the country, one in town, and the third 'auf der Bastei', and there she found him.

I entered unannounced, while he was sitting at the piano. I told him my name, he was very friendly and asked me whether I wanted to hear a song which he'd just composed. Then he sang, with a strident voice, so that I could feel the melancholy, 'Kennst du das Land'. Afterwards he said, 'It's nice, isn't it? *Wunderschön*. I'll sing it once more', and he was happy when I applauded. 'Most people are moved about something good, but they are not artists, artists are full of fire, they don't cry', he said. Then he sang a song by you [Goethe] that he had recently composed 'Trocknet nicht, Tränen der ewigen Liebe', [Don't dry, tears of eternal love]. He accompanied me home, talking about the beauty in art. He talked so loudly, often stopping in the street, that one needed courage to listen. He talked with great passion and I was so astonished that I often forgot to look down at the road. People were astonished when they saw him enter with me; we were having a big dinner party. After dinner he sat down at the piano without being asked, and played long and wonderfully; in such excitement his spirit creates the inconceivable, and his fingers achieve the impossible.

Nine years later Carl Friedrich Zelter wrote a different letter to Goethe, when he had tried to see Beethoven who had left for the country – it was the summer of 1819 – and no one knew where he lived.

He wrote to one of his girl friends from Baden, but he isn't in Baden. He is said to be impossibly *maussade* [difficult]. Some people say he is a fool; that's easy to say, God forgive us all! The poor man is said to be completely deaf. Lately he went into a restaurant, sat there absent-mindedly and after an hour asked the waiter, 'How much do I owe you?' 'Your Honour hasn't ordered yet, what should I bring you?' – 'Bring me what you like and don't bother me!' The Archduke Rudolf is said to be his patron and gives him 1,500 florins annually, and with that he has to get along, as all *Musenkinder* [children of the Muses]....

And Carl Maria von Weber, who saw Beethoven in 1823, was moved to tears when Beethoven unexpectedly embraced him 'six or seven times', exclaiming 'You are a *Teufelskerl*, yes, you are the devil of a fellow!' 'We spent lunch together, happily. This rough, reticent man treated me like a lady – in short, this day will always remain one of the strangest of my life.' Weber ends his report, 'How sad is his deafness. One has to write down everything for him.'

Grillparzer who spoke at Beethoven's grave in 1827 understood him well. 'Beethoven avoided people after he had given them everything and received nothing in return. He remained lonely because he never found a second ego. But to his grave he retained his human heart for all people.'

90 Beethoven house in Heiligenstadt Pfarrplatz

A BLAST OF WIND AND SLEET

For a long time Viennese writers, musicians and musicologists have been busy retracing the 'sanctified' places where their great composers lived and created. Some feel that 'to tread on classical soil' may bring about a sort of contact with the mysterious processes of creation. Others feel a touch of guilt at the thought of how shabbily the great composers had been treated in this 'world capital of music'. The case of Mozart, the greatest musical spirit of all, is the best known; he left only sixty florins in cash and there was scarcely enough money for a 'third-class' funeral. A 'blast of wind and sleet' made the mourners turn back, and the body was unceremoniously dumped into a mass grave. After Mozart's death, the emperor's exchequer granted Mozart's widow a yearly pension of two hundred florins, hardly enough to keep body and soul together.

Grillparzer was the first to explain the official neglect for Mozart. Mozart had greatness and genius, and Vienna's bureaucracy and the *Bürgertum* (the middle classes) always resented these qualities. Mediocrity is considered safe; genius means danger. Mozart was dangerous; so were Beethoven, Bruckner, Mahler. Actually Mozart's poverty and his lonely, dramatic funeral (often incorrectly

'Huic ergo parce deus': the last notes that Mozart wrote

91   Courtyard of the Deutsches Haus, where Mozart lived in 1781
92   (*overleaf left*)   Andromeda Fountain by G.R. Donner, in the old Town Hall
93   (*overleaf right*)   Fountain, the Widow of Sarepta, in a city convent

called a 'pauper's funeral') helped to make him a legend among the little people of Vienna very soon after his death. He had been a fine musician (they thought of him as a 'musician' rather than a 'composer'); he had been poor and struggling; he had had a nagging wife, as so many others; they could identify themselves with this poor fellow who died at the age of thirty-five. In 1833, only forty-one years later, Heinrich Laube, manager of the Hofburgtheater, wrote, 'Mozart is the only one ... who delights the simplest understanding'.

The cause of Mozart's death remains a mystery, with some 'baroque' authorities claiming that he did not die of a feverish infection (as many experts assume) but of quicksilver poisoning. The poisoner was said to be his arch rival, the composer Antonio Salieri, about whom Beethoven's friend, Anton Schindler, wrote, 'He [Salieri] has feverish fantasies – there is something he wants to confess'. The following year, after Salieri's death, Beethoven's nephew Karl noted, 'There is much talk here that Salieri is the murderer of Mozart'. There was always (and still is) much gossip in Vienna's musical circles. Whether Salieri murdered Mozart is as unproved as whether Lully murdered Robert Cambert.

IRATE LANDLADIES, UNSYMPATHETIC NEIGHBOURS

The experts have diligently retraced Mozart's steps to the twelve 'sanctified' places where he lived in Vienna. At the Hamberger House on the Wasserkunstbastei he visited his older friend Haydn, on the eve of Haydn's departure for London in 1791, and said, 'This will probably be our last farewell in this life.' It was. On the second floor of the Camesina house – the Swiss-Italian Alberto Camesina was one of the prominent stucco workers in Vienna – Mozart composed *Le Nozze di Figaro*, the most exhilarating expression of the art of opera, in a room whose ceiling is adorned with stucco nymphs and Amorettes, a fitting room for the creator of *Figaro*. There Haydn made his first visit to the young Mozart. Mozart's father Leopold later wrote:

On Saturday evening Herr Joseph Haydn and the two Barons Tindi came to see us. The new quartets were played... these are somewhat lighter but they are nevertheless admirably composed. Haydn said to me, 'I, as an honourable man, swear to you before God that your son is the greatest composer I know, either personally or by repute. He possesses not only taste but the most profound knowledge of musical composition.'

The Kärntnertor-
theater

It was in a particularly dark and depressing house at 26 Währingerstrasse
that Mozart wrote the magnificent symphonies in E flat major and G minor.

Beethoven's life-long pilgrimage through rented rooms, among irate land-
ladies and unsympathetic neighbours, has created a large local literature and
countless legends. Sixty-nine 'sanctified' places have been established. A difficult tenant, Beethoven would sometimes rent two or three dwellings at a time,
but was soon thrown out when he began to play the piano at two in the morning,
or poured a pail of water over himself in the middle of a room because he was hot.
Once he wrote music on the freshly painted window frames because he had run
out of notepaper.

Beethoven wrote the *Eroica* at the un-heroic Biederhof in Döblinger Haupt-
strasse, then a quiet country house, and his Fifth Symphony at 8 Grinzinger-
strasse in Heiligenstadt. At the *Three Ravens* inn in Vorderbrühl, a Wienerwald
wine-garden popular among musicians, who used to drink and play music there,
Beethoven wrote his 'Mödling Dances' for them. Though he did not like the
Viennese, Beethoven loved Vienna – the city, the Wienerwald, the *genius loci*.

95 Garden-house in the courtyard of a baroque house in Ulrichsplatz

In 1809 he even executed a draft agreement when his aristocratic patrons, Archduke Rudolf and the Princes Lobkowitz and Kinsky (of the 'Society of Cavaliers') persuaded him to refuse an invitation to the court of the King of Westphalia in Cassel. It says, 'Beethoven has such deep patriotic feelings for his second homeland that he never ceases to regard himself as an Austrian artist and for the same reason can never take up his residence in another country.' That would seem to settle a problem that still bothers many Viennese; that Beethoven was, technically, a foreigner. But one's native land does count. In the autumn of 1826, a few months before his death, when Beethoven was staying with his brother Johann at his country home in Gneixendorf, near Krems, he wrote to his publishers, Schott and Sons, 'The country in which I am living at the moment reminds me in some ways of the Rhine country which now, because I left it so long ago in my youth, I long ardently to see once more . . .'.

Haydn, who came from Lower Austria and spent much of his life in Eisenstadt, in the Burgenland province, decided towards the end of his life to live in Vienna. At 19 Haydngasse, when he was in his late sixties, he composed his last masterpieces, the great oratorios the *Creation* and the *Seasons*. Goethe called them 'an ideal language of truth'. The house is now the Haydn Museum. There the old man received visitors, 'sitting in an armchair, wearing a powdered wig with side locks, a white tie with a gold clasp, a richly embroidered waistcoat of white, heavy silk, a magnificent jabot, the brown gala dress, embroidered cuffs, black silk breeches and white silk stockings, while a silver buckle adorned his shoes.'

A more recent composer who came from faraway and completely grew into Vienna was Johannes Brahms. Elderly people in Vienna can still remember their grandfather or grandmother telling them of how they had seen Brahms walking, at about noon, from his home in 4 Karlsgasse, the 'Brahms House' in the Wieden district, a corner of 'Old Vienna' that has now gone. (It is now a wing of the Technical University.) From Christmas 1871 Brahms lived there for many years. From his window he could see St Charles' Church, the masterpiece of the great baroque builder, Johann Bernhard Fischer von Erlach, and the house 'To the golden Moonlight', where Schubert had lived. It was a small world – of music – in Vienna. Across an open space, now Ressel Park, Brahms could see the neo-Renaissance Musikverein building where he always sat in the

Brahms' *Cradle Song*

directors' box at the Sunday Philharmonic concerts. 'Strictly speaking,' wrote the recorder of the Society of the Friends of Music, 'there ought to be a gangway leading to the Musikverein that should be called the Brahms Bridge, and to which only Brahms should possess the key.' Brahms would have lunch at the 'Red Hedgehog Inn', usually in the company of friends, most of them professors at the nearby School of Music, and his biographer Paul Kalbeck. Their table was in a corner of the second-floor dining room. Downstairs in the *Schwemme*, a sort of popular tavern, Anton Bruckner and *his* friends were served the same food at somewhat lower prices.

At the Musikverein the Vienna Philharmonic under Hans Richter performed for the first time, in March 1897, Brahms' Fourth Symphony, his last. This work well explains the influence of the Austrian countryside and Vienna on the creative powers of a non-Viennese composer. Brahms wrote most of it in Mürzzuschlag, Styria, where he loved to walk in the woods. The sensitive romanticist from Hamburg whom Wagner called, not very tactfully, 'the chaste Johannes', discovered in Vienna's cheerful melancholy the mood that he could not find in the depressing *Schwermut* of the sombre north German landscape. With his German, contrapuntal knowledge of composition and his sensitivity to Vienna's everpresent melancholy, Brahms created a synthesis of north and south, of the baroque and the romantic.

97 (*top*) 'The Red Hedgehog'; (*below*) Brahms on his way to the inn
98 (*overleaf left*) Johann Strauss monument in the Stadtpark
99 (*overleaf right*) Kursalon in the Stadtpark, where Eduard Strauss conducted his 'Promenade concerts'

194

OPERETTA

The 'Viennese operetta' is a cherished local institution, and merely to express doubts about whether it still exists is considered heresy among enraged *Lokal-patrioten*. But the operetta was not invented in Vienna. Jacques Offenbach created the first operetta in France. *Fair Helen*, performed in Paris in 1864, remains the model of the literary, piquant, charming form of operetta, with fine melodies and subtle orchestration. Johann Strauss's *Indigo*, the first Viennese operetta, was performed seven years later; it is a rather shallow opus with skin-deep characterisation, banal lyrics and sugary sentimentality. Strauss, however, later wrote the finest operetta of all, *Die Fledermaus*, and ever since 'operetta' has been associated with Vienna, and also with a certain fin-de-siècle style of life.

The golden era of the Viennese operetta lasted only from 1874 *(Die Fleder-maus)* until after 1905 *(The Merry Widow*, by Franz Lehár). The greatest composers of this genre were, besides Strauss and Lehár, Karl Millöcker, Emmerich Kálmán, Oskar Straus and Robert Stolz. Of the vast Viennese production about a dozen operettas have survived. The glory of the operetta died everywhere with the monarchy. The world of Offenbach did not survive the end of the Second Empire; Gilbert and Sullivan reached their zenith during the Victorian age; in Spain, the republic brought an end to the *Zarzuela*; and in Vienna, the operetta never managed a comeback after the collapse of the Habsburg monarchy. In the 1880s, six theatres in Vienna performed operetta (Theater an der Wien, Carltheater, Bürgertheater, Raimundtheater, Stadttheater and Volksoper). No one was surprised when Franz Jauner, the manager of an operetta theatre, was in 1875 appointed *Direktor* of the Court Opera. The stars of the operetta – divas, charmeurs, comics, dancers – were among Vienna's most popular artists. The highbrows went to the Opera; *das Volk*, the people, went to hear an operetta. They never tired of the romantic nonsense and the trite sentimentality of the libretti – improbable love stories in which princes and dukes condescended to accept the favours of pretty commoners in an escapist atmosphere heavily drenched in champagne.

Today only two theatres, the Volksoper and the Raimundtheater, perform operetta in Vienna; there is no young generation of artists specialising in this dying art form. 'People from all over the world come to hear operetta in Vienna,' says Marcel Prawy, the leading operetta expert of Vienna's Volksoper who also introduced the American musical there to Viennese audiences, 'the same people who travel to Egypt to see the pyramids – monuments of a period of history that is gone for ever.'

THE VIENNA PHILHARMONIC

The number of concerts given annually in Vienna fluctuates almost as much as the number of restaurants in Paris; probably as many as fifteen hundred concerts take place every year. Vienna's musical life is organised in the style of the erstwhile *k.k.* (*kaiserlich-königlich*, or Imperial-Royal) bureaucracy – with rulers, a chancellery, ministers, secretaries of state, ambassadors; a musical state within the state. The title of hair 'ambassador' is bestowed upon the members of the Vienna Philharmonic. Arriving from an overseas concert tour, they have been received at the airport by the president of the republic, the federal chancellor, the minister of culture and education (who rules the musical state) and other high dignitaries. These hundred-odd members of the Philharmonic are treated with the sort of courtesy that is elsewhere extended to visiting statesmen.

Vienna has always loved its great orchestras. The baroque *Hofkapelle*, which so delighted Emperor Leopold I, had over a hundred members, mostly Italians, and received from the emperor an annual subsidy of sixty thousand florins. (By comparison, the court musicians of Leopold's great contemporary and rival, King Louis XIV of France, were not subsidised, and depended on their concerts for their income. Louis XIV preferred to spend *his* money on women – wives, *maîtresses en titre*, and untitled lady friends.) But Leopold – pious, austere, frail, 'rather ugly-looking' with his typical 'Habsburg lip', had no interest in women; he was emperor *dei gratia*, and God would not have liked it. On one occasion his *Hofkapelle* musicians went on strike just before a concert which the emperor himself was to conduct. A *castrato* singer, the spokesman for the orchestra, arrogantly demanded higher wages for everybody – or else. Leopold's advisers implored him to punish the '*Kanaillen*' (scoundrels) but he said, 'We must yield to them – having lost part of their manhood they may also have lost part of their brains.'

Among Vienna's concerts the regular Sunday afternoon subscription concerts of the Vienna Philharmonic are very special, rather nostalgic events. Ten or twelve times a year the subscribers, members of what was once known as 'the

101 Bishop Georg Slatkonia, first director of Maximilian I's *Hofkapelle*

good middle classes' (to emphasise that a new, not-so-good middle class had now attained a certain pseudo-status) meet at the gilt-pilastered Musikverein Hall for the Philharmonic *Feierstunde* (festive hour). There they are among their own kind – academic dignitaries, leaders of industry, doctors and *Direktoren*, a few members of the aristocracy, and many members of impoverished bourgeois families. The Philharmonic concerts are one of the last links with 'the good old days', the days of the bourgeois society before 1914.

The Vienna Philharmonic has undergone many changes since the great days of Nikisch, Mahler, Strauss, Furtwängler, but it still consists mostly of Vienna-born musicians, which is both its strength and its weakness. The 'Philharmonic style', which consists of a special sensitivity to beautiful tone, an inherited feeling for its classical and romantic repertoire, and the sweet mellow sound of the strings, is handed down from one generation to the next, from 'professor' to pupil. The *Professoren* bring in their favourite pupils to continue 'the tradition'. But no city on earth, even Vienna, can supply enough first-rate musicians for all the sections of a modern orchestra, and the Philharmonic's brass and woodwind sections have become sadly deficient compared to those of other celebrated orchestras. A significant break with the tradition was made last year when a gifted violinist, a Hungarian refugee, was elected by the members of the orchestra to be one of its four concert masters.

Vienna's musical bureaucracy consists of a hierarchy of court councillors, section chiefs, *Ministerialräte*, spies, former members of the state police, and honorary errand boys. Occasionally a musical dictator emerges who wields almost unlimited powers; Gustav Mahler and Herbert von Karajan have been the most forceful personalities in the past seventy years. During his ten years as *Direktor* of the Court Opera, Mahler established artistic standards for opera performances that have never been attained since, in Vienna or elsewhere. They were the golden years of the Vienna Opera. 'Mahler,' said Bruno Walter, 'was able to penetrate into the heart of the music, and to recreate the composer's dramatic vision from his music.' He was a ruthless perfectionist who hated the Viennese propensity toward compromise and made enemies everywhere. 'Mahler's heart was full of kindness but he could be cold and forbidding', wrote Bruno Walter. 'I'm beating my head against the wall but at least I'm making a hole in it', Mahler once said to Paul Stefan, the Viennese critic.

102 Custodian's lodge of the Upper Belvedere, where Anton Bruckner spent his last years

Mahler was finally driven out by an uneasy coalition of the high bureaucracy, the mob, and a collection of mediocrities who had no understanding of greatness, but he is still a legend in Vienna. All his successors were measured against his exalted memory; there are old opera lovers in Vienna who remember Mahler well. The last of his successors, Herbert von Karajan, lasted seven years as *Direktor* until he too was driven out by a similar combination of bureaucrats, mob rule, and the local aversion to any exceptional talent. In 1962, the 'first' Karajan crisis, as it is now called in operatic circles, was climaxed by a humiliating ultimatum which the conductor handed to the Austrian government. He demanded complete 'autonomy' for the State Opera, as a final attempt to eliminate the artistically stifling influence of the bureaucrats.

Vienna did not surrender to the Turks in 1529 or 1683 but it surrendered to Karajan in 1962. In return, the dictator promised to make Vienna the capital of his musical empire, reaching from Milan to Salzburg to Berlin, the first Austrian empire since the downfall of the Habsburgs. Two years later Karajan announced that he was not going to conduct in Vienna again. In the dramatic fight between him and the bureaucrats, each side relied on a network of unpaid informers and enthusiastic spies, intriguers and *aficionados*, just as in the days of Metternich. In the baroque musical atmosphere of Vienna rumours grow fast, cliques spread, and everything possible is done to keep people from creating and performing music. ('No other European city can compete with Vienna so far as cross-my-heart-and-hope-to-die-secrets, false and true rumours, slander, and vilification are concerned', writes Hilde Spiel, the Viennese author.)

Music is still considered art for art's sake by the Viennese but commercialism is increasing. American, British and German recording companies make important opera recordings in Vienna, where the cost is lower than elsewhere and where union rules are relatively relaxed. A former ballroom, *Sophiensäle*, was turned into a recording studio with excellent acoustics and first-rate technical equipment. Vienna provides the orchestra (the Philharmonic or the Wiener Symphoniker), and the chorus of the State Opera. The protagonists – conductors, singers, chorus directors, top technicians – are usually brought in from the outside. They too enjoy the intangible assets of Vienna's musical life. Conductors are surprised when the orchestra asks them to extend the contractual rehearsal time, at no extra cost to the recording company, because they *like* to rehearse.

103 Schweizer Tor in the Hofburg

These recording artists are not noticed by the press, though they would rate much space if they appeared at the Opera. Commercial activities occur in a vacuum, without touching the city's musical heart.

Vienna's concert life is dominated by the rather conservative Gesellschaft der Musikfreunde, founded in 1813, whose 'honorary members' include nearly all the great composers since Beethoven was so honoured in 1814 – Berlioz, Brahms, Bruckner, Donizetti, Dvořák, Massenet, Mendelssohn, Rossini, Schumann, Richard Strauss, Verdi, Wagner and others, but *not* Mahler and Schönberg – or the younger, more modern-minded Konzerthausgesellschaft. There are also several small, rather specialised circles and avant-garde groups. Almost anybody gets a hearing, even some who do not really deserve it. In the past years Vienna's music bureaucrats have reluctantly accepted the harsh fact that the overseas tours of the Spanish Riding School, the Vienna Boys Choir and the regimental band of the Deutschmeister are more in demand than the tours of the august Philharmonic or of the State Opera. (The Deutschmeister, founded in 1714 as the brass band of the Emperor's House Regiment, kept their 'imperial' uniforms after 1918 and continued as a professional band. The Spanish Riding School, established under Emperor Maximilian II, in 1580, is the world's oldest and greatest school of classical riding. Its performances of courbettes, levades and caprioles in the beautiful baroque riding hall, built by J. E. Fischer von Erlach during the reign of Emperor Charles VI, whose portrait hangs in the court box, are truly baroque shows, a magnificent blend of tradition, art and elegance.)

THE FESTWOCHEN

During the annual *Festwochen* (festival weeks) Vienna becomes one large musical stage. The biggest European festival, the *Festwochen* is also the only one on the Continent primarily arranged for the city's local population; foreigners are cordially invited but not terribly missed. The city-wide family party begins with dancing in the streets and ends four weeks later with widespread exhaustion. (Vienna's Theatre Almanac of 1794 reports, 'During the summer months one will meet serenaders in the streets almost daily and at all hours ... they consist of trios and quartets, most frequently from operas, of several vocal parts or wind instruments, frequently an entire orchestra ... the most ambitious symphonies are performed ... within a few minutes the musicians are surrounded by a crowd of listeners who rarely depart before the serenade comes to an end ....')

In 1966, over a thousand performances of opera, straight plays, concerts, serenades, took place during the *Festwochen*, many in outlying districts where hardly any foreigners attend. At 32 Nussdorferstrasse, where Schubert was born, a *Schubertiade* (an afternoon of Schubert's music) recalled the gatherings of his friends who met to play games and listen to his music. Mozart was honoured by serenades at the courtyard of Deutsches Ordenshaus, one of the 'sanctified' places where he once lived; Beethoven's serenades took place in the suburban square of Heiligenstadt. It may be commercial exploitation of the past but it certainly takes place in an authentic setting. Several years ago, al fresco performances of *Le Nozze di Figaro* were given in the courtyard in front of Schönbrunn Castle. During the third act – when the wedding takes place in Count Almaviva's palace – the baroque façade of the castle was dramatically lit up, to became a spectacular part of the scenery. It was baroque – and beautiful.

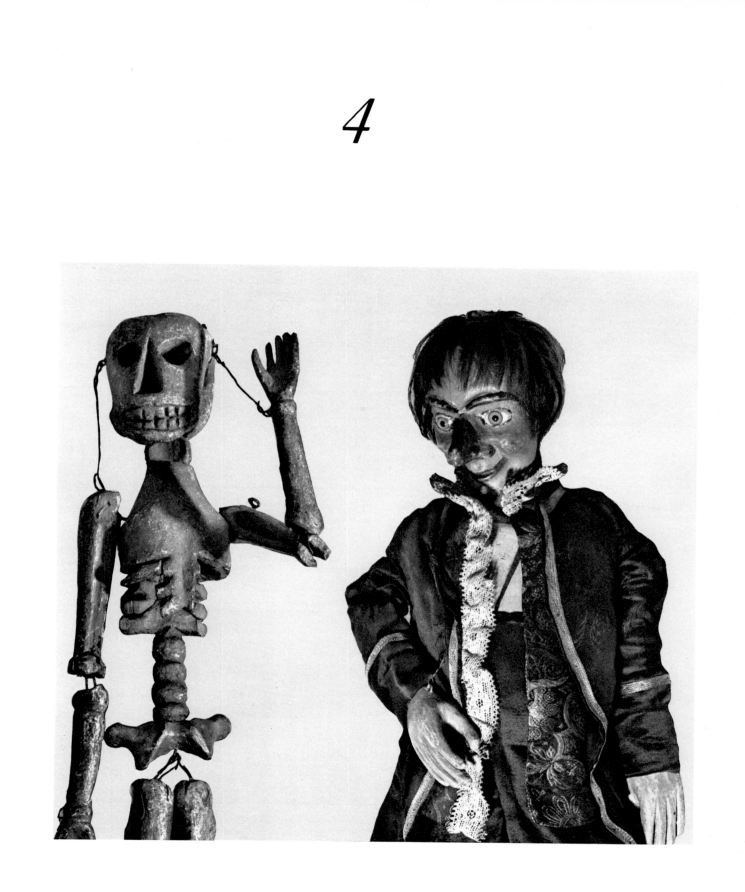

4

Theatre and Literature

I COULD NOT PARDON THE LIBERTY

'Spectacles are necessary', said Josef von Sonnenfels, Maria Theresia's minister of justice. 'Spectacles' began in the 1620s when the Jesuits staged their Miracle and Passion plays, in Latin, with humorous, folksy, German-language *intermezzi* for the local audiences who might get bored with the well-known biblical stories. Ever since, two parallel strains have appeared on Vienna's stages: the high road of the Good Lord, the metaphysical world of mythological gods and fairy kings; and the considerably lower road of our world, with ordinary mortals, comics and clowns. The finest integration of the two strains is the Schikaneder-Mozart masterpiece, *The Magic Flute*, with Sarastro and the Queen of the Night representing the supernatural forces of good and evil, the world of Tamino and Pamina seeking the highest ideal of humanism – and Papageno way down on earth. The wonderful duet of Pamina and Papageno ('*Bei Männern, welche Liebe fühlen*') is an unbelievably beautiful synthesis of two different worlds.

Many Viennese writers wrote 'folk comedies', plays for the low road with their earthy popular jesters. In 1712, Josef Anton Stranitzky, 'licensed tooth breaker and mouth doctor', was granted the privilege of letting German comedians perform in the newly built theatre near the Kärntnertor, next to today's State Opera. A great showman, by the end of his life Stranitzky was managing all the theatres in Vienna except for the two court theatres – the Opera and the Theatre Près de la Cour (today's Burgtheater). Not bad for a former dentist! Stranitzky brought back to the stage the medieval 'Hanswurst', a robust, comical character who was at the same time social critic, practical philosopher and sharp parodist. The people loved him. While the court went to hear Italian opera and French

106   The old Burgtheater

211

farces, and the Church produced Latin plays, most people went to see the baroque, exuberant Hanswurst, with whom they could easily identify. The Hanswurst, the Viennese version of Jack Pudding, grew so popular that even members of the court and the nobility would occasionally slip away for an evening of *real* fun. Among them was Lady Mary Montague who reports (in a letter supposedly written to her friend Alexander Pope) on 14 September 1716, 'I never laughed so much in my life', though the play, a local 'Amphitryon', shocked her Puritan soul.

> It began with Jupiter's falling in love out of a peep-hole in the clouds and ended with the birth of Hercules... But I could not pardon the liberty the poet has taken of larding his play with not only indecent expressions, but such gross words as I don't think our mob would suffer from a mountebank; and the two Sosias fairly let down their breeches in the direct view of the boxes....

PARTOUT COMME CHEZ NOUS

The sudden death of Emperor Charles VI in 1740 stopped the fun. Hanswurst comedies were no longer permitted, but Vienna did not lose its reputation as the city of comedians. When the Hanswurst was expelled by Imperial decree, a naive, shrewd Austrian peasant named Kasperl appeared on the stage whose function was to amuse and to satirise. The court took a dim view of Kasperl's antics. After a performance, the Emperor Franz said to the manager, Marinelli, 'I must admit I did not laugh. The man makes such vulgar grimaces! But do not tell him. I do not want to offend the man who amuses my Viennese so well.' Goethe's friend, Carl Friedrich Zelter, disagreed. In 1819 he wrote, 'My stomach still hurts from laughing. The actor and the audience together make the play... Such gypsy pleasure cannot be described. The theatre is always crowded, if not at the beginning of the performance, certainly at the end, when the people come back from the Prater.'

During the winter Marinelli produced his comedies in the suburban Leopold-stadt Theatre, in summer-time in Baden near Vienna. While the 'serious' opera reached its climax with Mozart's *Don Giovanni*, the popular theatres in the suburbs were performing travesties of the ancient, mythological subjects. To enjoy travesty one has to know the original, and since the popular Viennese playwrights made fun of the world of Homer, Vergil, Horace and Ovid, it must

Josef Anton Stranitzky as
Hanswurst

be assumed that there was widespread knowledge of Latin and Greek. (The
Vienna *Festwochen* have resurrected the popular farces with the *Pawlatschen-
theater*.) In 1782 a writer named Blumauer had a great success with a travesty,
Adventures of The Pious Hero Aeneas (the year Mozart's *Abduction from the Seraglio*
was first performed). Carl Ludwig Gieseke had a smash hit, the farce *Der Tra-
vestierte Aeneas* at the Theater an der Wien in 1801, where four years later the first
performance of Beethoven's *Fidelio* was a flop.

Most of the popular farces were performed at the 'popular' houses: the Frey-
haustheater in the Wieden, the Leopoldstädter Theater, and the Josefstädter
Theater. The genre came to an end in 1835, when *Silenced Olympus or The Cold
Bath in the Underworld* was given at the Leopoldstadt, but by that time Vienna's
reputation as a great place for fun in the evening was well established. 'Most
Austrians are born jesters, and their dialect contributes to the fun', Ignaz Franz
Castelli, the poet, wrote in 1861. 'I have never laughed so much as in Vienna.'

Satire flourishes in times of oppression and strict censorship. During the tough
Metternich regime, playwrights and satirists used the antique frame to make fun
of the hated regime. (But the censors were strict; Schiller's *Don Carlos*, with
Marquis Posa's moving plea for 'freedom of thought', was banned from the stage
by Count Stadion, the secretary of state.) Travesties in Hellenistic costume
showed, much to the delight of the Viennese, that things were hardly better on

Mount Olympus than in Vienna. Juno nagged Jupiter, Cerberus could be bribed, Pluto was a stingy 'capitalist', Adonis married Venus, which created complications, Alceste pawned her children, and the physicians of Admetus let their patients die while 'murmuring Latin formulas and behaving with shameless commercialism'. All this was presented under the motto, '*partout comme chez nous*'. The Viennese thoroughly enjoyed it: things were terrible in Vienna, but then they could have been much, much worse – which has been the philosophy of the Viennese for at least a thousand years. In *The Abduction of Princess Europa* Merkur says, 'If we had no hope left, half the people on earth would be no longer alive' – exactly what the Viennese said at the end of the second world war when many thought that things could hardly be worse.

FERDINAND RAIMUND: SOMETHING DARK AND SINISTER

The combination of playwright-and-actor, known elsewhere too, has always been particularly popular in Vienna. Schikaneder – actor, manager, librettist and playwright – amused his public with his baroque clown, a Tyrolian character called Wastl. ('The Viennese prefer Wastl and the Kasperl, and ignore the court theatre and the Italians', the critic J. G. Seume wrote in 1801.) Ferdinand Raimund, the great playwright-actor of the Biedermeier era, had been infected by the Viennese passion for the stage when he was a confectioner's apprentice (another very Viennese profession) and sold pastries in the gallery in the old Burgtheater. As a poet he always walks the borderline between reality and unreality, the earthly and unearthly world. He was neither satirist nor social critic but rather 'the Viennese *Volksgeist*' (folk spirit), as Hofmannsthal called him. Grillparzer, whose plays were performed on the stage of the celebrated old Burgtheater (where Raimund's plays appeared only after his death) admitted that there was 'some genius' in Raimund's plays.

'Something dark and sinister always stands next to Raimund', wrote Hofmannsthal. 'Sometimes it is people's jealousy, their meanness and envy, sometimes again it is melancholy that dims his spirit. His language is baroque, a mixture of common and noble elements, partly elevated, partly the voice of Vienna's Hanswurst.' The titles too of Raimund's plays have a very Viennese sound: *Der Diamant des Geisterkönigs* ('The Fairy King's Diamond') for instance,

107 Actors in the Viennese comic tradition: (*top left*) Johann Laroche as Kasperl; (*bottom left*) Ferdinand Raimund; (*top right*) Johann Nestroy; (*bottom right*) Alexander Girardi

in which the Emperor Franz I appeared on the stage, in proper satirical disguise; or *Der Bauer als Millionär* ('The Peasant as Millionaire'); and his finest play, *Der Verschwender* ('The Spendthrift'). In all his works Raimund created a synthesis of farce, fancy and baroque comedy; his sentiment, his resignation, his despair softened by moments of cheerfulness are typically Viennese. So was his end. Lonely, sensitive and 'easily frightened' (as Hofmannsthal, an easily frightened man himself, described him) he committed suicide, after an unhappy private life, 'while the balance of his mind was disturbed'. (Hofmannsthal himself died in 1929, as he was on his way to the funeral of his son, Franz, who had committed suicide two days earlier.)

JOHANN NESTROY

Raimund's great rival playwright and actor was Johann Nepomuk Eduard Ambrosius Nestroy, parodist, moralist and satirist who began, again in true Viennese style, as a bass-baritone at the court opera (he had some success as Sarastro in *The Magic Flute*) and became a brilliant comedian at the Theater an der Wien in 1831, five years before Raimund's death. Their rivalry delighted the Viennese and created endless arguments and legends in this stage-struck city. Many of the critics sided with Raimund who was a noble figure, representing the 'good old' (Biedermeier) days. The audience were fans of Nestroy, the somewhat sinister comedian who wanted 'to make them laugh' but at the same time exposed human frailty. The best Nestroy lines are timeless, topical and true, as are the lines of Shakespeare. Nestroy was a philosopher at heart (though professors of German literature or philosophy would hardly agree with that statement). Philosophers, especially in German-speaking countries, are supposed to be 'serious', and Nestroy's method was laughter. But he made people laugh (often against their will) about man's shortcomings – very serious things. His characters come from the suburbs – modest artisans, shopkeepers, shoemakers, little fellows who are good and bad. They are never idealised, always true; they are terrified of their landlord; they dream of *Backhendl* (chicken fried in breadcrumbs, the traditional Sunday and holiday dish that gave the Biedermeier era the name '*Backhendlzeit*'). Nothing escaped his satirical observation and sardonic wit. In *Unverhofft* Nestroy debunked 'the threadbare Viennese *Gemütlichkeit*'

108 Window of a hatmaker's shop in the early nineteenth century

(which Dr Hanns Sachs, a pupil of Sigmund Freud, later defined as 'a special weakness of character that avoids sharp conflict and ignores strong convictions'); in *Freiheit im Krähwinkel* Nestroy satirised the revolution of 1848, which took some courage. Everybody in the audience knew that the silly, ridiculous people of Krähwinkel were really the Viennese, and everybody laughed and applauded enthusiastically; this farcical play was the most important literary product of the revolution. It ran throughout July 1848, while the revolution continued throughout Europe.

Two years later Nestroy wrote *The Old Man with the Young Wife*, which he called a *Volksstück* (popular play), but by that time censorship had been re-established and the play was not performed in Nestroy's lifetime. The censors considered it dynamite. The plot describes the escape of a political prisoner in 1850, and the behaviour of the people towards him. In his masterpiece, *Judith and Holofernes*, Nestroy attacked another cherished Viennese institution, anti-semitism, by the brilliant device of disguising Viennese characters as Jews and holding the Jews up for laughter, while actually exposing the Viennese for their weakness and meanness, their outward charm and lack of inner conviction.

Perhaps not unexpectedly, Nestroy was also much disliked in Vienna. The liberals called him a reactionary; the conservatives damned him as an anarchist. As a baroque philosopher he did not take himself seriously, never set up a 'system'. His aim was to hold up man's imperfections and his weapon was wit. Goethe once called Voltaire 'France'. Egon Friedell, the author of the brilliant, three-volume *Kulturgeschichte der Neuzeit* (The Cultural History of Modern Times), called Nestroy 'Vienna'. (Had Nestroy lived, he might have returned the compliment. On 18 March 1938, five days after Hitler's arrival in Vienna, three Austrian Nazis came up to Friedell's apartment, wanting 'to take him along'. Friedell, still wearing his dressing gown, excused himself for a moment, stepped into the other room and leaped from the fourth floor, crying 'Hallo!' to warn the people in the street, so that he would not hurt anyone.)

Nestroy's plays often dealt with the past or with the future, but his characters are timeless. Though he was the greatest Austrian satirist, abroad he is the least known because his idiom cannot be translated. His language is the Viennese mixture of Czech, Hungarian, Croatian, Italian, French and many German words, all buried under the fluffy Viennese *Schlagobers* dialect.

109 Staircase in the old Sternhof where Nestroy lived

It has been Vienna's good fortune that in times of spiritual or moral decadence there has almost always been a satirist and social critic around, usually on the stage, to debunk the Viennese legend and tell the people the awful truth. The Viennese have always accepted criticism, as long as it is presented by one of their own people and in an amusing manner. Nestroy's contemporaries did not really understand him; they thought he was a marvellous comic and laughed at his satire without realising its deeper meaning. (Satirists never have an easy life in Vienna. Karl Kraus, the great twentieth-century moralist in Vienna who fought a one-man battle against everything that was rotten in Austria, was often ridiculed, but thirty years after his death there has been a Kraus renaissance in Vienna. And now Helmut Qualtinger, the leading contemporary satirist and co-author of *Der Herr Karl*, spends much of his time away from the city which he hate-loves and debunks.)

ALEXANDER GIRARDI

Twenty years after Nestroy's death, a great comedian, Alexander Girardi, became the darling of Vienna. Unlike Raimund or Nestroy, he did not write his own material, but he continued their tradition, creating human beings on the stage and making witty and barbed remarks. He performed several parts in Raimund's plays which Raimund had originally written for himself; perhaps the most famous was Valentin, the carpenter in *The Spendthrift*. The memory of Girardi's '*Hobellied*' ('Plane Song') still brings tears to the eyes of many old people in Vienna. His '*Fiakerlied*' became the theme song of the 'Girardi era'; in Vienna, historical epochs are more often called after actors than rulers. When Girardi, as the immortal *Fiaker* (the driver of a two-horse coach) sang, 'Anyone can become a *Fiaker*, but only in Vienna do they know how to drive', the Viennese of all classes had a lump in their throat. Yet Girardi was no sentimental fool; he was just a very good actor. (Like many 'typical' Viennese he was not born in Vienna but came from Graz in Styria.) He used to say that he played a Viennese 'for the benefit of the Viennese … not what they are but what they would like to be'. He created a fashion and a type, wearing a straw hat (later to be called 'a Girardi', which was fashionable in America during the Prohibition, when Girardi was long dead) and an elegant stick; and when he walked in

110 Motor-car made for the Duke of Cumberland, exiled in Vienna

Kärntnerstrasse, the gay and charming *bon vivant*, doffing his straw hat to a pretty woman, he looked exactly what every Viennese wanted to be – *ein echter Wiener*, a genuine Viennese.

A TYPICAL AUSTRIAN FATE

Except for some blessed, short periods of time, the 'world capital of music' never was a city of literature. The muses who loved Austria did not give the people everything; Austrians have never been very good at expressing themselves with words. Schubert and Johann Strauss expressed the spirit of Vienna in their melodies, Fischer von Erlach and Johann Lucas von Hildebrandt achieved the same in their baroque buildings, Johann Michael Rottmayr and Moritz von Schwind in their paintings, Georg Raphael Donner and Balthasar Permoser in their sculptures. But only during the *Vormärz* did there emerge a definite Austrian literature which was not part of the German literature. During this period Grillparzer, Raimund, Nestroy, Nikolaus Lenau and Adalbert Stifter lived and worked in Vienna. They never formed a 'group'; all of them remained fierce individualists, each going his lonely way, suffering from melancholy, the Austrian writer's occupational disease, and often from morbid hypochondria. Misunderstood or ignored by their own people who took little interest in literature, they sensed their isolation and were depressed by it. Nestroy fought a losing battle against his attacks of despondency; Lenau's depression ended in madness; Raimund and Stifter both committed suicide. Grillparzer's tragedy has been called 'a typical Austrian fate', for he did everything wrong. He did not marry the girl he had loved all his life; only as an old misanthrope did he move in with her and her sister. As a thirty-five-year-old poet, already famous, he made a pilgrimage to Goethe in Weimar which did not turn out very well: 'To see the idol of my youth, the author of *Faust, Clavigo* and *Egmont* as a stiffly formal minister who offered tea to his guests was a terrible disappointment. I would have preferred it if he'd been rude to me and thrown me out.'

Grillparzer's revolutionary poems were found in his drawer – after his death. He was too late for everything. Like all Austrian writers of his time, he had been deeply aroused by the authoritarian Metternich regime with its severe censorship and the ubiquitous secret police.

JUNG WIEN: VIENNA'S GAY APOCALYPSE

The next wave of literary rebellion, this time against bourgeois narrow-minded-
ness and the cultural decay of the 'Ringstrasse' style, came around the turn of the
century, when the fin-de-siècle group 'Jung Wien' (Young Vienna) began to meet
at the Café Griensteidl, and later at the 'Central', 'Herrenhof', 'Schottentor'
and 'Bastei'. As always in Vienna, the personalities were better known than their
works. A great many Viennese who had never read a book or seen a play would
know the exact location of the *Stammtisch*, the table where Arthur Schnitzler,
Richard Beer-Hofmann and Hermann Bahr used to sit at the Café Griensteidl.
In *The World of Yesterday* Stefan Zweig writes about Hugo von Hofmannsthal's
first appearance in this hallowed inner circle:

Hermann Bahr often told me of his astonishment when he received for his magazine an
essay signed 'Loris'. Never had he seen among all the contributions one that dispersed in
such spirited language a similar wealth of thought with such apparent facility. Who is
'Loris'? who is this unknown author? Bahr asked himself. Certainly an old man who in
years and years of silent meditation had distilled his wisdom and cultivated in mysterious
solitude the sublime essence of language into an almost voluptuous magic. And such a
sage, such a blessed poet was living in the same city, and he had never heard of him! Bahr
wrote at once to this unknown man and made an appointment at the Café Griensteidl,
the headquarters of the group. Suddenly a slim *Gymnasiast* [high-school student] who wore
short pants and certainly did not shave, approached Bahr's table, bowed and said in his
high-pitched boy's voice, 'Hofmannsthal! I am Loris.' Even years afterwards Bahr became
excited when he remembered his astonishment. At first he had refused to believe it. A
Gymnasiast, with such art and understanding, such depth of feeling and knowledge of life!

Later Arthur Schnitzler invited the young *Gymnasiast* to read for him a play in
verse. Schnitzler told Zweig that he had been deeply impressed. 'I had the
feeling of having encountered a born genius for the first time in my life. Never
again during my entire lifetime was I so overwhelmed.'

The writers of the 'Young Vienna' group had many things in common to make
them friends: their feeling for style and beauty, their infatuation with poetry,
their deep love of Vienna. They would read their works to one another and
listen to each other's suggestions. They were enthusiastic letter writers and their
correspondence, much of which was later published, is an astonishing comment
on the workings of the creative mind. They wrote introductions to each other's
books; Hofmannsthal, still a teenager, wrote a beautiful verse prologue to the

published version of Schnitzler's satirical comedy *Anatol*, in which he lovingly and artfully recreated the Vienna of 1760:

> *Mit verschlafenen Kaskaden*
> *Und verschlafenen Tritonen*
> *Rokoko, verstaubt und lieblich,*
> *Seht ... das Wien des Canaletto*
> *Wien von siebzehnhundertsechzig ...*

The stars of the Café Griensteidl were literary all-rounders: poets, playwrights, essayists, novelists and critics. Bahr was an influential drama critic and his reviews helped Schnitzler to be accepted by the exalted Burgtheater. Once Bahr discovered the unusual talent of an unknown Italian actress who was performing the title role in Sardou's *Fedora* at the suburban Carltheater. Her name was Eleonora Duse. (Another time Bahr sarcastically criticised a young actress of pronounced non-talent. He was duly challenged to a duel by her brother, a young officer. The duel was fought with pistols; fortunately the two duellists missed each other. A few days later the actress wrote to Bahr and bitterly complained that first he had ruined her career and now had tried to murder her brother; this was too much, she said, and she was giving up the stage and going home.)

Many poets and writers of the 'revolutionary' Young Vienna school were embarrassed by their solid, bourgeois family background. Their fathers and uncles were prosperous merchants, industrialists, factory owners. Some broke away by changing their names. Hofmannsthal's great-grandfather, a Jewish silk merchant named Isak Löw Hofmann, had come from Prague to Vienna in 1788, became a silk millionaire and was ennobled by Emperor Franz I. Herr Hofmann changed his name to Herr von Hofmannsthal and had an impressive coat of arms designed that showed a mulberry leaf, the symbol of silk, and the tablets of the law. (Did Hugo von Hofmannsthal think of his ancestor when he created the amusing character of the recently ennobled Herr von Faninal in *Rosenkavalier* who is proud of his new rank?) The son of the silk millionaire had become a Roman Catholic and married an Italian girl; and *his* son, the father of the poet, had married an Austrian Catholic. Hugo was raised as a Catholic but always remained conscious of his Jewish heritage. He wrote 'Ganz vergessener Völker Müdigkeiten kann ich nicht abtun von meinen Lidern' (I cannot brush from my eyelids the weariness of a forgotten people).

111   Hofmannstahl's baroque house in Rodaun

Egon Friedmann, whose papa was a silk manufacturer, became the cultural historian Egon Friedell. Herr Richard Engländer turned into the bohemian coffee-house poet, Peter Altenberg, and when even that sounded too bourgeois, he called himself just 'P.A.'. Yet Vienna's writers did not scorn the comforts of wealth and the things money could buy. Schnitzler, Beer-Hofmann, Bahr and Hofmannsthal had beautiful homes, gardens, servants. But they were not happy. The great romantic epoch was over. They were living at a time of decadence and were acutely aware of it. They became introspective and precious, caring more about style than content; they avoided reality. Hofmannsthal in his beautiful prologue to Schnitzler's *Anatol*, said that he saw himself *'frühgereift und zart und traurig'*, precocious and delicate and wistful.

In the cold, desperate years after the first world war, the coffee-house remained the writers' real home. There they forgot their worries and fears. Trebitsch writes that Roda Roda, Ralf Auernheimer, Stefan Zweig, Jakob Wassermann and he himself were fanatical chess players. The grand old men of 'Young Vienna' were still around, though somewhat removed from the daily routine of the coffee-houses. Hofmannsthal, Vienna's greatest twentieth-century poet, had retired into his private dream world. In his essay 'Hofmannsthal und seine Zeit' (Hofmannsthal and His Time), Hermann Broch, now considered one of Austria's greatest philosophers, says, 'He [Hofmannsthal] walked as an exotic prince, without companions ... through a reality which his loneliness deepened and widened into a dream, to become an unworldly solace in his isolation.'

The atmosphere of the world of yesterday was vividly recreated not long ago when the correspondence between Hofmannsthal and Schnitzler was published. It began in 1891, when Schnitzler was twenty-nine and 'Loris' was seventeen. In the earlier letters, Schnitzler addresses the young man as 'Dear Friend' and Hofmannsthal respectfully writes *Geehrter Herr* (Esteemed Sir). Both were enthusiastic bicyclists who were forever discovering new tours in the vicinity of Vienna. In one letter Schnitzler suggests a beautiful excursion, '... you go from Tini by way of Heiligenkreuz-Alland-Neuhaus-Pottenstein-Vöslau. Or: Rohrerhütte-Königstetten, very hilly, you will have to push. Or: Rekawinkel-Hütteldorf. ... I would be delighted to ride with you.' And Hofmannsthal admits that 'bicycling makes me very happy'.

In many letters there are mentions of meetings at the coffee-house; 'I'll see

112   The Arsenal, destination of a Schnitzler-Hofmannsthal bicycle ride

you after seven at the Griensteidl', Schnitzler writes. And another time, 'It would be too bad if I couldn't come at ten to the Café Central, where we can talk for an hour.' Hofmannsthal tells his friend that he would like to make two excursions, one to the Arsenal, and another to the tower of St Stephen's Cathedral. Two weeks later 'Arthur' answers, 'Will you be at the Café Central on Saturday night? When shall we go to the Arsenal? And when shall we see each other?' Other meetings are arranged, 'under the arcades of the Opera', at 11 a.m. at the Café Central, late at night at the Café Pucher – 'tonight almost certainly at the Pucher – do call for me there at about ten-thirty'.

Though Hofmannsthal was twelve years his junior, Schnitzler was so impressed with the young poet that he sent him his manuscripts asking for Hofmannsthal's judgement, and rewrote some parts of *Anatol* after Hofmannsthal had suggested changes. On 15 February 1903, Hofmannsthal and Beer-Hofmann wrote a joint letter to Schnitzler, having just read the manuscript of *Der Reigen* (better known in England and America by its French title, *La Ronde*). They addressed Schnitzler as 'Dear Pornographer' and wrote alternate paragraphs. 'Much will depend on who is going to publish this smut', wrote Hofmannsthal. 'Illustrations à la Coshell would make this *cochonnerie* the laughing stock of Europe. If you find a serious publisher then it will be all right because this is your best book, you *Schmutzfink* [dirty fellow].' Beer-Hofmann adds, 'You are bound to get so much money for it (in advance, because if you are paid afterwards it might be confiscated) that this will please you more than the trouble you are going to have with all the gossip. Whether I would publish it, I don't know. Probably I would ask *you* . . .'. Hofmannsthal writes, 'I would publish it, against a considerable advance, and under *your* name. (The advance would be payable in *my* name.)' Beer-Hofmann ends, 'This letter may be used as a preface.'

Reigen, a chain of terrifying and poetic satirical dialogues on the decadence of Vienna before the first world war and on the mating habits of the Viennese, reveals the full mastership and maturity of Arthur Schnitzler, the most important playwright of the fin-de-siècle (that era called by Broch 'Vienna's gay apocalypse'). Schnitzler's characters have the inimitable Viennese mixture of lightheartedness and *Schwermut*, of exhilaration and haunting nostalgia. He was born in 1862 in Vienna and came from a highly cultured Jewish family. When he was young, anti-semitism in Vienna was merely a lower-class, vulgar phenome-

non that had not yet inflicted intelligent people; it was 'not done'. Unlike some Jewish writers who came later – Karl Kraus, Stefan Zweig, Egon Friedell – Schnitzler was not perturbed by racial discrimination. With a doctor's insight into the tragedies of life he was able to write comedies about psychological conflicts with detachment and always with a touch of poetry. The Viennese now recognise themselves in Schnitzler's plays. In *Anatol*, for instance, he writes about a young Viennese poet who believes himself to be in love with a woman but is really only in love with himself. A great many young men in Vienna have since considered themselves Anatols. Schnitzler's other famous creation is the Viennese *femme fatale*, married, attractive and unfaithful, slipping out of her bourgeois home late in the afternoon, veiled and mysterious, to spend the blue hour with her lover, knowing the risks and willing to pay for them. (In Trieste,

Schnitzler's influence caught up with Italo Svevo, who in turn influenced Alberto Moravia, whose family comes from there.)

Schnitzler expressed in his poetry what Schubert had expressed eighty years earlier in his music. 'So much of what we now live through and suffer started around 1900, and amazingly much of it in Vienna', writes Hans Weigel, the critic; 'for instance, what we call "modern literature", which shows itself, quite inconspicuously, in Schnitzler's one-act plays which act out a strange game with reality and set a question mark against the reality of the observed world. But this literary revolution was unannounced and unobserved. In music and psychology there were Viennese schools; painting and architecture had their trends and scandals; but the "Young Vienna" literature around 1900 spread only accidentally across the borders of the country ... Schnitzler's perceptions are new though he presents them often with conventional means.'

Of all modern Austrian playwrights, Schnitzler is now the most popular, more often performed than at the time of his death. Psychologists and critics give various reasons for this Schnitzler renaissance: Schnitzler's 'death wish', his loneliness, his psychological insight, his penetrating analysis of a decadent society make him alive, modern, very close to our consciousness. No one knew this better than Sigmund Freud who wrote to Schnitzler on 8 June 1906 (one of Freud's letters published in *Die Neue Rundschau*, with notes by Heinrich Schnitzler, the son of the writer, now director of the Theatre in the Josefstadt): 'I have often asked myself, wondering from where you were able to draw that secret knowledge that I had to acquire through laborious investigation of the subject, and in the end I came to envy the poet whom before I had only admired ....'

THE PRESS: KARL KRAUS

Vienna is the city of such 'intimate' writers as Schnitzler and Hofmannsthal but the Viennese have never had an intimate relationship with books, such as, for instance, the Parisians have, or the Londoners, or the Berliners. The Germans are proud to be called the nation of *Dichter und Denker* ('poets and thinkers'). The Austrians are resigned to being the nation of *Geiger und Tänzer* ('fiddlers and dancers'). The delight of spending the evening at home with a book is not popular in this city of sensuous extroverts who love to be out, to be surrounded by

music, to drink young wine at their favourite *Heuriger*, or, best of all, go to the theatre. There are over twenty major libraries in Vienna but many Viennese have never been inside one. The National Library, established in 1526, now occupies a beautiful building by Fischer von Erlach. Wilhelm Hausenstein called this great hall 'the nonplusultra of the Viennese baroque, with its columns made of stucco lustro, pink, dove-gray, beige, pearl-gray ... gilded panels way up to the frescos, perhaps the most important wall coverings created by the Austrian High Baroque'. The library contains over one and a half million printed volumes and rare special collections (such as the papyrus scrolls and the theatre collection).

The great libraries are often ignored. 'In its book production Vienna mirrors itself as in a small hand mirror, but in its newspaper production it stands in front of a large dressing-room mirror, and appears as a literary person from head to toe', the satirist Ferdinand Kürnberger wrote in 1873. Vienna's newspapers were once the best in Europe. They created a style and a fashion and were widely, and unsuccessfully, imitated in Germany. The 'small' literary genre of the *Feuilleton* is a Viennese invention. 'Nothing is more significant for Vienna than the hegemony of the *Feuilleton*', wrote Franz Servaes in 1908. The *Feuilleton* is a short, light, pointed essay which presents in a small frame – rarely more than two thousand words – a graceful reflection on a topical or not-so-topical event, combining style and poise, information and entertainment, and at best a certain depth and wisdom. The language is cultivated, and the style is lucid. The early masters of the Viennese *Feuilleton* – Ludwig Speidel, Eduard Hanslick, Daniel Spitzer, Ferdinand Kürnberger – wrote little close-ups of Vienna and the Viennese, producing literary gems which have shown astonishing durability. A strong mutual bond existed between the newspaper and its readers, as between performer and audience. The newspapers were a substitute for books, and journalists fulfilled the function of authors elsewhere. Identification with the reader went so far that the papers printed exactly what the readers expected, creating a definite language, which was in turn imitated by the readers.

The most important paper of the final half-century of the Habsburg monarchy was the *Neue Freie Presse*, founded in 1864, the unofficial mouthpiece and sounding board of the monarchy under Franz Joseph I. (The official mouthpiece, *Wiener Zeitung*, had a small circulation.) The often pompous-sounding

114 Garden of the Döbling villa where Josephine von Wertheimstein held her literary salon until the 1890s

editorials that Moritz Benedikt wrote for the *Presse*, the brilliant *Feuilletons*, the literary and musical reviews, were the Bible of the bourgeoisie in the vast empire of Austro-Hungary, from Craców to Trieste, from Budapest to Czernowitz, from Mährisch-Ostrau to Meran. The *Presse* was the daily encyclopaedia of all the things a member of the bourgeois and aristocratic society, of the middle class and intelligentsia, was expected to know – and say. It gave the readers a pleasing sense of security to find their own thoughts and aspirations, ideas and ideals expressed and reflected every morning when they opened their paper. In an era that proudly called itself 'liberal', the *Neue Freie Presse* remained conservative (and often hypocritical) where the institutions of the monarchic establishment were concerned.

The most sardonic, most widely quoted, most brilliant critic of the *Presse* was Karl Kraus, the Viennese moralist, satirist, playwright and poet who used an inimitable mixture of allusions, puns, pointed sentences, new words and new meanings to ridicule people, symbols, actions, gods, and literature; he had bitter contempt for Schnitzler, Hofmannsthal and Sigmund Freud; he was immensely egotistical but even his enemies and victims respected his integrity and intransigency. At the time of his death in 1936 he was admired only by a small clique of fanatical followers. Now he is compared to Kierkegaard, Kafka and Eliot, and is recognised as one of the great innovators of the German language.

TWO TWENTIETH-CENTURY NOVELISTS

The two great Austrian novelists of our century are Robert Musil and Heimito von Doderer. Both had known the monarchy, had perhaps sung Haydn's beautiful national anthem *Gott erhalte unseren Kaiser* (taken from his String Quartet in C major, opus 76, No. 3). They had seen their fathers and elderly friends leave for the front, wearing their elegant light-blue tunics. Many of them had not returned. These writers had witnessed the collapse of a civilisation and were resigned to the fact that they would not see a new one. Robert Musil, an Austrian of partly Czech descent, has now emerged as one of the great figures of world literature. His monumental, unfinished novel, *Der Mann ohne Eigenschaften* (The Man without Qualities), is a complex satire on Vienna on the eve of the first world war. It is one of the longest novels in literature; Musil admired Dostoievsky,

Tolstoy and Balzac, and he continued in the great tradition. But he was Austrian and he deals with the favourite theme of Viennese literature, the conflict between *Sein*, what one is, and *Schein*, what one appears to be. The novel is a magnificent exercise in the Austrian counterpoint between thoughts and behaviour; Ulrich, the passive hero, tries to be himself but is unable to achieve this and eventually submits to the indefinable pattern of the world. ('I am not the kind of author who tells his readers what they want to hear because they know it anyway', Musil wrote in a letter in 1940, two years before his death. 'My attitude and my work tend rather more towards the severe, and my readers have gradually come to me, not I to them.')

The last of the important Austrian novelists, Heimito von Doderer, died late in 1966. His greatness is not yet fully appreciated; it has always been 'an Austrian fate' to be discovered only posthumously. His novels, *The Demons*, and *Die Strudelhofstiege*, are wonderfully rich chronicles of Vienna and the Viennese; his last, vast work, called simply *Roman No. 7* (Novel No. 7) is unfinished.

LINA LOOS: THE COLD LIGHT OF DEFEAT

Between the two world wars there was a new generation of educated citizens in Vienna – people who were not afraid of doing a little hard thinking, who listened to Karl Kraus, the great magician of the language and the conscience of the literary epoch. These people were more interested in what their writers had to say than what they were. The pleasures of sensuousness gave way to meditation, discussion, the formation of new thought. Suddenly there were groups and circles that *cared* about literature; people were keeping in touch with literature abroad. A few old men from the 'Young Vienna' days were still around, and they were joined by Robert Musil, Franz Werfel, Robert Neumann, Stefan Zweig, Anton Wildgans, Alexander Lernet-Holenia, Alfred Polgar, Egon Friedell, Felix Braun, Hermann Broch, Max Mell, Franz Theodor Czokor. The 'Viennese School' of novelists, essayists and playwrights had both depth of thought and brilliance of expression; for once the form did not dominate the content. For a few happy years Vienna became *the* literary city in German-speaking Europe; Austrian literature was not a sub-species of German literature.

It did not last; in retrospect it looks like the last flickering of the candle before

Adolf Loos, by Kokoschka

the storm of Nazism blew out the light. The writers and their readers dispersed, went into exile, were taken to concentration camps. The few who stayed back were cut off from the currents of world literature. It was not only the end of a literary era but of a whole literature-minded society.

In a recently published collection of letters, *Du Silberne Dame Du*, written by and to Lina Loos, the first wife of Adolf Loos, the last flickering of the candle brilliantly illuminates the atmosphere of literary Vienna during the first half of the twentieth century. Lina Loos was born in 1882 in the building of 'Casa Piccola', one of Vienna's most famous coffee-houses, whose owner, the South-Tyrolean Obertimpfler, was Lina's father. (Napoleon's war council met at the Casa Piccola in 1809. In 1820 it was the scene of Metternich's police raids against the 'Carbonari', members of the secret Italian society which was fighting for Italy's liberation from the Habsburg yoke.) Lina Loos was called the most beautiful woman in Vienna when in 1902 she married Loos, who had proposed to her when she was sixteen. Loos, a fanatic of lean, unadorned beauty, had shown her two boxes, one made of gold with many baroque ornaments, and a simple, unadorned box of birch wood, and had asked her to choose one. Lina took the wooden box, and Loos sensed that she shared instinctively his theory of 'ornament and crime'.

The marriage did not last. Lina became a celebrated diseuse (in Berlin she

115 Living-room designed by Adolf Loos

was compared to Yvette Guilbert), an actress (in New York she was hired by Heinrich Conried to perform the part of Luise in Schiller's *Kabale und Liebe*), a gifted writer, and the friend of the poets and writers and musicians of her era: Peter Altenberg thought of himself as 'Lina's Tristan', and Egon Friedell was always in love with her. The neo-romantics and expressionists, fin-de-siècle writers and Bauhaus creators gathered around Lina Loos; Franz Werfel and Alma Mahler-Werfel, and the playwright Georg Kaiser; Berta Zuckerkandl, the sister-in-law of Georges Clemenceau; the great Viennese dancer, Grete Wiesenthal; the gifted actress, Margarete Köppke (who committed suicide); August Strindberg's daughter, Kerstin; and Franz Theodor Czokor, the Catholic poet and playwright, one of the few non-Jewish Austrian intellectuals who voluntarily went into exile in 1938 'because I could not stand the inhumanity and meanness of the Viennese around me'. Czokor co-edited the letters which Lina Loos, the 'Silver Lady', had written and received. Czokor calls these letters 'epistulae ex Ponto':

They lead from the dreamy *Wienertum* of yesterday by way of the civil war of February and July 1934, the end of Austria in 1938, into the world of 1945, when the people came out of their broken houses with broken hearts, to meet again in the cold light of defeat. Only very few had kept a clean, unbroken conscience because they had dared brave the depreciation of human values in these dark years... Lina Loos was one of the very few....

One of Czokor's letters, of 17 June 1939, to Lina Loos is from Osiedle Ostoja, Poland, where he had found temporary exile until Hitler's *Blitzkrieg* forced him to run again. The letter had to pass the Nazi censors in Vienna and is written in a sort of private code:

My dear.... Your letter contains nothing but sad news. Ö. [Ödön von Horvath] is dead, and so are G. and K., and all like Egon [Friedell]. Strange that his sickness [read: suicide] is now so widespread there [in Vienna]. I feel as though we stand at the grave of a whole world, which had so much merry melancholy and dreamy seriousness. Remember the novel *Radetzkymarsch*? Its author [Joseph Roth] followed Ödön whom he loved. In a bistro in the Sixième Arrondissement he collapsed; to the people who wanted to help him, he said, 'Don't bother. It won't last long.' It did last four long, painful days until he died. And T. [the playwright Ernst Toller] hanged himself in a New York boarding house. Dori [the poet Ferdinand Bruckner] in his obituary rejected such a death for people who want to give an example, as T. did. The 'cat' [nickname of a Viennese actress] found a refuge at her sister's place in Huelva, Spain; Maria K. [Maria Klöpfer, wife of a Viennese actor] found peace at the bottom of the Lake of Lugano. 'Even the trees seem artificial here', the other Rudi [the actor Rudolf Forster] writes from Hollywood; he asked me to send him a certain poem about Vienna written by Anton Wildgans which he loves very much. Yes, strange wishes reach me here from everywhere ... And I walk as in a dream through the southern district of Warsaw where my friend Józef Wittlin [the famous Polish novelist] lives, and the street reminds me of our Iglaseegasse in Döbling, and now the streetcar No. 39 – your streetcar! – comes around the corner, and I shall see the vineyards of the Wienerwald – but no, it's only my loneliness that has led me astray ... here the streetcar No. 39 goes to Wilanow, the sad pleasure-castle of Jan Sobieski ....

Lina Loos died in 1950 after a terrible sickness, of which she never said a word even to her closest friends. Czokor remembers that as a school girl she was once asked what she wanted to be in life, and had answered, 'a martyr'.

By the time the literary Vienna had recovered from the shock of the second world war, had rediscovered Franz Kafka and Karl Kraus, and produced a few new talents, the centrifugal forces were already too strong for the young people to resist. Many new talents left Vienna to live in Germany, Switzerland, France, Spain. Today the state, private sponsors, the city, industry, try to stimulate literary production by arranging contests and awarding prizes. The Austrian Society for Literature keeps in touch with literary currents abroad – both in the East and the West. But the literary world has become very small. Vienna's publishing world is again a 'hand mirror', as Kürnberger wrote in 1873. Many Austrian writers prefer to be published in Germany or in Switzerland, where the leading literary groups are established. In fact today Vienna is journey's end rather than a junction for the flow of ideas. In London, Paris, Munich, Zurich, people and ideas are on the move but not in Vienna, which tries so hard to be a focal point and bridge. There are discussions of writers, artists and intellectuals from East and West, but they seem to take place in a sound-proof room into which no word can penetrate from the outside. Most Viennese are hardly aware of it.

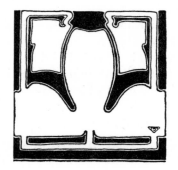

5

Coffee, Wine and Cakes

MASTERPIECES AND CIGAR SMOKE

Kolschitzki's first coffee-house was established in Vienna in 1684, one year after the Turkish siege and eighteen years after the first local opera performance. Both the opera and the coffee-house have baffled Viennese historians by their apparent indestructibility. Admittedly the coffee-house had long periods of decline, and its fall was often predicted, but after two hundred and eighty-four years the institution is still gloriously alive. Somehow it has remained, an island of free thought and free speech, an oasis of solitude or companionship, of meditation or conversation, the haven of the individualist and the refuge of the non-conformist, the last catacomb where Man can go underground with his secret thoughts and inner aspirations.

The coffee-house is not a Viennese invention. The first coffee-house was opened in Constantinople in about 1540, and from there the pleasant institution came to Europe, in about the middle of the seventeenth century. Oxford had its first cafés as early as 1650. Two years later, one Daniel Edwards, a merchant, opened a coffee-house at St Michael's Alley in London. Later, writers and dandies would meet at Tom's and Button's or at Farr's and Will's. The oldest café in Paris is the Café Procope in the Rue des Fosses-Saint-Germain; it still exists and is popular with students from the Sorbonne. In Venice the first coffee-house was opened in St Mark's Square.

But the Viennese coffee-houses were to become the most famous of all. Sixteen years after Kolschitzki had started the trend, there were already thirty such establishments in Vienna. The owner needed an Imperial privilege but quite a few people served Turkish coffee illegally. In 1704 a chronicler wrote, 'Vienna

118 Girl with a coffee-grinder

is full of coffee-houses where the novelists ... get together, read the news in the papers, and talk about it'. Billiard tables were added in 1780, and signs informed the patrons that smoking was permitted. One Johann Evangelist Milani opened his coffee-house in Kohlmarkt and put up chess tables. Among the habitués was Mozart's brilliant librettist, the poet Lorenzo da Ponte. Milani was always there, cutting a splendid figure in his white tails, with *Dreispitz* and pigtail, and looking like Guglielmo or Ferrando in da Ponte's and Mozart's *Così Fan Tutte*. 'One studies, one plays, gossips, sleeps, negotiates, barters, intrigues', writes a chronicler. 'At night, Milani wants to close and implores the guests, *corpo dio maledetto*, to leave, but no one does.' Ladies were served 'frozen cream' in the 'garden', a section of the sidewalk in front of the coffee-house, separated from the street by a low barrier and a couple of potted trees. Unlike the French sidewalk café which merges with the street the Viennese coffee-house always likes to preserve the illusion of privacy.

By the end of the eighteenth century, the Viennese coffee-house had become the cradle of Vienna's literature; ever since, 'coffee-house' and '*littérateurs*' have remained synonymous in this city. There has always been one outstanding literary café – only one. Writers and scientists first met at the dim, shabby, bohemian-like Kramer's Coffee-House in Schlossergassel, near Graben. Here, according to Friedrich Nicolai, one could read newspapers from Hamburg, Frankfurt, Bayreuth, Cologne, Leiden, and also Hungarian and English papers. The first local *literati* – Ayrenhoff, Blumauer, Alxinger, Ratschky, Retzer, Rautenstrauch – met there to read each other their works and to discuss them. They were not exactly men of modesty.

The Biedermeier created the 'Nobelcafé', a luxurious place for rich bourgeois where even archdukes might occasionally drop in. At the Café Jüngling, 'Christians, Jews and Macedonians' were seen sitting together. A string trio under young Joseph Lanner played music, and later a young man named Johann Strauss played second fiddle. But Vienna's poets felt nothing but contempt for the elegant Nobelcafés which were bright and ostentatious. Ideally, a coffee-house should be *gemütlich* and comfortable but must never 'look new'; it must have a special atmosphere but not necessarily crystal chandeliers.

During the *Vormärz* days, a new generation of writers and composers moved to Ignaz Neuner's Café at the corner of Spiegelgasse and Plankengasse. 'At

Neuner's men of spirit found their real home and a second reality, a world of the printed word, of unwritten masterpieces talked into the air and the cigar smoke, an empire with its own laws, a classless society', writes Hilde Spiel, the contemporary coffee-house historian and novelist. Grillparzer, Lenau, Raimund and Stifter regularly went to Neuner's, and less famous scribes gathered round the luminaries. Here all the fixtures were made of pure silver; there were silver door latches and silver coat hangers and seventy-two silver hat-hangers, and silver-rimmed meerschaum pipes for the habitués. There was also a special ladies' room with red damask walls where smoking was not permitted.

After the 1848 revolution Neuner's closed. To the authorities the Kaffeehaus had always been suspect. Austrian intrigues and Balkan revolutions have been plotted around Vienna's coffee-house tables. Metternich's secret police always searched the coffee-houses first when they had reason to expect some trouble. (Ninety years later, Hitler's Gestapo almost ruined the coffee-houses where Vienna's Catholics and Jews, clericals and liberals, and other 'enemies of the régime' would gather to hear the latest news or to digest disturbing rumours.)

THE CAFÉ GRIENSTEIDL: DON'T GIVE ME ANYTHING

In 1873, Ferdinand Kürnberger, a writer, reported that Vienna's newspapers sent free copies to all the coffee-houses and bribed the headwaiters 'to put them into the hands of the habitués'. By 1900 there were over seven hundred coffee-houses in Vienna. Around the fin-de-siècle the 'Young Vienna' circle – poets, satirists, essayists, critics, actors, politicians – gathered at the Café Griensteidl, at the Herberstein Palais, near the Hofburg. It was the meeting place of *littérateurs* and their hangers-on, 'well-bred burghers' sons whose thinking was concerned with aesthetics, not with ethics; the idea was to find the form since the subject was given; the subject was forever Vienna', write Julius Bab and Willi Handl. But there were some real writers too. Around 1890, one could have met there on almost any afternoon Arthur Schnitzler, Richard Beer-Hofmann, Felix Dormann, Felix Salten, and perhaps young Hugo von Hofmannsthal. Hermann Bahr from Linz, Upper Austria, became the leader and spokesman of the 'Moderne', an impressionist-psychological group of poets and philosophers. Richard Specht, the music critic, and a member of that august discussion group, later wrote, 'If someone had written down their conversations and published them as a book, he might have created one of the most candid, charming, artistically fascinating documents of the modern psyche.'

The atmosphere of the Café Griensteidl was beautifully and satirically described in its epitaph. Until 1897, when the Palais Herberstein was turned into an apartment building and the Café Griensteidl had to be closed, Karl Kraus – critic, moralist, essayist, playwright, who has been called 'Vienna's Rochefort' – had been one of its habitués. Like many 'genuine' *Wiener*, Kraus came from Moravia. He was a short, slim man with very bright blue eyes, who often wrote for Viennese newspapers under the nom-de-plume 'Crêpe de Chine'. Later he became a purist, a fanatic of good writing and of the German language, the violent partisan of Shakespeare, Nestroy and Offenbach. He broke with his erstwhile friends at the Griensteidl when he published his famous essay 'The Demolished Literature', a brilliant, satirical obituary on the great coffee-house, which he called

a literary traffic centre ... where even the *Marqueure* took part in the literary activities of their guests ... They seemed to be members of the writers' union rathers than the waiters' union ... Headwaiter Franz could even remember the face of a *passant* [a passer-by who dropped in once in a while, not several times a day, like an habitué]. Franz would always hand any guest the right newspaper, even if he had not seen the guest for twenty years. He had been a friend of Grillparzer and Bauernfeld; he remembered how naturalism had come from Berlin directly to the Café Griensteidl, where it was triumphantly greeted as a strong reaction against aesthetic defea ism... Since then the waiters had loved modern art, serving strange colour compositions of ice creams and parfaits, and introducing absinthe ....

Realism was soon followed by symbolism, the era of 'clinically observed conditions of the psyche [*Seelenzustände*], the escape from urgency, the interpretation of life...'. According to Karl Kraus the Griensteidl must have been a unique place. It had 'mountains of newspapers', and a complete set of Meyer's Konversations-Lexikon, the famous German-language encyclopaedia. This made visits to the café obligatory for writers doing some research. They also used the café's writing paper, but apparently many of them did not bother to order anything. ('There was the poet who would say to the headwaiter, "Don't give me anything", and after a while Heinrich, the headwaiter, would say to the underwaiter, "Herr Doktor has nothing as usual" ', writes Kraus.)

119 Franziskanerplatz reflected in a restaurant window

Karl Kraus, by Kokoschka

In the same obituary Kraus wrote sarcastically about 'the gentleman from Linz' (Bahr) whom he called 'a sort of latter-day Goethe ... his popularity is limited to the first four tables. Beginning with the left mirror table his popularity wanes. . . '. Kraus also attacked Hofmannsthal and Schnitzler ('When he writes about death, do not get frightened – his pistols are loaded with apathy ... to die is nothing but to live and not to see anything is everything'). Kraus also wrote about 'those who carry theatrical gossip from one table to the next while others imitate the Parisian bohemian ... And now all of them are thrown out and our literature enters a period of homelessness'.

THE CAFÉ CENTRAL: COULD IT BE HERR BRONSTEIN?

It was not really that bad. Even during the final years of the Griensteidl some writers had already moved into the nearby Café Central in Herrengasse, which became the headquarters of Egon Friedell, Alfred Polgar, Franz Blei and Anton Kuh. Friedell once claimed that he accomplished more at the coffee-house than a businessman did at his office. Satirists, essayists and journalists met in a large,

Egon Friedell

vaulted room of the Central which was called the 'Arkadenhof'. The Griensteidl
had been the home of neo-romanticism and impressionism. The Central became the breeding ground of expressionism. Its great commentator was Alfred
Polgar, who described the Central's geographic location 'at the latitude of
Vienna and the longitude of solitude', and called the Central 'not a coffee-house
but a *Weltanschauung* [a philosophy of life] ... Its inhabitants are mostly people
whose antipathy to other people is as strong as their yearning for human beings.
They want to be alone but always need company ... In this blessed place even
faceless people are credited with personality ...'. At the Central the prominent
writers were always surrounded by nondescript 'bohemians' whom Kuh, a
super-bohemian, scorned as 'banks clerks with an ethical background'. And
there was a generous assortment of 'Viennese Schopenhauers', such as the
Hungerkünstler Ottfried Krzyzanowsky who could go without solid food for days,
and was nourished by the stale coffee-house air. He became a local legend but
never wrote a line.

Into this 'refuge from *Angst* and reality', as it has been defined, there came such sturdy realists as Dr Sigmund Freud, unafraid of *Angst*, and Dr Theodor Billroth, the celebrated surgeon and a great friend of Johannes Brahms. Also present were Victor Adler (profession: Socialist) and Adler's political enemy, Karl Lueger (profession: demagogue and mayor of Vienna). At a rear table, somewhat removed from the undercurrents of local political and literary life, there might be Professor Thomas Garrigue Masaryk and Karl Kramář who, as Anton Kuh said, 'were manufacturing *k.&.k.* [Imperial-Royal] high treason against the *k.&.k.* monarchy'. (Masaryk later became the first president of Czechoslovakia; Kramář was sentenced to death for high treason, was pardoned, and became Czechoslovakia's first prime minister.) In the chess room, a gloomy Russian conspirator by the name of Bronstein played endless games with local virtuosi. Later he went to Switzerland and became world-famous under the name of Leon Trotsky. When the October revolution in Russia was reported to Count Czernin, the Austrian foreign minister, he refused to believe it. 'It can't be true', he said. 'Who could have made the revolution in Russia? Could it be Herr Bronstein from the Café Central?'

CAFÉ HERRENHOF: THE SCHWEBEZUSTAND WAS HERE PERFECTED

While the literati lived and quarrelled at the Café Central, the painters congregated at the Café Pöchhacker near the old Künstlerhaus and also at the Café Museum near the Secession. Actually, most of these so-called 'painters' were cartoonists and caricaturists, just as many of the self-styled 'poets' were satirists and essayists. The Café Museum had been decorated by the great Adolf Loos; it is still popular with artists and musicians in Vienna. Even before the Café Central died in 1925, the habitués had moved to the nearby Café Herrenhof, just a block down in Herrengasse. Between the two world wars the Herrenhof became the refuge of many a hopeless talent or gifted creator of *Galgenhumor*, the cynical 'gallows humour' that was brought to perfection there. It was a strange, unreal time. The intellectual sons of wealthy Jewish businessmen talked about literary magazines which they were going to, but never did, publish; of marriages that never took place; of books and plays that were 'planned' but never written. 'The *Schwebezustand* [a feeling of being suspended in space and time] so dear to the heart of the Viennese was here perfected', remembers a chronicler. The Herrenhof became a waiting room between the end of the monarchy and the beginning of 'the next epoch' that many people were expecting after the rise of National-Socialism in neighbouring Germany. Everybody was afraid of the future and no one did anything about it. No one at the Herrenhof wanted to face reality; everybody escaped into their unreal world of bizarre humour. Only *Hungerkünstler* Krzyzanowsky was no longer with them. While the people at the Central thought he was at the Herrenhof and the Herrenhof habitués thought he was at the Central, he had literally died of hunger in his small, cold, rented room.

Between the two world wars, in 1925, there were over 1,250 coffee-houses in Vienna. Some of them had been banks and savings institutions which had failed, whereupon the premises were turned into coffee-houses. There were special coffee-houses for pianists and others for string players, for operetta composers and for serious composers, for stamp collectors and court councillors, for radicals and conservatives. Almost each self-respecting soccer club had its coffee-house, and almost each unrespected ministry.

Coffee-house life in Vienna ended abruptly in March 1938 when the Nazis took over. They preferred the atmosphere of German-style beer gardens and of prison canteens. During the second world war the coffee-houses were almost deserted. There were no people worth meeting, no newspapers worth reading; many habitués had been taken to concentration camps. Many light bulbs were turned out. There was no heat. Both the atmosphere and the coffee had become *ersatz*.

After the war, an effort was made to bring the Café Herrenhof back to life, but it had lost its will to survive. Perhaps it sensed that it was now out of tune with the post-war generation. (Vienna's coffee-house habitués have always agreed that a coffee-house is a living organism with a 'soul' of its own.) It cannot have been an accident that Vienna's writers, painters, artists, bohemians and hangers-on moved into the small, shabby Café Hawelka in Dorotheergasse, a quiet side-street of Graben. The Hawelka had once been the afternoon refuge of the *Kleinrentner* (small pensioner) who could afford just one small cup of coffee and who spent the whole afternoon there reading the papers. Its owner, Leopold Hawelka, a man with artistic ambitions, began to

126 Wine-producer's house in Gumpoldskirchen

collect paintings, to subscribe to 'mountains of newspapers', and to attract the 'men without qualities', as Musil would have said, the human beings without identity.

The Hawelka is the perfect place for them, looking as it does like the stage set from a Genet play. But into this non-existentialist place there came the novelists (Doderer, Lernet-Holenia, Czokor), satirists (Qualtinger, Weigel, Merz), painters (Moldovan, Fuchs, Lehmden), and some aristocratic art patrons (Schwarzenberg, Sayn-Wittgenstein, Czernin). Only the Burgtheater actors, an exclusive folk, prefer the more elegant Café Savoy. But they are not really missed at the Hawelka.

PRIVACY AND ANONYMITY

During the final days of the Habsburg monarchy, the great era of the Viennese coffee-house, there was one in every town of the remote provinces of Austria, from Trieste to Cracow, from Czernowitz to Prague, from Budapest to Innsbruck, from Troppau to Temesvar. There was the same aroma of freshly made coffee, the latest issue of the *Neue Freie Presse*, the local gossip and the news from Vienna. But there was a difference between a Viennese coffee-house elsewhere and one in Vienna. The café's visible appurtenances – comfortable benches, marble tables, soft lights, dark walls stained by generations of smokers – could be exported, but somehow not its inimitable atmosphere. The coffee-house was a strong colonising influence throughout the Habsburg empire, but the original remained in Vienna. 'The Viennese', writes Hilde Spiel, 'led a *Schein*-existence at the coffee-house; one was not at home yet one was not outside in the fresh air. One was "reachable" but one could leave any time. One could invite friends but one was not responsible.'

Stefan Zweig once called the Viennese coffee-house 'our best educational establishment for all that is new'. The coffee-house always stimulated new ideas; it was Vienna's club that anyone could join who had the money for a cup of coffee (or at least a friend who would pay for his coffee). This modest due entitles the guest to hours of solitude or companionship, whichever he prefers. There is no time limit; after a while the 'piccolo', an apprentice waiter in a midget's tuxedo brings a tray with several glasses of fresh water, and removes the earlier

127 Old *Heuriger* in Sievering

tray from the table – a friendly gesture imported from the bazaars of the Balkan, a sign of hospitality, not a subtle hint that you should vacate your table. It offers living space and privacy, light and heating (which some habitués cannot always afford in their own home during the winter), reading matter and a discussion partner, card and chess games. It is the guest's message centre and mailing address, a place for his business appointments, and a powerful erotic catalyst. It is a place where the guest can feel at peace with himself, surrounded by privacy and anonymity, clouds of smoke and piles of newspapers, understanding and tolerance. At a time of widespread *Angst*, when the pleasure of conversation has become almost extinct, the coffee-house conveys a reassuring sense of the past, a feeling of permanence beneath the change, of comfort and security in the midst of recurrent disaster.

THE HEURIGER

Intellect and emotion, often conflicting in Vienna, have separate establishments there. The refuge of the intellectual is the coffee-house; the haven of the emotional is the *Heuriger*, literally 'this year's', meaning 'the place where this year's wine is drunk'. It is the most dearly beloved Viennese institution; no intellectual powers are needed for its enjoyment. Located in the garden or inside the kitchen of the small vineyard-proprietor who grows his own grapes and makes his own wine, a *Heuriger* consists of a few crude benches and unpainted wooden tables, a walnut-tree or a linden. But more important are the intangibles – the smell of jasmine or lilac, the view of Vienna below, or the lights of the Kahlenberg in the rear – for the *Heuriger* is one third wine and two thirds *Stimmung*. The mood is induced by the deceptively mild white wine that 'goes down like water' but has a very different after-effect. The potent young wine causes a typically Viennese gamut of reaction, beginning with a strong feeling of euphoria which soon deteriorates into sentimentality which in turn gives way to depression and, in the final phase, to abrupt violence.

Psychologists, satirists, poets and students of the Viennese *Volksseele* – 'the people's soul' – are often astonished by the violent effect of a few glasses of young wine. A prominent student, Helmut Qualtinger, co-author and performer of 'Der Herr Karl', the famous fictional character personifying the Viennese *Volks-*

seele, spends many nights at the Prater and at the *Heuriger* studying the people's unfathomable soul. ('Qualtinger,' writes Hans Weigel, 'is the Austrian version of the angry young man; his anger is neither coquetish nor sterile, but formidable like the frame of his body, a holy anger. He remains indispensable to all who rise *in tyrannos* – against the tyrants – politicians, industrialists, theatrical managers, bureaucrats, journalists . . .'.)

At the *Heuriger*, after a litre of the young wine – or of *Sturm*, or 'storm', as the wine is called when it has been fermenting feverishly for three weeks and affects you with the force of a hurricane – the Viennese is happy to be unhappy. He pours his aches, his heart, his tears out into the wine, and the wine is a patient, responsive listener. At the *Heuriger* he feels no *Angst*, no loneliness, surrounded as he is by congenial fellow drinkers who are also trying to forget *their Angst* and loneliness. All of them practise the therapy of talking into their glasses. Happy to be out of their dark, narrow apartments, they go to the *Heuriger* all year round, at five in the afternoon, immediately after work. ('To sell one's own wine in Vienna is not considered dishonourable for the burgher', Aeneas Silvius Piccolomini wrote in 1438. 'Many keep vineyards, attracting drunks and loose women, and they serve them gratis some food to make them drink even more, but their wine is bad.') Nothing is served gratis any more; people now bring sausage and bacon and hard-boiled eggs wrapped in paper, and provide their own entertainment. Perhaps the owner or an itinerant musician will play the zither. The best thing that can be said about the wine is that it is 'fresh'. The local *Weinbeisser* (literally, 'wine biters') do not taste the wine as the French or Germans do, by letting it roll round and under the tongue; they 'bite' the young wine which is hard and high on acid. But after the fifth glass one does not notice it any more. For a while all men are brothers, as in Schiller's 'Hymn To Joy'.

DEMEL'S

In a very different tradition to both the coffee-houses and the *Heuriger* is Vienna's most famous pastry shop. In fact, Demel's is far more than a pastry shop; it is a way of life, the graceful Viennese manner of living, now almost gone. Relatively few changes have been effected at Demel's since it was founded ten years after the American Declaration of Independence. It was not Vienna's first

Ducking a baker, whose *Semmel* where short-weight in the Danube

pastry shop. Five years before Columbus discovered America, a Viennese baker discovered the *Kaisersemmel*, or 'emperor's roll', which he stamped with a picture of Emperor Friedrich III. Many Austrians consider his discovery greater than Columbus's. The first sugar-blowers appeared in 1514 at the court of Emperor Maximilian I. Three hundred years ago, an unknown Viennese who ought to have a monument took the cream off the milk and whipped it into *Schlagobers*, which has since given pleasure to millions of people and became the title of a ballet by Richard Strauss. Other Viennese inventions are the *Indianer*, a chocolate cream-puff filled with whipped cream, and the *Faschingskrapfen*, a glorified doughnut. Over two million *Krapfen* were eaten during the Congress of Vienna in 1815. When a girl broke a *Krapfen* in half and gave it to her young man, he was hooked: the broken *Krapfen* was considered a token of engagement.

A few years ago Demel's won the Prize of Honour in a city-wide window display contest, with a delicious assortment of *Torten* and pastry, made from

128 Biedermeier glass with a view of Kohlmarkt

century-old recipes, and the inscription, 'Your charming great-great-grand-mother went to Demel's'. It was true. In 1786, a sugar-baker's apprentice from Württemberg named Ludwig Dehne opened his pastry shop across from the stage door of the old Burgtheater. (The present owner, Baron Friedrich von Berzeviczy, still keeps the old metal containers that were used to bring coffee and ice-cream to the boxholders at the Burgtheater.) In 1799, Dehne's widow Antonia was appointed court caterer. One of Dehne's grandsons sold the shop to his first assistant, Christian Demel who moved it in 1887 to its present location in Kohlmarkt, across the square from the entrance to the Hofburg.

Emperor Franz Joseph I loved Demel's *Faschingskrapfen*, and Empress Elisabeth often sent out for 'something sweet' at coffee time. Demel's 'Eis-Salon' became the 'in' place for archdukes, diplomats from the nearby Ballhaus-platz, officers and spies. International intrigues began over a Sicilienne (rasp-berry and vanilla ice-cream soaked in Malaga wine with dried grapes), and Schnitzlerian passions came to their inevitable end over small mountains of *Schlagobers*, said to have a soothing effects in moments of tragedy.

The Habsburg Empire is gone, but Demel's still rules Vienna's pastry empire. There is a Victorian touch about the front room (*das Gewölbe*), its laden buffet and old-fashioned chandeliers. Demel's waitresses, many of them now elderly ladies, once came directly from their school; until not all that long ago they used to wear black, high boots and marched to church on Sundays in closed formation. The 'abbesses', as they are called by the habitués, treat the customers with maddening nonchalance. At Demel's haste is considered definitely plebeian. A house rule says, *Herrschaften haben Zeit*, ladies and gentlemen never hurry. The kitchens have sinks of dark stone, made in 1888. There are no electric beaters; all cake mixtures are lovingly beaten by hand. Everything is made 'in the house'; if it were possible, they would beat their own butter and grind their own flour. They make their own chocolate, bake their own sandwich breads, make small notches into chocolate-covered coffee beans to make them look like real ones. Practically everybody is a specialist.

I have often watched people who come to Demel's for the first time. They usually have an incredulous look on their face – like children in front of a lighted Christmas tree. They seem bewitched as they stare at the sweets, the desserts (*Guglhupf* and *Streuselkuchen*) on large tables, the dozens of *Torten* on the shelves.

At Demel's they make over a hundred different *Torten*. For decades now they have collected the best recipes from the far-flung provinces of the Habsburg Empire. The great Danube Federation, the dream of many statesmen, has come true at Demel's. There are Gubanen from Gorizia, Potizen from Serbia, Dalken from Bohemia, Aranygaluska from Hungaria. They have also borrowed fine confections from France (madeleines and brioches), Italy (pizza and sfoliatelli), England (crumpets and ginger cake), Germany (Baumkuchen or 'tree cake'), Russia (kulic, a large brioche), and from America (delicious fresh fruit salads).

At Christmas time, during the carnival season and around Easter, the shop windows are filled with marzipan trains and sugar waterfalls, nougat castles and chocolate mountains. Apparently, Vienna's gingerbread-makers have lost none of their skill since they founded their own guild in 1661. The sugar-bakers were restricted by law to the use of 'burnt sugar, burnt almonds, biscuits and zwiebacks', and the chocolate-makers, cake-bakers, marzipan-formers and candymakers also had their own guilds. At Demel's they still speak of the 'golden epoch' of Vienna's pastry-making, when every sugar-baker was a trained sculptor.

6

The Jews

THE VIENNA SCHOOL OF MEDICINE

Of Vienna's best-known contributions to modern civilisation – the waltz, the operetta, the pastry and psychoanalysis – psychoanalysis is today the least-known in the city where Sigmund Freud created it. About a dozen physicians practice it, some only as a sideline. Vienna's Psychological Institute is small and has few students, almost no Austrians among them. Vienna's official medical school today pays little attention to mental sickness; one studies the body but not the soul.

It was not always that way. The Viennese school of medicine, founded in the late 1830s (together with the famous schools of geology and geography, patronised by Metternich) was developed by great pioneers of modern medical science – Carl Freiherr von Rokitansky, the founder of pathological anatomy, Joseph L.Skoda, the brilliant diagnostician, I.P.Semmelweis, the discoverer of puerperal fever, who was almost defeated by the conservatism of the Viennese medical establishment until both Rokitansky and Skoda came to his help. The Vienna school of medicine reached world-wide fame before the first world war. Among its greatest names were Josef Hyrtl, Ferdinand Hebra, Theodor Billroth (known to chamber-music players as the close friend of Brahms, to whom the composer dedicated his two String Quartets, opus 51), Anton Eiselsberg; great neurologists (Krafft-Ebing, Wagner-Jauregg) and analytical psychologists (Alfred Adler and Sigmund Freud). The decline of the school began after the first world war and was hastened by the Nazis who drove out many great scientists. After the last war, the tradition was carried on by the surgeons Leopold Schönbauer and Wolfgang Denk, the internal-disease specialists Karl Fellinger and Ernst

Lauda, the gynaecologists Hermann Knaus and Tassilo Antoine, the orthopediatrist Lorenz Böhler – but gone are the days when American millionaires and Indian maharajas came to Vienna for treatment. During the second world war and the occupation, Vienna's doctors were cut off from their colleagues elsewhere and grew out of touch with the phenomenal medical advances of those years; 'ever since, it has been hard to catch up', one great Viennese doctor said.

It is not true, as some people claim, that 'there is no need for psychotherapy in Vienna'. The amount of mental sickness is, relatively, as large here as in New York or Paris or London. In Vienna it is often said that 'the Americans overdo the Freudian business'. The Viennese certainly underdo it. One prominent local analyst admits that a Viennese has to be terribly sick to come to him; no one ever consults him about minor problems of adjustment, marriage, children.

Freud might have enjoyed analysing the reasons for the neglect of psychoanalysis in the city where it was created; he would have carried out his investigation with his usual scientific detachment and sardonic wit, to explain why the Austrian government takes no notice of the one Viennese who probably did more than any other citizen of Vienna to influence modern thinking in the past hundred years. Freud spent seventy-nine years of his life in Vienna and considered himself a Viennese (though he was born in Moravia). He hesitated to leave the city even when his life was threatened by the Nazis, but deep in his heart he disliked Vienna for the very reasons that explain Austria's official neglect of Freud today: the opposition of the Roman Catholic Church, and anti-semitism.

THE MOST JEWISH CITY IN EUROPE

The history of the Jews in Vienna (which Goering in 1938 called 'the most Jewish city in Europe') begins before the Christian era when, after the destruction of the Temple in Jerusalem in 87 BC, members of the Tenth Roman Legion were transferred from Judea to the Roman *castellum* of Vindobona. They brought with them Jewish women as slaves and mistresses and the women, who knew no other faith, educated their children as Jews. Excavations have produced oil lamps made of clay with the sign of the Jewish *menorah*. The Roman Emperor Caracalla gave the Jews in the Roman frontier fortifications Roman citizenship.

For the next thousand years there is no documentary evidence of Jews on the Danube; only after the tenth century are Jews mentioned in restrictive decrees and special confiscatory laws. They were forbidden to acquire land and to carry out most trades; rulers and local governors hired Jews to carry out unpopular actions such as the collection of taxes. If something went wrong they were made scape-goats. The Catholic Church forbade Christians to lend money on interest, and the Jews became money-lenders, sometimes operating with funds belonging to Christians. Creditors are rarely popular with their debtors, and when the debtors happened to be powerful princes, they would often settle accounts with their Jewish creditors by expelling them. All debts were automatically liquidated, and the Jewish assets were taken over by the rulers. In order to be able to meet their special taxes and make forced contributions, the Jews demanded higher interest rates which, in turn, made them more hated. Almost all persecutions against Jews in Vienna were *propter pecuniam*, for financial reasons. The oldest debt certificates found in Vienna, dated 1303 and 1306, mention an annual interest rate of 130 per cent.

In 1371, the Dukes Albrecht II and Leopold III carried out a complete confiscation of all Jewish assets, cancelling all interest payments to Jewish money-lenders and all repayment of capital. The legal position of the Jews became increasingly insecure. 'Each endorsement of existing rights had to be bought with great financial sacrifice', writes the Viennese historian, Hans Tietze. Occasional contributions were turned into permanent taxes. In 1406, the Jewish ghetto was burned down and plundered. The *Klosterneuburg Chronicle* estimated the robbed Jewish assets at over one hundred thousand florins, of which only a small part was restituted, in spite of strict orders from Duke Leopold. In 1419, the theological faculty of the Vienna university hinted darkly at 'an alleged understanding between Jews and Hussites', noting 'the luxurious style of living of . . . a large number of Jews' and 'their damnable books'. No other proof was given.

Duke Leopold needed popular support in his campaign against the Hussites and eventually yielded to public pressure. In May 1420 all the Jews in Austria were arrested and their assets confiscated. Some were put in underground prisons and given the choice of conversion or death. On 12 March 1421 – and ever since the month of March has become particularly sinister in the history of the Jews of Vienna – two hundred and ten Jews were burned at the stake 'on the meadow in Erdberg', after rejecting conversion. The *auto-da-fé* was a public holiday, with people coming from far away to enjoy the spectacle. (The last public execution in Vienna took place in 1878, and again thousands of people attended.) The Jews held their holy books in their hands and chanted; it was the opinion among the inquisitors and the mob that the chanting made the Jews insensible to pain. The Jews' houses became the property of the duke who gave them to his friends or sold them to the town of Vienna. All outstanding Jewish claims were to be paid, with no interest, to the ducal chamber. The duke thus became a public benefactor and made a nice profit.

Later, certain 'court-exempted' Jews *(Hofjuden)* were permitted to return. Emperor Friedrich III received an assurance from Pope Nicolas V that Jews might again settle in Vienna, '*pro necessitate vitae Judeorum et commoditate Christianorum*', since he needed the Jews for his fiscal and financial transactions. In 1625, Ferdinand II permitted a new Jewish ghetto in 'Unteren Werd', the second Viennese district now known as Leopoldstadt. The ghetto had one hundred and thirty houses and lasted forty-five years. In 1670, the Jews were again expelled, once more some were exempted, and others later returned. Charles Patin, a doctor from Paris, wrote in 1673: 'The small suburb which the Jews once inhabited has been rebuilt, and the church has been consecrated after every trace of the old superstition had been destroyed'. The Jewish houses were sold, and the proceeds were distributed among the prominent citizens. A certain family named Lueger was given three thousand florins. In 1897, a descendant of the family, Dr Karl Lueger, became mayor of Vienna and a celebrated leader of anti-semitism.

132   Plaque in Judenplatz celebrating the expulsion of Jews from Vienna in 1421
133   Plaque commemorating the Jewish resistance 1938-45

STÄTTE ... ZUFLUCHT
am 29. V 1944
STÄTTE ... ERRETTUNG
bis
STÄTTE ... TRUTZES
DIENSTE
WIDERSTANDES

OESTERREICH

Towards the end of the nineteenth century Vienna became the birthplace of both modern anti-semitism and modern Zionism. There had been a growing influence of Jewish bankers, industrialists, politicians, writers, musicians. (It is interesting to note that the most prominent anti-anti-semite was Emperor Franz Joseph I, whose letters show his profound distaste for anti-semitic politicians such as Lueger.) In 1898, Jakob Wassermann, the Jewish novelist, wrote, 'the banks, the press, the theatre, the literature, the social life are all in the hands of the Jews'. In this atmosphere one Georg von Schönerer began to spread ugly racist ideas ('Jew or Christian, it's all the same, the nastiness lies in the race') among the pseudo-intellectuals, the *petit bourgeois*, the *Hausmeister*, as Vienna's concierges are called, the student fraternities. (Yet in *Mein Kampf* Hitler notes Schönerer's failure to understand 'the importance of the lower strata of the population' and admires Lueger for his 'correct estimation of the various social forces'.)

When Theodor Herzl, a member of the Café Griensteidl group, prominent feuilletonist and Paris correspondent of *Neue Freie Presse*, published his book *Der Judenstaat* (The Jewish State) he admitted he had been motivated not so much by Vienna's anti-semitism as by the case of Captain Alfred Dreyfus. Herzl founded the first Zionist publication, *Welt*, 'but in the Viennese circle in which he lived, the citadel of ideas of assimilation, the "Judenstaat" created dismay or laughter', Hans Tietze wrote in 1933 in *The Jews of Vienna*. 'With the exception of Max Nordau and Count Heinrich Coudenhove-Kalergi, all Herzl's older friends considered his plan (for a Jewish home in Palestine) either ridiculous or mad.' One of the worst detractors was Karl Kraus who refused to contribute 'one crown for Zion'. Self-criticism has always been a Jewish characteristic and among Vienna's Jews, self-criticism often became self-hatred. One of the few exceptions was Richard Beer-Hofmann who sought a Jewish renaissance in the heroic history of the Jews; and Martin Buber, the religious philosopher, who was born in Vienna in 1878 and based his teachings on German philosophy and Jewish mysticism. Tietze calls Buber's work 'the last creation to come out of the specific position of Vienna's *Judentum*', and concludes that *das Wiener Judentum*, 'the Jews of Vienna ... are an integral part of Vienna'. The final chapter to *das Wiener Judentum* was written by the author of *Mein Kampf*. There were some 350,000 Jews in Vienna before the Nazis came there; today there are less than 10,000.

Anti-semitism has survived Nazism in Vienna; prominent Austrian anti-Nazis who fought against Hitler and spent years in Dachau concentration camp are anti-semites 'on principle', though 'some of their best friends are Jews'. It is an atavistic phenomenon, inherited from former generations who instinctively disliked the Jews, because they 'tried too hard', were 'too able', or 'too industrious', or simply because they were different.

SIGMUND FREUD

Anti-semitism and the opposition of the Catholic Church may have something to do with Sigmund Freud's unpopularity in his own city, but there are other, more important, typically Viennese reasons. The Viennese use Freudian terms as often as other people without realising that Professor Freud down in Berggasse 19 created them. (The apartment where he wrote *The Interpretation of Dreams* and nearly all his subsequent works is now a fashion knitting workshop; Freud would have been amused to know that among the present tenants in the house are one Herr Bormann and one Herr Kafka.) Hundreds of Viennese streets are named after obscure citizens but none after Freud. In 1956, at the hundredth anniversary of Freud's birth, it was proposed that Berggasse (not named after Alban Berg, the composer, but after a small mountain, or *Berg*, which it ascends) be renamed in his honour. The city administration turned down the idea. Ignorance about Freud is widespread even among doctors in Vienna. 'We never thought much of Freud here', one doctor confided to me recently. 'No wonder he went to America after the first world war.' This doctor would be quite surprised to learn that Freud remained in Vienna even after the *Anschluss* in the spring of 1938, when his books had been burned in Berlin, and he was at the top of several Nazi black-lists. He was in physical danger but he decided to stay and calmly continued his work. Three friends came from abroad – Ernest Jones, Princess Maria of Greece, and Dorothy Burlingham. They kept watch over Freud, one of them always remaining nearby, but they could not prevent a group of Viennese SA men from entering the apartment. They asked Frau Freud for five thousand schillings. Frau Freud came into her husband's study and told him about the visit of the blackmailers. Freud quietly looked up from his work, told her to pay the money and said, 'That's more than *I* ever got for a visit.' At last he consented to leave for London, but before the Nazis let him leave Vienna, all the books of the Psychoanalytischer Verlag had to be brought back from Germany to Vienna where they were burned. To his last day in Vienna, Freud felt that he had his roots in this city, which, however, never returned his loyalty.

Some writers have tried to create a connection between Freud's work in Vienna and the city's peculiar atmosphere of frivolous eroticism, in the same way that there exists a definite relationship between Vienna and Schubert, or Vienna and Johann Strauss. In his *History of the Psychoanalytical Movement* Freud writes that there is no basic connection between his researches and Vienna's loose sexual morals. Vienna's sexuality is an urbane, irresponsible phenomenon (as Schnitzler so beautifully showed), very different from Freud's bitterly serious 'tyranny of the libido'.

Neither is there any relation between Freud's work and the Jewish element in Vienna. Freud probably had a love-hate relationship with Vienna, as have so many other prominent Viennese; and Vienna simply ignored him. Patients from all over the world came to his study in Berggasse but there were almost no Viennese among them. They did not trust Freud. 'Vienna did all it could to take no part in the development of psychoanalysis', Freud has written. When he became famous the Viennese tax authorities informed him, '... it is well known that your fame attracts wealthy patients from abroad'. Freud called this letter 'the first official recognition of my work in Austria'.

Dr Hanns Sachs, a pupil and friend of Freud, and a member of the Group of the Seven Rings (with Freud, Rank, Abraham, Eitington, Jones and Ferenczi) talks in his intimate memoir of Freud's daily routine in Berggasse. The apartment had formerly been occupied by Victor Adler, a close friend of Freud's who had organised Austria's Social-Democratic Party. Freud's study was the erstwhile nursery of Adler's son, Friedrich, who in 1916 assassinated Count Stürgkh, the Austrian prime minister. There Freud saw patients from nine to one. After lunch with his family and a one-hour walk, on which he often visited second-hand bookstores, Freud had consultations and saw more patients until 7 p.m. At nights he worked alone in his study, except on Wednesday's when he went to the meetings of the Psychoanalytical Society, and Saturday night when he lectured at the university. He smoked as many as twenty 'Trabuco' cigars a day.

Sachs remembers that Freud's early lectures attracted from five to fifteen students, rarely more.

After Freud was appointed *Privatdozent* (university lecturer) he had to wait twelve years before he was made an unsalaried professor *extraordinarius*. Freud's case is now a matter of published records, a curious, very Austrian mixture of many components. Anti-semitism, professional intrigues in high academic circles, and personal jealousies play a certain role, and the case is further complicated by bureaucratic conservatism and the heritage of the Metternich system.

Towards the end of the nineteenth century when Freud's researches were becoming known (*The Interpretation of Dreams* was published in 1899), anti-semitism was still considered somewhat vulgar in Vienna, practised only by racists like Schönerer or demagogues like Karl Lueger; members of the intelligentsia kept away from it. At Vienna university, anti-semitic slogans were popular with members of some of the student fraternities, the nationalistic, duelling, beer-drinking groups. Members of the faculties had no special love for their Jewish colleagues, perhaps because so many gifted Jewish professors were famous specialists and heads of clinics; but the Jewish professors had attained their positions in spite of such latent anti-semitism. Certainly there was a strong anti-Jewish feeling among the clerical bureaucrats at the ministry of religion and education who had the right to confirm or reject the proposals made by the professorial college of a faculty.

The professors several times proposed the appointment of Dr Sigmund Freud as professor *extraordinarius*. The ministry ruled that this was not possible (in the case of Freud *and* several other candidates) 'on budgetary grounds', an excuse which is popular with bureaucrats everywhere. The professorial college stubbornly repeated its proposal. This was due less to widespread enthusiasm for Freud's researches but rather to the bitter struggle that was going on between the university and the ministry. The bureaucrats claimed that a man could be appointed as professor only when he had been 'a diligent teacher'. The medical college claimed that a man should get the appointment if his scientific work would benefit the faculty and the university.

On 12 June 1897, the medical college decided to propose once more to the ministry that Freud be appointed professor *extraordinarius* – that he would get the

title *and* the salary. The vote was twenty-two for and ten against. It had been preceded by a report written by Professor Richard Krafft-Ebing, who had held the chair of psychiatry since 1880. Professor Krafft-Ebing (whose *Psychopathia Sexualis* pioneered a new approach in sexuality) wrote on Freud's research:

> Freud ... has proved that a principal factor in the genesis of hysterical and neurasthenic conditions which hitherto had been unexplained in their causes (aetiologically), consisted in anomalies and occurrences within the field of sex life, and that only their discovery and elimination could help in individual cases, a fact demonstrated in particular as regards so-called compulsive ideas and phobias.
>
> The novel character of these researches, and the difficulty of checking them, prevent as yet a definite judgement on their significance. It is possible that Freud is overrating them, and goes too far in generalising the results he has obtained. In any event, his researches in this field prove an extraordinary gift and capacity for guiding scientific investigation into new channels....

Krafft-Ebing's appraisal of Freud was supported by other medical luminaries, among them Professor Hermann Nothnagel, but Freud remained pessimistic about his chances. He thought it was 'unlikely that the minister should act upon the proposal' and he was right; the war between the bureaucrats and the professors continued for another five years, and ended only in 1902 with his appointment.

THE HEURIGER THERAPY

In the city of Freud, the people have always disliked any kind of analysis. The seemingly light-hearted but really melancholy Viennese do not like to ask themselves searching 'Freudian' questions.

> In many countries a neurosis is a personal problem [says a Viennese analyst]. In Vienna it is a mass phenomenon that goes back to mass persecution. In recent years some very uncomfortable facts have become known here and the young people are beginning to ask their fathers some unpleasant questions. The father's silence is often interpreted as an admission of passive guilt, and a sense of passive guilt is widespread in Vienna. Suppose you lived here in those years but yet you did not do anything really bad – you were not even a member of the Nazi Party. But one day you failed to leave open the door through which a Jewish friend *might* have walked out and saved his life ... A nation-wide trauma exists. If these people started to analyse themselves, thousands of them would jump out of the window.

The attitude has not changed in recent years. A large number of Nazi trials in Austria have ended with acquittals though the judges had indicated to the jurors that they considered the defendants guilty. Forty-three former SS men working at the Auschwitz camp are said to be living peacefully in Austria. Among them are three doctors who took part in 'selections'.

The *Heuriger* therapy is the answer. It is cheaper than analysis, less upsetting than talking to the priest in the confessional. A fatalistic strain has run through the Viennese soul since time immemorial. Since there is nothing one can do about so many things, why worry? The Viennese philosophy is expressed by the words of the beautiful song from Johann Strauss' *Die Fledermaus*: '*Glücklich ist, wer vergisst, was doch nicht zu ändern ist*', Happy is he who forgets what cannot be changed. And that is the reason why the Viennese put up a beautiful monument to Johann Strauss who makes them forget – but no monument at all to Sigmund Freud who makes them remember.

Today the Iron Curtain stretches beyond the fringe of the Marchfeld where the Habsburgs founded their empire. It is less than an hour's drive from the heart of Vienna to the electrified barbed-wire fences of the Czechoslovak border or to the minefields along the Hungarian frontier. The past and the present are inseparable in Vienna and the Viennese are aware of it. Once again their city is the eastern frontier fortress of the Western world. 'Let us eat, drink and be merry, for tomorrow we die.' '*Es wird ein Wein sein und wir wer'n nimmer sein.*' 'There'll be a wine, but we won't be here anymore.'

Notes on Illustrations

1 SELF-PORTRAIT OF ANTON PILGRAM FROM THE PULPIT IN ST STEPHEN'S CATHEDRAL

Anton Pilgram (*c.* 1460 - *c.* 1515) worked in St Stephen's from 1511 until 1515. During this time he set up the pulpit, a new stone support for the organ (cf. plate 71) also decorated with a self-portrait, and he finally halted work on the truncated north tower (cf. plate 24). His two self-portraits have probably contributed as much to his fame as his magnificent pulpit.

In 1511 'Master Antony of Brno' was appointed Master of Works of the Cathedral in Vienna; he also succeeded in wresting the commission for the new organ support from a respected member of the Vienna guild to whom it had already been promised. This led to a quarrel with the guild, who refused to appoint Pilgram their head, as was customary for the Master of Works. Petitions went to the Emperor Maximilian I, and Pilgram seems to have come out of it badly. He spent the last years of his life in Vienna, at war with the Viennese, working on the Landhaus (House of the Estates) of Lower Austria (cf. plate 33) and on his pulpit (*c.* 1514-15).

2 'SCHUBERTIADE' BY LUDWIG MOHN, *c.* 1820-5. NATIONAL LIBRARY

A Game of Ball at Atzenbrugg, or *The Feast at Atzenbrugg*. Coloured etching after a drawing by Franz von Schober (landscape and architecture) and Moritz von Schwind (figures).

Franz von Schober (1796-1882; remembered as the poet of Schubert's song *To Music* and later a close friend of Liszt) was among the first of the group of Schubertians who joined with the young composer in *Schubertiaden* (cf. page 150). Schober's uncle was steward at Atzenbrugg castle, a property some miles from Vienna, and each year from 1817 the Schubertians would make an excursion there and stay for three days. Schubert is here seated in the foreground in his shirt-sleeves smoking a long pipe, with Schober on his right. The violinist is Kraissl, another Schubertian who was a landscape-painter and musician. Moritz von Schwind, who painted the figures, did not join the group until the early 1820s.

3 DEATH WEARING THE CROWN OF THE HOLY ROMAN EMPIRE, FROM THE TOMB OF EMPEROR CHARLES VI BY B. F. MOLL IN THE KAPUZINERGRUFT

The Imperial vaults under the Capuchin Church were founded by Emperor Matthias and his Empress Anna in the early seventeenth century; today there are 138 metal coffins of Habsburg emperors and their families, Franz Joseph I being the last to be buried there. (The burial customs of the Habsburgs involved complicated dismemberment: their bodies are buried under the Capuchin church, their hearts in a chapel in St Augustine's, and their entrails under the Cathedral.) The present form of the Imperial Vaults is largely due to the Moll brothers who were responsible for the masterly lead coffins of many of the eighteenth-century Habsburgs.

The tomb of Charles VI was made originally in 1742 by Johann Nikolaus Moll (1709-43), a pupil of G. R. Donner, but was reworked in 1753 by his brother Balthasar Ferdinand (1717-85), who was responsible for the four figures of Death, wearing royal and imperial crowns, at the corners.

4 ARCHDUKE CHARLES MONUMENT IN THE HELDENPLATZ BY ANTON DOMINIK FERNKORN

The Heldenplatz (Heroes' Square) of the Hofburg takes its name from the statues of Austria's two most celebrated generals, Prince Eugene and Archduke Charles, by A. D. Fernkorn (1813-78).

Archduke Charles (1771-1847) was the first commander to defeat an army led by Napoleon, at the battle of Aspern outside Vienna on 21 and 22 May 1809. His victory made him a popular hero, but he held no further command, probably because his brother the Emperor mistrusted his popularity and his ability. It was the news of his death in 1847 that first gave the sculptor Fernkorn the idea of making an equestrian monument, immortalising the dramatic (if apocryphal) moment in the battle of Aspern when Charles siezed the standard of his regiment to rally his troops. Fernkorn also became preoccupied with the idea of achieving what Leonardo had planned, but never carried out, a monumental equestrian figure, cast in bronze, supported only on the hind legs of the rearing horse. During the next few years Fernkorn made many studies of horses, particularly in the Spanish Riding School in Vienna. In 1853 he received an official commission to carry out the monument, and the work on the great bronze statue occupied his time from 1853 to 1859. He had already gained great experience in bronze-casting in Germany and, simultaneously with the commission, he was appointed director of a new Imperial Bronze Foundry. Part castings were made in 1857, and in 1859 on 26 March the main casting using over seventeen tons of metal was successfully carried out. Little over a year later the monument was unveiled, and Fernkorn was knighted. The monument did not win universal approval. Although the extraordinary technical achievement was acknowledged, it was described as 'a statuette blown up into a colossus' and the board who commissioned it wanted the companion statue of Prince Eugene to have 'greater monumental repose and dignity'. The sculptor had been inspired by David's *Napoleon Crossing the Alps* in the Archduke Charles monument, and he was now required to model his work on Velasquez' equestrian portrait of Don Baltazar Carlos. First designs for the second monument began in 1859, but Fernkorn had exhausted his strength on the first work and the monument to Prince Eugene, which was unveiled in 1865, was completed by his pupil Pönninger. In 1866 after several strokes Fernkorn went into a private mental home and from 1868 he spent the last ten years of his life in the provincial lunatic asylum in Vienna.

5 THE OLD DANUBE

The stream of the Danube splits into many branches as it crosses the plain north of Vienna. The earliest town was built on a southern arm of the river, but gradually the main stream moved further north away from the city. An unsuccessful attempt had been made to regulate the river under Emperor Rudolph II in 1598, but it was not until the nineteenth century, after floods had twice engulfed the city – in 1830 and 1862 – causing considerable loss of life, that an effective regulation of the Danube was carried out (1869-75). Branches of the old courses of the river were cut off, fed by an underground stream, and it was on the sandy shore of an island (the Gänsehäufl) between two of these that the nature-healer Florian Berndl started a fresh-air and sun-bathing cult towards the end of the century. Berndl's sand packs and sun cures were not taken seriously, and he earned the name of 'the half-savage', but the Viennese were quick to catch on to the amenities of the 'old Danube' and in 1908 the council took over the Gänsehäufl as a public bathing-place, and the 'Berndl-Colony' moved to 'New-Brazil' further downstream in the Lobau. The old Danube has now been developed with many facilities for bathing and sailing, and the Gänsehäufl has a new swimming-pool, built in 1950. Other parts of the old Danube area, particularly round the Lobau, still retain their wild character.

6 THE BURGGARTEN

The area between the Hofburg and the city walls was one of the most strongly fortified places in Vienna, and withstood attacks in the two Turkish sieges. After Napoleon had occupied Vienna in 1809 he ordered these fortifications to be destroyed, and in 1818 the area was laid out as an Imperial garden. The grandiose projects fifty years later for an Imperial Forum (cf. p. 125) cut through the middle of the garden, and although the Forum was never realised, the Heldenplatz (cf. plate 4) and the new wing of the Hofburg, planned by Karl Hasenauer in the 1880s and eventually completed at the beginning of this century, cut off the smaller Burggarten (Palace Garden) from the Volksgarten (People's Garden). The photograph is taken from the glasshouses in the Burggarten looking towards the new wing of the Hofburg on the right.

7 GARDEN FAÇADE OF THE STARHEMBERG-SCHÖNBURG SUMMER PALACE

After the final victory over the Turks in 1683 the nobility of Vienna embarked on a vast programme of building, each family having its winter palace in the central city, and a summer palace in the suburbs. The suburbs were then largely rural, and the summer palaces were each beautifully landscaped in a spacious park, forming a belt round the inner city. One of the few to survive with at least part of its garden is a charming small palace attributed to Lucas von Hildebrandt, built in 1705-06 for Count Starhemberg.

The palace was acquired by the Schönburg family in the nineteenth century, and is still in their possession, now an oasis not in the fields surrounding Vienna, but tucked away among the houses of the fourth district. Palace and garden, having survived the destruction of 1945, are now scheduled for demolition. If not saved, they will be an addition to a list of monuments destroyed since the war that is already much too long, and includes, in the neighbourhood of the Starhemberg-Schönburg Palace alone, the palace of Archduke Rainer (which was built in 1710-11 and had an early eighteenth-century riding school building in its park) and the church of St Florian (1725), the former replaced by an office block, the latter (unnecessarily as it now turns out) to facilitate construction of a new underground railway line.

8 SCHWEIZERHOF (SWISS COURT) OF THE HOFBURG

The Hofburg, or Imperial Palace, as it stands today is a monument to the rule of the Habsburgs in Vienna. Ottokar II of Bohemia started to build a new palace, to the south of the Babenberg palace, about 1275; but in 1276 he was defeated on the Marchfeld by Rudolf of Habsburg, and from that time until the declaration of the Republic in 1918 the Hofburg was the palace of the Habsburgs.

The Schweizerhof is still in essentials the core of the medieval moated palace. (The ditch for the moat is still clearly visible on the north-west side of the building.) Old views of Vienna show the Schweizerhof with a chapel leading off it crowned with towers at each corner; the towers are gone, and the facing of the court dates in the main from the middle of the sixteenth century, but the courtyard and chapel are still easily recognisable in the old paintings and prints. The Swiss court remains the heart of the palace complex that has grown up round it on every side.

9 HOUSE IN SIEVERING WITH OLD GAS LAMP

In 1688 the first public street-lighting was introduced in Vienna. Until that time everyone in the streets of the city after dark was obliged to carry a lantern with him. Now a corps of lamplighters was founded, whose job it was to collect the lamps at dusk from various inns, which served as filling stations, and set them up at strategic points throughout the city. An ordinance of Leopold I laid down that anyone who maliciously destroyed a public lantern should have his right hand cut off.

The first gas light in Vienna was the work of an enterprising chemist, Joseph Moser, who lit the window of his Löwenapotheke with gas lamps in 1816. Immediately this became one of the sights of the city, and even Emperor Franz I made an excursion to see it.

Street-lighting by gas was introduced in 1841 by the English Imperial-Continental Gas Association, and the new lamplighters became familiar figures, with their white overalls and long bamboo poles. But by the end of the century their days were numbered. In 1893 the first electric street lights were lit on the Kohlmarkt, and a few years later electric lights were added to the gas lamps lighting the Ringstrasse. Today all the old gas lamps that have survived, like the one illustrated in the old main street of Sievering, have been converted to electricity.

10 STAIRS AND FRONT COURTYARD OF SCHÖNBRUNN PALACE

The palace of Schönbrunn was conceived as a Habsburg palace to rival Versailles. Until the second Turkish Siege there had been an Imperial summer residence there, built orginally as a hunting lodge by Maximilian II in the 1570s. This had been completely devastated by the Turks, and in 1692 plans were drawn up by J. B. Fischer von Erlach (1656-1723) for a grandiose palace for the future Emperor Joseph I on the crown of the hill (where the Gloriette now stands), with a triumphal staircase leading up to a statue of Joseph. These plans were considered too extravagant, and in 1696 work started according to a new, more modest plan of Fischer's.

During the first half of the eighteenth century considerable changes were made to Fischer's building, and Schönbrunn's present appearance owes as much to his son Joseph Emanuel (1693-1742) and to Nikolaus Paccassi (1716-90), who carried out a major reconstruction in 1744-9. These later changes gave the palace a less dramatic appearance, but it retained a great sense of grandeur, both in the front with its massive wings stretching forward into the vast courtyard, and at the back, with the subtly articulated straight façade, constantly changing its appearance as seen from different parts of the garden (cf. plate 49). The staircase in the front is now quite modest, but is remarkable for its gently curving flights and the fine wrought-iron balustrades and lamps (cf. also plate 45).

11 MINORITENKIRCHE. TYMPANUM OVER THE SOUTH-WEST DOOR

The Franciscan *Fratres Minores* were called to Vienna in 1230, and their first church was completed in 1251. In 1339 work was begun on a new Gothic west façade, and the west porch is documented as the work of 'Frater Jacobus Parisiensis' (Brother James of Paris). The tympanum over each of the three west doors was divided into three parts; in the centre door (*c.* 1350 but much restored), ascribed to Brother James, a Crucifixion scene is divided between the three fields, Christ on the Cross in the centre, with the mourning women on the left, and St John and the soldiers on the right; the decoration of the north door has been destroyed and the door walled up; the south door (which is illustrated here) shows the stigmatisation of St Francis, with two Poor Clares on the right.

12 STAINED-GLASS PANEL FROM ST STEPHEN'S CATHEDRAL. DIOCESAN MUSEUM

This panel, showing an angel swinging a censer, probably belongs to a scene from the Life of the Virgin, forming part of a window in the north chancel of the Cathedral. The glass dates from about 1340-50, and was restored in 1900-01.

13 HEILIGENKREUZERHOF

From medieval times the great monasteries and abbeys of Lower Austria owned lands in the capital. On these properties courts were built with their own chapels, and later often a wine-cellar and tavern where the abbey's wines were sold. The most impressive of the surviving courts is that belonging to the Abbey of Heiligenkreuz.

In 1662 the Abbot Klemens Schäffer rebuilt the chapel, and five years later properties that had belonged to the abbey since the thirteenth century were rebuilt into one court nearly three hundred feet long. In 1746 further changes were made, but the court still preserves traces of the medieval buildings and Abbot Schäffer's plan. Most of the court has always been taken up by apartments. The restricted space in the inner city has meant that since very early days the Viennese have lived in apartments rather than houses. Even the palaces of the nobility accommodated lodgers on all but the principal floors, and in the houses of the middle classes the owner would generally occupy only the '*Belletage*'. The vast number of civil servants at court, who had to be housed by the citizens, no doubt also contributed to this situation.

14 FRANZ XAVER MESSERSCHMIDT, 'AN ARCHVILLAIN'. BAROQUE MUSEUM

F. X. Messerschmidt (1736-83) is one of the most remarkable Austrian sculptors of the eighteenth century. His early work follows on the classicist baroque of G. R. Donner (cf. plates 92, 93), but after he had been debarred from the professorship at the Vienna Academy because 'his unstable temperament would have a bad effect on his pupils', he retired to Bratislava, and worked chiefly on his sixty-four 'character heads'. This was the heyday of physiognomic studies (carried sometimes to such lengths that one disciple of the movement stole Haydn's head from his grave, and kept it to try and discover the secret of his genius) and Messerschmidt was also a friend of Dr Mesmer, the inventor of animal magnetism. In this climate of thought Messerschmidt's works and his strange ideas have their place. A visitor to him at the end of his life reported that he modelled the heads on grimaces he made in the mirror. The sculptor claimed to see ghosts, and also to be plagued by spirits, especially by the spirit of human proportion, who was jealous of his discoveries. The grimaces he made in the mirror relieved the pain and banished the spirits. The character heads cover the whole range of human expression from the most grotesque to nobility and resignation.

15 CORNER TILE WITH THE IMPERIAL ARMS, FRAGMENT OF A STOVE, c. 1500. MUSEUM OF DECORATIVE ARTS

This tile is one of few surviving fragments of a Renaissance stove from the sacristy of St Stephen's. The deeply hollowed shape helped spread the heat more effectively by presenting the maximum surface area to the air. The relief on the inner part of the tile shows Samson strangling the lion.

16 STATUE OF EMPEROR CHARLES IV FROM THE SOUTH TOWER OF ST STEPHEN'S CATHEDRAL, c. 1360-80. HISTORICAL MUSEUM

The south tower of St Stephen's, which reaches to a height of 448 feet from the ground, was started probably in 1359 and completed after three-quarters of a century in 1433 by Hans Prachatitz. The tower was conceived to be richly decorated, and the programme included the over-lifesize (7ft 3ins) statues of Emperor Charles IV (1316-78) and his wife Blanche de Valois, with companion statues of Duke Albrecht II, the Wise, and his wife. The statues were replaced on the Cathedral in 1870-1 by copies so that the soft sandstone would not suffer further deterioration from weather and grime. Behind the statue can be seen panels from the mid-fourteenth-century St Michael's window from the Cathedral.

The 'rebuilding' of St Stephen's after the middle of the fourteenth century was due to Rudolph IV, the Founder, who was eager to emulate his father-in-law Charles IV, and to establish the claims of the Habsburg line to a position of importance in the Empire. He founded Vienna University (1363) and had St Stephen's raised to the status of a collegiate church. He had intended that it should be made a cathedral, with a burial-place for the Habsburg dukes in the choir.

17 HEAD OF ST JOHN, FROM THE FORMER DOROTHEER-KLOSTER, c. 1430. HISTORICAL MUSEUM

A chapel dedicated to the Blessed Virgin and St Dorothy was founded on a site just to the east of the Hofburg by Duke Albrecht II in 1357; and was completed by his son Rudolph IV. During the first half of the fifteenth century the foundation was enlarged to become a priory of Augustinian canons, and a new church was built, dedicated to Sts Dorothy, Catherine and Agnes, which was completed in 1459. The Crucifixion group, of which this fine terracotta head of St John is a survival, dates from this period of construction. In the late eighteenth century the buildings were secularised and became the Versatzamt (state pawn office), forerunner of the present 'Dorotheum', the state-run auction rooms and pawn office, which still occupies the same site.

18 STAIRCASE OF THE FORMER TOWN PALACE OF PRINCE EUGENE (NOW MINISTRY OF FINANCE)

The winter (town) palace of Prince Eugene was one of the many to be built in the decades following the defeat of the Turks. The central part was built by J. B. Fischer von Erlach in 1697-8 and the palace was later enlarged by Lucas von Hildebrandt, when the Prince acquired neighbouring properties. The grand staircase was designed by Fischer and the statues are by the Venetian sculptor Giovanni Giuliani (1663-1744).

The grand staircase was a feature of all baroque palaces in Vienna, more notable perhaps, for being more unexpected, in the winter palaces with their comparatively plain façades fronting on the narrow streets of the city. It exemplifies the strongly theatrical element in Viennese baroque, the curtain rising on a grandiose stage set, which makes some elaborate allegorical reference. As in the prince's summer palace (cf. note 51), the themes here are the conquering power of Hercules and the glory of Apollo.

19 ST PETER, FROM A HOUSE SIGN 'THE TWELVE APOSTLES' IN GLAZED EARTHENWARE, 1567. HISTORICAL MUSEUM

Until the middle of the sixteenth century the houses in Vienna were distinguished not by numbers but by names taken from the house signs (generally sculptured reliefs or figures). In 1566 the first numbering of houses was made, from 1 (the Imperial Palace) to 1205; this was the basis of the system that lasted until 1862-3, when all houses were renumbered according to streets. This gave the City Council the opportunity to introduce a brilliantly logical and simple system, which makes it very easy to find any house in Vienna – if you can find the street: all radial streets (from the city centre) are numbered from the centre outwards, all others in a clockwise direction in relation to the centre, no. 1 on the left, no. 2 on the right. (The former have rectangular signs, the latter oval.)

Very few of the medieval house signs still exist. The house 'The Twelve Apostles' was in the Hafnersteig (Potters' Steps) near the oldest surviving houses in Vienna, and the figures of Christ and the twelve apostles are made in brightly coloured earthenware, reminiscent of late Gothic stove tiles. At the end of the war all thirteen figures were intact, but only four of the apostles along with the figure of Christ, have found their way into the Historical Museum of the City of Vienna.

20 JACOB SEISENEGGER, 'THE PAPAL NUNCIO MUSSO PREACHING IN ST AUGUSTINE'S. HARRACH GALLERY

On 15 July 1560 the papal nuncio preached in St Augustine's Church in the presence of Emperor Ferdinand I and Archdukes Maximilian and Charles, urging the Emperor to reopen the Council of Trent. The event was commemorated in a painting, dated 1561, by Jacob Seisenegger (1505-67), done for Count Harrach, recently appointed imperial high-chamberlain. This was the first important painting acquired by the Harrach family, who later built up one of the finest private collections in Europe. This is still intact and is open to the public in their Vienna palace.

21 HOUSE IN GRIECHENGASSE (NO. 9) INCORPORATING A TOWER FROM THE MEDIEVAL FORTIFICATIONS

The houses around the Griechengasse (Greeks' Alley, so-called since the eighteenth century from the colony of Greek traders with the Ottoman Empire who lived there, but known in medieval times as Sauerkraut Gassel) are the oldest in Vienna, and the little house-tower of no. 9, built into remains of the city wall probably on Roman foundations, is famous as the only surviving secular building in the city from before 1500. In the foreground of the photograph are the houses of the Hafnersteig (cf. plate 19) and in the background the Fleischmarkt (Meat Market).

22 ROMAN HEAD. WERTHEIMSTEIN VILLA, DÖBLING

This head of a Roman was found built into a stone bridge over a stream in a Döbling vineyard. It was probably in Döbling, which includes the wine-growing suburbs of Grinzing, Sievering and Nussdorf, that the first vines introduced by the Romans were grown in Vienna.

23 INTERIOR OF ST STEPHENS'S CATHEDRAL WITH DETAIL OF THE TOMB OF EMPEROR FRIEDRICH III

In the long reign of Friedrich III (1439-93) much that the Habsburgs had long striven for was attained; but paradoxically the Emperor's life cannot be considered very successful, since his achievements did not really bear fruit until the reign of his son Maximilian I. Friedrich's election as Holy Roman Emperor established the Habsburg claim to be the first family in Europe (his motto AEIOV is usually interpreted as *Austria Est Imperare Orbi Vniverso*,) and from then on there are Habsburg emperors as long as the Empire lasts. In St Stephen's many of the plans of Rudolph IV (cf. note 16) were accomplished: six years before Friedrich came to the throne the great south tower of the church had been completed; the first years of his reign saw the completion of the roof (cf. plate 69), and plans were approved for building the companion tower on the north side. In 1469 the church was made a cathedral. Two years previous to this, work on the north tower began, and in the same year the Emperor commissioned his tomb from Niclas Gerhaert van Leyden. Gerhaert made plans for the red marble tomb, and was himself responsible for the portrait of the Emperor carved on the top surface, which was finished about 1470. The sarcophagus was finished by about 1485, but the balustrade, which is richly decorated with sculptures, was not completed until 1513, long after Friedrich's death. In 1485 Friedrich had been forced to abandon Vienna when it was besieged by the Hungarian king Matthias Corvinus, and he died at Wiener Neustadt, where he is buried. The final completion of the tomb was the pious work of Maximilian, who had recaptured Vienna in 1490 after the death of Matthias Corvinus.

24 'CAPISTRAN PULPIT' OUTSIDE ST STEPHEN'S CATHEDRAL, AND THE NORTH TOWER

Although the famous sermons of Abraham a Sancta Clara were delivered from the pulpit of the Augustinerkirche, the pulpits of St Stephen's were the chief platform in the city for important preachers.

The exterior pulpit takes its name from the Franciscan saint John Capistran (1386-1456), who came to Vienna in 1451 and roused the people to a crusade against the Turks. The pulpit itself, which dates from around 1430, may well have been the one that was replaced by Anton Pilgram's new pulpit in the early sixteenth century (cf. plate 1). The figure of the saint with his banner by Johann Josef Rössler was added in 1737.

Work on the north tower (Eagle Tower) of St Stephen's finally came to a halt in 1511, and although a survey in 1523 established that the tower, for which detailed plans existed, could be completed, it was decided to build no further and the tower was capped by a Renaissance lantern. It is from this tower that the Pummerin sounds.

25 CHURCH OF ST RUPRECHT

This church is traditionally supposed to be the most ancient in Vienna, with a foundation dating back to Roman times. (It now seems likely that St Peter's, though not founded by Charlemagne as legend would have it, is an earlier foundation.) In outward appearance the Ruprechtskirche is certainly the oldest in Vienna, giving a consistent impression of a late Romanesque church, with parts of the nave and tower that date from the eleventh century or earlier.

26 CHURCH OF SANKT MARIA AM GESTADE (ST MARY'S ON THE BANK)

The Marienstiege (St Mary's Steps) which leads up to the church formerly led up from an arm of the Danube, and it was here that the fishermen docked, and built a small wooden chapel of St Mary. The foundation stone for a new church was laid in the twelfth century by the Babenberg Duke Heinrich Jasomirgott, but this church was burnt down in 1262, and the present Gothic church with its remarkable seven-sided tower and lantern was built during the fourteenth century. The Turkish siege of 1529 damaged the tower, and this was repaired, but by the end of the eighteenth century the church had fallen into complete disrepair, and when Napoleon occupied the city was used by French troops as a magazine. Later it was to have been pulled down, but was saved at the instance of Emperor Franz I, who had it restored in 1817-24.

27 TOWER OF ST MICHAEL'S CHURCH

The Michaelerkirche was founded in 1221 by Duke Leopold VI, and the late Romanesque decoration of the original church is still visible on the choir (cf. plate 84). The church suffered several times from fire and the octagonal tower (up to the level of the balcony) dates from 1340-4. In 1590 part of the tower was damaged in an earthquake and it was rebuilt with two more storeys; the pointed top was added in 1598. This tower, rising above the buildings of the Hofburg, would have been one of the chief landmarks in the city during the second Turkish Siege. To the right of the picture the square tower of St Augustine's can be seen.

28 SALA TERRENA OF UPPER BELVEDERE

The decoration of Prince Eugene's summer palace (cf. note 51) is conceived as a glorification of the prince. In the entrance hall to the Upper Belvedere his achievements as a general are celebrated: the ceiling, decorated with allegorical stuccos by Santino Bussi (1663-1737), is borne on four thick columns, each surmounted by a trophy and representing a Turk supporting pediment and ceiling. The statues are by Lorenzo Mattielli (1688-1748).

29 FRANZISKANERPLATZ (FRANCISCANS' SQUARE)

The Franziskanerplatz dates as a whole from 1624, and although some of the houses were rebuilt at a later date it preserves the general appearance of a seventeenth-century square. It was created by the Franciscans, whose new church and convent was built 1611-22, and who wanted more space for carriages to draw up and stop outside the church. The church and convent (cf. plate 119) occupy the south-east side of the square; to the north-east, with a high chimney, is one of the oldest houses in the city (the Dompropsthof), used from the middle of the sixteenth century as a residence for the bishops of Vienna. Next to this house on the west side is the house where Dr Paul de Sorbait (cf. page 66) lived, and wrote his celebrated report on the plague. In the centre of the square is the Moses Fountain (1798) by J.M. Fischer.

During the Turkish siege of 1683 the cloister of the Franciscans was used as a hospital for wounded soldiers.

30 PESTSÄULE ON THE GRABEN

The *Pestsäule* (Plague Memorial) on the Graben was built in thanksgiving for the end of the plague of 1679. Originally a wooden column was erected, but this was replaced (1682-94) by an extraordinary work in white marble, designed jointly by Fischer von Erlach, the court architect, and Lodovico Burnacini, the court theatre engineer and designer. This was conceived as a column floating on clouds, on which the Holy Trinity and the Nine Choirs of Angels were seated, with the kneeling figure of the Emperor and a group showing Faith Triumphant over Pestilence below. The statue of the kneeling Leopold I crowned by an angel, who emerges from a cloud of putti, is by Paul Strudel (1648-1708), the most notable Austrian sculptor of the late seventeenth century.

31 ST LEOPOLD'S CHURCH ON THE LEOPOLDSBERG

On the site of this church in a little chapel of St George mass was read by Marco d'Aviano, the legate to the relieving armies, with King Sobieski of Poland as server, on the morning of 12 September 1683. In the evening the Turk had been routed.

Earlier there had been a castle and chapel on the spot built by Margrave Leopold III (1096-1136), who was canonized in 1485 and in whose honour Emperor Leopold I rededicated the chapel after the defeat of the Turks and renamed the hill. (Confusingly, it had previously been the Kahlenberg, and the present Kahlenberg, a favourite spot for Wienerwald trippers, had been called Sauberg or Schweinsberg. The Battle of the Kahlenberg took place on the old Kahlenberg, now Leopoldsberg.)

Emperor Leopold had started rebuilding the chapel after the plague of 1679; it was repaired and completed after 1683 and enlarged into the present church by Antonio Beduzzi, Burnacini's successor as court theatre engineer, in 1718-30.

32 FEDERAL CHANCELLERY IN BALLHAUSPLATZ

The Chancellery in Ballhausplatz (Tennis Court Square) is most closely associated with Metternich, the brilliant Rhinelander who dominated the Congress of Vienna in 1815, and from that time until his resignation in March 1848 shaped the course of European history from this house. It was originally built as the Court Privy Chancellery in 1717-19 by Lucas von Hildebrandt, and enlarged by Nikolaus Paccassi in 1766. The square takes its name from the Imperial tennis court, which was first erected near this site in 1525, and after various removals was rebuilt again next to the Chancellery, where it remained until the nineteenth century. 'Ballhausplatz' came to be a synonym for Austrian government policy, equivalent to 'the White House' or 'Downing Street'.

33 HOUSE OF THE LOWER AUSTRIAN ESTATES (LANDHAUS) IN HERRENGASSE

In 1513 the Estates of Lower Austria commissioned the Cathedral workshop (Anton Pilgram was then Master of Works, cf. plate 1) to carry out their new parliament house. The small Gothic council chamber dates from this first phase of building (1513-18), and it has been suggested that Pilgram was himself responsible for the ribbed vaulting of the room.

In 1848 the Landhaus became the starting point of the Revolution in Vienna. Early on the morning of March 13 four thousand people, mostly students, marched to the Herrengasse, where the Estates were in session, to solicit their cooperation in a petition to the Emperor, demanding the abolition of the secret police and the dismissal of Metternich. A huge crowd, swelled by workers from the suburbs who had downed tools and forced their way through the city gates, refused to disperse, and eventually the Pioneer Regiment was called in.

Four men were shot dead, the first of many hundreds of victims of the revolution, which lasted until the end of October.

34 FORMER CIVIC ARSENAL (NOW CENTRAL FIRE STATION), AM HOF
The old arsenal am Hof, dating from the fifteenth century, was damaged during the siege of 1683 and was rebuilt in 1731-2 by Anton Ospel (1677-1756), the imperial fireworks engineer. The sculptural decoration on the façade is by Lorenzo Mattielli (1688-1748).

The arsenal was another focal point of the 1848 revolution: the day after the riot at the Landhaus it was stormed by the students, who set up the headquarters of their National Guard there.

35 STATUE OF FRANZ JOSEPH I IN THE BURGGARTEN
The statue of Emperor Franz Joseph I was erected in the Palace Garden (cf. plate 6) after the Second World War. It stands away from the palace hidden under the trees.

36 VOTIVKIRCHE, 1856-79, BY HEINRICH FERSTEL
On 18 February 1853 an unsuccessful attempt was made on the life of Emperor Franz Joseph I, and his brother Archduke Ferdinand Max decided to build a votive church to commemorate this delivery. The winner of the competition for the design was the twenty-seven-year-old Heinrich Ferstel. The building was in the form of a French High Gothic Cathedral, but on a small scale. Building lasted from 1856 until 1879, when the church was dedicated as the opening ceremony in the Imperial Silver Wedding Festivities (cf. endpapers).

Ferstel (1828-83) was the son of an official in the National Bank, and became one of the leading exponents of the 'Ringstrasse style'. His buildings, like those of the other 'Ringstrasse' architects, typify the theory that the style should mirror the function of a building. Unlike Friedrich Schmidt, whose works were mainly ecclesiastical, and therefore Gothic (cf. plate 60), Ferstel's, after the Votivkirche, were principally secular and showed strongly the influence of his studies in Italy. They included the new Austro-Hungarian Bank (1856-60, Italianate Romanesque combined with early Renaissance and using modern techniques of iron construction), the Museum of Decorative Arts (1868-71, Italian Renaissance with extensive application of sgraffiti and terracotta decoration) and the University (1873, completed after the architect's death in the grand manner of the Italian Renaissance). In 1877 Ferstel founded the Vienna Cottage Association, under whose aegis numerous villas were built in the suburbs in various extravagant (and appropriate) designs (cf. plate 61). Ferstel was knighted in 1879.

37 MAIN STAIRCASE OF THE BURGTHEATER
The new Burgtheater was built 1874-88 by Gottfried Semper and Karl Hasenauer (cf. plate 57). The interior, lovingly restored after the war, is notable for the corridors and foyers with portraits of actors and actresses and also for the magnificent main staircase, with ceiling frescoed by Gustav and Ernst Klimt, and others.

Katharina Schratt appeared regularly at the Burgtheater between 1883 and 1900.

38 ROMAN RUINS IN THE GARDEN AT SCHÖNBRUNN
The gardens of Schönbrunn, originally laid out by Jean Trehet in 1705, underwent major changes in the reign of Maria Theresia, as did the palace itself (cf. plate 10). In 1765 Ferdinand von Hohenberg (1732-1816) started replanning the garden, and this was completed by about 1780. In 1775 the 'Gloriette', closing the vista from the entrance of the

palace to the top of the hill, was completed, and the Roman ruins were built in 1778. These were planned to give the impression that the level of the ground had risen, so that only the top parts of a great arched temple were visible. A bearded river god and a nereid sport in the pool in front of the ruins.

39 TROPHIES CROWNING THE REICHSKANZLEITRAKT OF THE HOFBURG
The Reichskanzleitrakt (Wing of the Imperial Chancellery) was begun in 1723 by Lucas von Hildebrandt. The architect wrote that he was 'in projecto to start a whole new wing at the Imperial court, to accommodate the court treasury, living quarters for the Imperial Vice-Chancellor, and the Imperial Court Council with all its Chancelleries'. The trophy in the photograph, which crowns the centre of the wing, depicts the Imperial arms with the chain of the Order of the Golden Fleece, surmounted by the Crown of the Holy Roman Empire and supported by figures of Fame.

40 GRILLPARZER'S ROOM FROM HIS FLAT IN SPIEGELGASSE. HISTORICAL MUSEUM
The reconstruction of Grillparzer's room, with all the original furniture, paintings, decorations, and even floorboards, gives an intimate picture of the simplicity in which the great man lived, and also shows a typical bourgeois flat in the mid-nineteenth century, with its *Biedermeier* furnishings. The piano was often played by Schubert when he visited Grillparzer, who was an excellent pianist himself.

41 ALOIS VON SAAR, 'VIEW INTO THE KÖLNERHOFGASSE', 1833. HISTORICAL MUSEUM
Saar's painting shows a view typical of old Vienna in the pre-March days, before the political upheavals, and the sweeping changes in the appearance of the city. The Kölnerhofgasse (Cologne Court Alley) had been in the Middle Ages the street where the prosperous North German merchants had their warehouses in Vienna, but the houses in Saar's painting date from later periods.

42 TOWERS OF VIENNA AT SUNSET
In the foreground is the tower of the Minoritenkirche (cf. plate 11), distinctive among the churches of Vienna for its little roof, replacing the top of the tower knocked off in the Turkish Siege of 1683; behind and to the right is the Town Hall built in Brabantine Gothic style by Friedrich Schmidt (cf. plate 60); in the distance are the hills of the Vienna woods.

43 THE DOME OF ST PETER'S CHURCH AND THE ROOF AND TOWERS OF ST STEPHEN'S
St Peter's is in origin the oldest church in Vienna, but the present church dates from the beginning of the eighteenth century. It was built by Gabriele Montani and Lucas von Hildebrandt in a markedly Italianate style, but it exemplifies a specifically Austrian solution to the problem of a church with dome and west towers: the church is built on an oval plan, set longitudinally, and the towers (here placed at an angle to the line of the façade) are made subordinate to the massive dome (cf. plate 96).

The first church of St Stephen's was dedicated in 1147, and was a Romanesque building with two towers at the west end to the sides of the nave. This church was destroyed by fire in 1258, and rebuilding began in the Gothic style. Since the towers and porch had survived the fire, these were preserved in the new Gothic church with its wide walls; but this meant that no new towers could be built at the west end, as would have been normal, and it was decided that these should be built at the side of the church. It was for this reason that the great south tower of St Stephen's could be built almost as a separate campanile, tapering from the bottom to the top of the spire. The north tower was never completed (cf. plate 24).

44 SCULPTURAL DETAIL FROM THE WEST PORCH OF ST STEPHEN'S CATHEDRAL
The west porch, known as the Riesentor (Giant's Door) belongs to the last phase of building of the Romanesque church, and was completed about 1240. There are a number of important Romanesque buildings in Austria with porches that are related in style, and the Riesentor of St Stephen's is probably the latest in date, and is undoubtedly one of the finest and most richly decorated, showing the fullest fantasy of late Romanesque sculpture.

45 FLIGHT OF STEPS ON COURTYARD FRONT OF SCHÖNBRUNN PALACE
See note on plate 10.

46 WROUGHT IRON GATES OF UPPER BELVEDERE
The wrought iron gates at the southern end of the Belvedere garden were made in 1728 by Arnold and Konrad Küffner. Each gate is topped by Prince Eugene's coronet, which is also incorporated in his coat of arms on the top of the two main gateposts. To either side a putto plays with a chain of the Order of the Golden Fleece.

47 COURT FAÇADE OF THE STARHEMBERG-SCHÖNBURG SUMMER PALACE
See note on plate 7. The two sphinxes at the gate date from the early eighteenth century.

48 WROUGHT IRON SCREEN IN THE DOMINICAN CHURCH
The Dominicans came to Vienna in 1226, and their first church was dedicated in 1237. This was badly damaged in the Turkish siege of 1529 – it stands right above the city wall (still visible here) to the east of the city – and was rebuilt in the first half of the seventeenth century in Italianate baroque style. The church has one of the most charming baroque interiors in Vienna, and especially striking is the rococo screen, thought to have been designed and carried out by two of the monks, Brother Martin Ecker and Brother Raymund Schrob, in 1769.

49 SCHÖNBRUNN. VIEW TO THE PALACE FROM BENEATH THE OBELISK
The layout of Schönbrunn Garden (cf. plate 38) makes attractive use of the contrast between high clipped hedges and, behind them, trees which are allowed to grow freely. Together they provide screens, so that as one walks in the gardens parts of the house, or other buildings in the park, constantly disappear, and reappear again in unexpected new perspectives. The obelisk and its wild rocks were erected by Hohenberg in 1777 near the Schöner Brunnen (Beautiful fountain) which gave the castle its name.

50 FRONT (SOUTH) FAÇADE OF THE UPPER BELVEDERE
The Lower Belvedere was built as a summer palace for Prince Eugene in 1714-16 by Lucas von Hildebrandt. After its completion Hildebrandt planned an Upper Palace at the top of the garden as a showpiece to contain ceremonial rooms and to house the Prince's collections. This 'Upper Belvedere' was built in 1721-2 and is Hildebrandt's finest work. The façade itself has beautiful decorative detail, but the proportions are governed by the fantastic roofline, reminiscent of a Turkish tent.

Lucas von Hildebrandt (1663-1745) was the son of a German captain in the Genoese army. He accompanied Prince Eugene on his campaigns in Piedmont in 1695 and returned to Vienna as the prince's architect. He built many palaces for the nobility both in the city and in the suburbs.

51 FRESCOED GARDEN ROOM IN THE UPPER BELVEDERE
The ceiling painting representing Apollo and Aurora, or Light Triumphing over Darkness, is by Carlo Carlone, the *trompe-l'œil* architecture is painted by Gaetano Fanti, an artist who worked a great deal in Vienna and was responsible among other things for the *trompe-l'œil* architecture in the dome of the Karlskirche. The room was decorated in the years shortly following the completion of the building in 1722.

There was a strict allegorical programme behind the decoration of both the Belvedere and Prince Eugene's town palace (cf. plate 28), although so much has been destroyed or misplaced that it is now hard to follow. The essential elements are the comparison of the Prince to Apollo (as in this painting) or to Hercules (cf. plate 52), and originally the eastern part of the Belvedere gardens illustrated Herculean themes, the western Apollonian. The essential concept was the glorification of the Prince as an invincible hero, and the defeat of the powers of evil.

52 'APOTHEOSIS OF PRINCE EUGENE', BY BALTHASAR PERMOSER. BAROQUE MUSEUM
The statue was commissioned by the Prince in 1718 from Balthasar Permoser (1651-1732), who had since 1689 been court sculptor to Augustus the Strong in Dresden. A portrait of the prince was sent to the sculptor and also, presumably, the allegorical programme he was to follow. A long poem by Augustus' court poet explains all the allusions: the Prince is seen as Apollo and Hercules (cf. plate 51). In his right hand he holds Hercules' club (helpfully supported by a putto), and with his right hand he modestly mutes Fame's trumpet. He wears Hercules' lion skin beneath the Order of the Golden Fleece, and on his right Eternity holds high a symbol of his everlasting fame composed of the sun, a serpent and a triangle. Below (not to be seen on the detail in the photograph) he treads on a Turk (a self-portrait of the sculptor) and there is a gorgon's head, indicating that all his enemies freeze in terror. Considering this exhaustive programme it is all the more remarkable that Permoser's statue of the Prince is so successful, the many figures with their twisting bodies forming a dynamic group, always bringing the eye to rest on the imposing face of the Prince.

53 GARDEN PAVILION IN THE UPPER BELVEDERE
A little pavilion at the side of the Garden, with, on either side, a figure of Plenty accompanied by a putto. The figures, erected here about 1850, originally formed part of the decoration of the Orangery (1714-16) in the Lower Belvedere.

54 COURTYARD OF BAROQUE HOUSE, ULRICHSPLATZ 2
The Neubau (7th District) still preserves a few baroque houses, of which this is the finest example, and one which gives an excellent idea of the typical town house of the well-to-do middle classes during the mid-eighteenth century. As in the centre of the city (cf. note 13) only the principal floor would have been occupied by the owners, with lodgings above, and shops below.

55 VIEW FROM THE TOWN HALL TO THE BURGTHEATER, VOLKSGARTEN AND HELDENPLATZ
Although Franz Joseph's letter of intent to build the Ringstrasse dates from 1857, it was not until the seventies that

construction work started on the western side. The Burg-theater, built by Karl Hasenauer to Semper's designs (cf. note 57), was begun in 1874, but not completed until 1888.

To the right of the theatre is the Volksgarten with the Helden-platz behind, backed by the only completed wing of the New Hofburg. This open space contributes more to the grandeur of the Ringstrasse-Hofburg complex than the buildings themselves, and it is fortunate that the plans to complete the Forum here came to nothing.

56 FOUNTAIN OUTSIDE THE PARLIAMENT

A new building for Parliament was built in the appropriate Classical Grecian style by the Danish architect Theophil Hansen in 1873-83. It stands on the Ringstrasse next to the Town Hall (appropriately built in late Brabantine Gothic style). The fountain in front of the Parliament by a number of hands is composed of a massive figure of Athene supported by two groups of rivers, the Elbe and Moldau, and the Danube and Inn, and by Allegories of Power. It was completed in 1902.

57 KUNSTHISTORISCHES MUSEUM AND MARIA THERESIA MONUMENT

The museums for the History of Art and for Natural History were built by Semper and Hasenauer between 1872 and 1881. Gootfried Semper (1803-79), the leading theorist of nine-teenth-century architecture, had previously worked in Dresden and Zurich, and had also come to London, where he designed several pavilions for the Great Exhibition of 1851, and advised Prince Albert on the design of the South Kensington museums. He came to Vienna in 1871 with plans for a great 'Imperial Forum' (cf. page 125), of which the museums were to form an integral part. In all his work in Vienna he was assisted by the Viennese architect Karl Hasenauer (1883-94), a pupil of Siccardsburg and Van der Null. Viennese intrigue made Semper's work increasingly difficult and in 1876 he left the city; he died in Rome three years later.

The Maria Theresia monument (1874-81) was designed by Kaspar von Zumbusch, and shows the Empress surrounded by equestrian statues of her greatest generals.

58 'ARCHDUKE LEOPOLD WILLIAM IN HIS PICTURE GALLERY' (DETAIL) BY DAVID TENIERS THE YOUNGER (1610-90). KUNSTHISTORISCHES MUSEUM

The nucleus of the present collections of the Kunsthistorisches Museum is formed by the collection of Archduke Leopold William (1614-62), to whom David Teniers was court painter and gallery director. This painting shows the Archduke and the artist in the gallery, and almost all the paintings are indentifiable and are still in the Kunsthistorisches Museum today. They include in the top row Giorgione's *Three Philo-sophers*, Veronese's *Adoration of the Magi*, Palma Vecchio's *Visi-tation*, Titian's *Diana* (now in Lord Harewood's collection), and below other pictures by these and other Italian artists, including (fourth row, centre) three wonderful Titians.

The Kunsthistorisches Museum is not a representative gallery of works of art, but reflects the personal tastes of many members of the Habsburg family whose acquisitions make up the collections. Together with Archduke Leopold William the most notable collector was Emperor Rudolph II, whose Breughels and other Dutch and German paintings are one of the glories of the museum.

59 STALLBURG (PALACE STABLES)

A century after the building of the Stallburg (1559-65) Archduke Leopold William brought his art collection back from the Netherlands, where he had been governor, and arranged for the upper arcades of the building to be walled

up so that the collection could be accommodated there. In 1721-8 Emperor Charles VI had the rooms completely redecorated as the Imperial Picture Gallery, but in 1775 the gallery's director wrote to Empress Maria Theresia that the Stallburg was 'a place never suited to such a purpose, since it is not provided with the necessary light, and is at every moment liable to the risk of fire'. A year later the Empress ordered the transfer of the paintings to the Upper Belvedere (cf. plate 50), and this was completed in the following year.

In addition to the gallery, part of the building seems always to have been used as stables (in 1700 it was referred to as 'the Palace Stables of the Spanish horses'), and there have been apartments for members of the Imperial family and for various government offices. In 1955-60 the arcades were laid free of the walling-up, restoring to its original form one of the finest Renaissance buildings in Austria.

60 CHURCH OF OUR LADY OF VICTORIES (MARIA VOM SIEGE) IN FÜNFHAUS, BY FRIEDRICH SCHMIDT

Friedrich Schmidt (1825-91) was one of the chief exponents of the Vienna Ringstrasse style and his Town Hall (cf. plate 42) is one of Vienna's landmarks. He was born in Württem-berg and at the age of eighteen became a mason in the Works of Cologne Cathedral, and was made Master in 1854. In 1859 he moved to Vienna to teach at the Academy, and in 1863 he became Master of Works of St Stephen's Cathedral, where he carried out extensive restorations. In addition to the Town Hall he designed a number of houses in the city and the Acad-emic Grammar School (English Gothic with open-beam roof), but his real speciality was neo-Gothic brick churches, of which some half dozen by him survive around the suburbs. Most of these are very sober, but Fünfhaus church (1868-75) runs riot inside and out. The inside is overwhelming with its brightly coloured frescos all over ceiling and walls (recently cleaned and restored); the outside has been described as a 'Karls-kirche translated into Gothic'. A closer analogy would be with the church of St Peter (cf. plate 43) from which the two towers set at an angle to the front are borrowed. Given this extraordinary amalgam (one legend attributes its origin to a dream of the architect in which he had a vision of the ideal synthesis of ecclesiastical styles) Schmidt's handling of the detail is remarkable, with flying buttresses, causeways from the towers to the dome, and elaborately articulated pinnacles on towers and dome alike.

61 VILLA IN RODAUN

This villa (already being pulled down when the photograph was taken) is an example of the 'cottage style' (cf. note 36) taken to its furthest limits: a villa with chalet reminiscences combined with a tower derived from one of mad Ludwig's castles.

62 OLD TEA-BOXES IN THE SHOP OF SCHÖNBICHLER IN WOLLZEILE

63 SECESSION BUILDING BY JOSEPH OLBRICH

The Secession building was constructed in 1897-8, and the first exhibition of the Secessionists was held there in November 1898. The building itself was designed by Olbrich, but its decoration involved other artists of the group. The metal doors were designed by Gustav Klimt and the decoration above and round them by Koloman Moser; the interior was renovated after wartime destruction, and redesigned according to plans by Joseph Hoffmann. The dome is composed of laurel-branches of gilt iron (the Viennese called it 'the golden cabbage'). Over the door the inscription reads 'To the Age its Art, to Art her Freedom'.

64 VIEW FROM THE NORTH TOWER OF ST STEPHEN'S
The centre of Vienna was a walled city until the mid-nineteenth century, and the building of the Ringstrasse left the central city intact as an isolated unit. As a result of this each new age has pulled down outdated buildings or replaced ones that were destroyed, and the styles of ten centuries are to be seen side by side. On the left of the photograph the modern upper storey of the Archbishop's Palace has been constructed above a seventeenth-century building with a history that goes back to the early Middle Ages, on the right the courtyard of the Zwettlhof (which has belonged to Zwettl Abbey since the thirteenth century) dates from the mid-nineteenth century and is in the traditional style of Viennese town houses.

65 'ZACHERLHAUS' IN BRANDSTÄTTE BY JOSEPH PLEČNIK
The Zacherlhaus, built 1903-05, is one of the most remarkable modern buildings in Vienna; clearly of its period (the decorative elements beneath the roof), it has a simplicity of line and clarity of articulation which anticipate works of a much later date. Plečnik was born in Ljubljana in 1872, and was a pupil of Otto Wagner in Vienna. In 1911 he left the city for Czechoslovakia, where he worked for the rest of his life. The statue of St Michael on the side of the house is by Ferdinand Andri.

66 EGON SCHIELE, 'MEIN WOHNZIMMER', 1911 (SIGNED AND DATED). HISTORICAL MUSEUM
In 1911 Schiele was staying in Neulengbach, a small town west of Vienna, and this painting shows his room there – furnished simply enough, though perhaps not quite according to the dictates of Adolf Loos.

67 BASSENA IN AN OLD HOUSE IN GRIECHENGASSE
The bassena, or communal pump, is now dying out in Vienna, and this is an especially interesting example, for the head modelled on the spout. The bassena, like the old village pump, was the social centre for the women of the house, for gossip and for disputes only to be settled by the Hausmeisterin (janitress). Viennese dialect still remembers this in phrases like 'She heard that at the bassena' (idle gossip), or a 'bassena case' (neighbours' quarrel) in the law-courts. The word is a typically Viennese mixture of French bassin and Italian bacino.

68 GUSTAV KLIMT, 'MUSIC', FROM 'VER SACRUM', 1901
Ver Sacrum was a periodical founded by the Secessionists in 1898, to which all the major artists of the group contributed. It is a wonderful source of architectural and decorative material of the period and has designs by Joseph Olbrich, Joseph Hoffmann, Koloman Moser, Otto Wagner, Alfred Roller and Adolf Böhm, as well as many drawings by Klimt, and poems by Rilke and Hofmannsthal. It survived only six years.

69 ROOF AND SOUTH-WEST TOWER OF ST STEPHEN'S CATHEDRAL
The two west towers of the Cathedral reach to a height of 215 feet, and rose imposingly above the original Romanesque church (cf. plate 44). But the ridge of Gothic roof, completed after 1440, is only twenty feet lower, so that west towers have taken on an entirely new function in the design of the west façade. The roof of the nave, built in the middle of the fifteenth century, was a masterpiece of Gothic wooden construction. This was entirely destroyed in the fire that gutted the Cathedral in 1945. It was replaced by a steel construction, but the original outside appearance of the roof, with its patterns of brightly coloured glazed tiles, has been faithfully preserved, and the Cathedral stands now as a monument not only to the great craftsmen who built it in the Middle Ages, but also to those who, since the war, have rebuilt it.

70 THE WIENERWALD
The Wienerwald (Vienna Woods) to the north-west of Vienna lies on the extreme eastern foothills of the Alps. It is now so much taken for granted as one of the greatest attractions of Vienna that it is hard to believe that in 1870 the government had arranged a contract for the cutting down of the trees. The woods were saved thanks largely to the efforts of themayor of Mödling, Joseph Schöffel, who carried on a fight with the government for three years until he achieved success in 1873.

71 SELF-PORTRAIT OF ANTON PILGRAM ON THE STONE SUPPORT OF THE ORGAN IN ST STEPHEN'S CATHEDRAL
It was this organ support that brought Pilgram to Vienna in 1511, and that led to his dispute with the masons' guild (cf. plate 1). As in the self-portrait on the pulpit Pilgram has shown himself leaning out of a window holding his compass and square; but here the window is high on the wall, and he looks right out watching what is going on below. It is signed and dated 1513.

72 'DREIMÄDERLHAUS', SCHREYVOGELGASSE
The Dreimäderlhaus has long been associated with Schubert, although no connection has ever been traced with the composer. The house, built in 1803, is a fine example of late Josephinian Classicism.

73 HEURIGER HOUSE IN SIEVERINGERSTRASSE
A small baroque wine-house (Heuriger) in Sievering, its exterior decorated in Classicist style, though a simpler less sophisticated version than the previous plate. Although there are again no specific connections it is typical of the houses out near the Wienerwald where Beethoven or Schubert met with their friends.

74 PORCH OF FRIES-PALLAVICINI PALAIS, JOSEFSPLATZ
The palace facing the National Library across the Josefsplatz was built in 1783-4 for Count Josef von Fries by Ferdinand von Hohenberg; the caryatid porch was sculpted by Franz Anton Zauner (1746-1822). Moritz von Fries (1777-1826), Josef's younger brother, made the palace a centre of Viennese musical life in the first years of the new century. He was co-owner of the bank of Fries & Co. (which he eventually ruined by his prodigal spending), he was an avid art-collector, and was a founder member of the Society of the Friends of Music. Beethoven was a regular guest at the palace on the Josefsplatz and often played the piano there. He dedicated two violin sonatas (Op. 23, 24, 1800) and a string quartet (Op. 29, 1821) to Moritz von Fries, as well as his Seventh Symphony (1816). Haydn's last quartet (1803) and Schubert's Gretchen at the Spinning-Wheel (Op. 2, 1821) were also dedicated to the count.

75 FESTSAAL OF THE LOBKOWITZ PALAIS
The Lobkowitz Palais on the former Schweinemarkt (Pig Market – the market was removed at the instance of the redoubtable Abraham a Sancta Clara, because the animals' squeals disturbed devotions in the nearby church of St Augustine) was built after the second Turkish Siege for the Dietrichstein family, and the ceiling of the Festsaal was frescoed with allegories of the arts during the early eighteenth century. At the time of Haydn and Mozart many of the nobility had their private orchestras, often employing musicians who also belonged to the court orchestra; but by the early years of the new century Prince Lobkowitz (1772-1816) was almost the only aristocrat left who still maintained his orchestra. A great admirer of Beethoven he put his orchestra at the composer's disposal, and it was in the Festsaal of his palace that the first

performance of the Eroica Symphony (dedicated to the Prince) was given, in 1804. The palace saw many other Beethoven performances, and the composer dedicated a number of his works to Prince Lobkowitz, including the Fifth and Sixth Symphonies (a joint dedication with his brother-in-law, Count Rasumofsky).

76 RASUMOFSKY PALAIS (NOW NATIONAL GEOLOGICAL INSTITUTE)
This neo-classical palace was built in 1806-07 by the Dutchman Louis Montoyer for the Russian Ambassador in Vienna Count Andreas Rasumofsky (1752-1836). One of the most spectacular events of the Congress of Vienna was the ball given in the palace by Tsar Alexander on New Year's Eve, 1814, made even more spectacular when the central heating caught fire and the palace burnt down. Rasumofsky was another of Beethoven's patrons, and a great admirer of the composer. The Russian Quartets (Op. 59) of 1806, two of which make use of a Russian folk melody, were dedicated to the count, and were probably written for Schuppanzigh's quartet, although Rasumofsky's own private quartet, in which he played second violin to Schuppanzigh, was not established until 1808. Ignaz Schuppanzigh (1776-1830) had been a friend of Beethoven's since the composer's early years in Vienna. He was the greatest violinist of his time and was largely responsible for the first public quartet concerts in Vienna, originally in the Heiligenkreuzerhof (cf. plate 13). The majority of Beethoven's quartets were first performed by Schuppanzigh.

77 OLD HOUSES IN GRIECHENGASSE
Among the old houses in the 'Greek district' (cf. plate 21) is the 'Griechenbeisl' (on the left of the photograph), now probably the oldest inn in Vienna. There has been an inn there since the sixteenth century and in the nineteenth it won great popularity among musicians, writers and politicians; Schubert went there regularly, and later it was a favourite haunt of Nestroy and of Grillparzer, of Brahms and Wagner.

78 THEATER AN DER WIEN, PAPAGENO TOR
The Theater an der Wien was opened as an 'Imperial-royal privileged Playhouse' on 13 June 1801 with a performance of *Alexander* by Franz Teyber. Since that time it was the scene of many more distinguished first performances. As well as *Fidelio*, Beethoven's Violin Concerto, and, in a memorable concert on 22 December 1808, his Fifth and Sixth Symphonies and Choral Fantasy received their first performance at the Theater an der Wien. Later it was the theatre where Nestroy enjoyed success after success, and it was for eighty years the real home of Viennese operetta. *The Merry Widow* received 483 performances there.
The classicistic porch at the side of the theatre, with the arms of Emperor Franz I and the group of Papageno and his children, dates from the building of the theatre, and is a memorial to the first Papageno and founder of the theatre Emmanuel Schikaneder.

79 ORGAN OF THE CHURCH OF THE MERCIFUL BRETHREN
A new organ gallery was built in the church of the Merciful Brethren in 1736; and during the years 1755-8 Haydn was organist at the church. A few years after this the gallery was enlarged and a new organ built.

80 BEETHOVEN'S HAMMERKLAVIER. KUNSTHISTORISCHES MUSEUM, COLLECTION OF MUSICAL INSTRUMENTS
This hammerklavier was made in 1803 by Erard Frères, and was presented to the composer by the makers in that year.

81 CEILING OF THE GREAT CONFERENCE HALL OF THE LOWER AUSTRIAN LANDHAUS
The Great Hall of the Landhaus (cf. plate 33) was built about 1570, and the ceiling (representing Austria's Greatness) was painted by Antonio Beduzzi in 1710. This hall was Vienna's first important public concert hall, and concerts were given there throughout the eighteenth century. It was here in 1822 that Franz Liszt, then eleven years old, gave his first concert and received Beethoven's kiss of dedication.

82 HEAD OF RIVER MARCH, FROM G.R. DONNER'S FOUNTAIN FOR THE NEUER MARKT. BAROQUE MUSEUM
Georg Raphael Donner (1693-1741), Austria's greatest baroque sculptor, was born just outside Vienna, and as a boy became apprenticed to a Vienna goldsmith. He went as a choir-boy to Heiligenkreuz Abbey near Vienna, and when he was thirteen was found to have been stealing candlesticks and the lids of pewter jugs, to engrave them during the night. This brought him to the notice of the Venetian sculptor Giovanni Giuliani, whose pupil he became. In about 1710 he returned to Vienna, and in 1715 he married. In the next twenty years he worked in Salzburg, in Bratislava and elsewhere as well as in Vienna, but his greatest works were crowded into the last five years of his life. The most important of these was the commission from the city of Vienna to build a fountain for the Neuer Markt.
In 1737 the council had discussed the project with the Italian Lorenzo Mattielli, who agreed to make a stone fountain for the sum of 600 florins. Donner then offered to make a metal fountain for the same price as Mattielli. The council preferred the native artist, whom they considered anyway to be the better sculptor. The original fountain consisted only of the figure of Providence above a wide basin, but the council were so pleased with Donner's work that the fountain was completed by the addition of four figures (on which Donner was assisted by J. N. Moll) symbolising the chief rivers of Austria. It is said that the figure of Providence was modelled on Donner's wife, and that the River March (illustrated in this plate) represents the 'pretty confectioner's wife of the Neuer Markt'.
The legend goes that when Donner first returned to Vienna he had lodgings in a house on the Neuer Markt, which belonged to a rich gingerbread-maker. This man had a pretty young wife called Simonae or Simonetta, with whom Donner fell violently in love. He modelled a wax bust of her which came into the hands of Prince Eugene, who offered the sculptor his patronage, from which moment he never looked back; and the *schöne Lebzelterin* was immortalised as the River March. In 1770 the statues on the Neuer Markt were removed on the orders of Empress Maria Theresia, and were to be melted down; they were luckily rescued by J.M. Fischer, who restored them, and replaced them on the fountain in 1801. Later in the century the originals were replaced by bronze copies, to prevent deterioration of the lead.

83 ROOFS OF THE ESTERHÁZY PALAIS AND THE HAARHOF
This view shows one of the oldest parts of Vienna. In the background is the Naglergasse, a street which follows the old boundary wall of the Roman encampment of Vindobona, and beyond this is the square am Hof, where the Babenberg Dukes had their court in the thirteenth century. The Esterházy Palais (right foreground) is built on the site of a hunting lodge of Margrave Leopold III (St Leopold), at that time on the fringes of the forest. The Esterházy Palais was the town house of Haydn's great patrons. Much of Haydn's time was spent at the family's castles in Eastern Austria and Hungary, but in the winter months the household moved to Vienna, and Haydn

directed many performances in the town palace. It was there in 1800 that he met Nelson, in honour of whose victory in the Battle of the Nile (1797) he had composed his 'Nelson Mass'.

84 GREAT MICHAEL'S HOUSE, KOHLMARKT 11
This large house next door to the church of St Michael was built about 1720. It gives a clear view of the great nave of the church with its late Romanesque arcading under the roof. The poet and librettist Pietro Metastasio lived and died in the house, and it was in the same house that Haydn lived in an attic room in 1750-5, studying with another resident of the house, the Neapolitan composer Nicola Porpora (1686-1766). While living there Haydn wrote his first mass and his first opera, *The Crooked Devil*.

85 ALLEGORICAL STATUES IN FESTSAAL OF THE AULA (OLD UNIVERSITY, NOW ACADEMY OF SCIENCES)
A new ceremonial building (Aula) for the University was erected 1753-5 by Jean Nicolas Jadot de Ville-Issey (1710-61). In addition to university functions the festival hall of the Aula was used for 'Kavalierskonzerte' (cf. page 168) and for other grand concerts, one of the most notable being on 8 December 1813, when Beethoven's Seventh Symphony and 'Wellington's Victory' were first performed.

Round the body of the pulpit, which is made of wood inlaid with mother-of-pearl, are gilt statues of the four Evangelists, and the top of the canopy is surmounted by a figure of St Francis Xavier with figures of Faith, Hope (with an anchor) and Charity (as a widow). Below the pulpit two putto angels battle with a putto devil.

The Aula became the students' centre during the 1848 revolution, and was in revenge used by the army as a barracks until 1857. Since that time it has housed the Austrian Academy of Sciences.

86 PULPIT IN THE JESUIT (UNIVERSITY) CHURCH
In 1702 Andrea Pozzo was given permission by the pope to leave Rome, and the last seven years of his life were spent in Vienna, where his masterpiece was the complete rebuilding of the interior of the Jesuit church (1703-05), with an astonishing virtuoso *trompe-l'œil* ceiling, complete with false domes, that outdoes even the celebrated ceiling of the Jesuit Church (Gesù) in Rome. The pulpit, by a local sculptor, formed part of Pozzo's plan for the complete refitting of the church, which, although originally built in 1627, is as a whole the most satisfactory late baroque church interior in Vienna.

87 THE AUSTRIAN: DETAIL FROM A NINETEENTH-CENTURY MECHANICAL ORCHESTRA. FOLKLORE MUSEUM
This mechanical orchestra with representatives of the various nations playing their instruments used to perform in the Prater at the end of the nineteenth century. The detail illustrated shows the Austrian playing the flute, the other figures in the group are a Frenchman playing the clarinet, a German (in the centre of the group as an innkeeper), a red-nosed English-woman playing the violin, and an American with a cello. Behind the main figures are grotesque figures: a devil behind the Austrian and his dog, two grotesque Italian comedians behind the German and a monkey conducting the orchestra behind the American.

88 JOSEPHINIAN HOUSES IN BALLGASSE, NOS. 6 AND 8
No. 6 Ballgasse was an inn *Zum Blumenstöckl*, the Flower-Pot, where Beethoven often went and met his friends. For a short time in 1819-20 the composer had lodgings in the house.

The neighbouring house (no. 8) was a lodging house for the city's furniture-makers.

89 VIEW TO VIENNA FROM THE UPPER BELVEDERE
This is the famous view of Vienna that was painted by Bellotto (cf. page 108) showing the layout of the Belvedere gardens and the lower building, the actual Palace of Prince Eugene.

90 BEETHOVEN'S HOUSE IN HEILIGENSTADT, PFARRPLATZ 2
This is probably the most famous of all Beethoven's houses, although the master lived here only a short time in the summer of 1817, and wrote no important music at that time. Its fame depends more on the charm of the house itself (although this may well owe its preservation to the tenuous Beethoven connection), which is a double house dating from the seventeenth century; in a niche on the corner there is a baroque statue of St Florian. The street to the left of the house is the Eroicagasse.

91 COURTYARD IN THE HOUSE OF THE TEUTONIC ORDER (DEUTSCHES HAUS), AND THE TOWER OF THE CATHEDRAL
The Knights of the Teutonic Order came to Vienna in the early twelfth century and their first house was built around 1220. It was rebuilt in 1667 by Carlo Canevale, and later enlarged several times. It was here that Mozart first lived when he came to Vienna in 1781.

In March of that year Mozart was summoned to Vienna by the Prince Archbishop of Salzburg: 'I have a charming room in the same house where the Archbishop is staying – Brunetti and Ceccarelli [other Salzburg musicians] are lodging elsewhere – Che distinzione!' Mozart lived in the Deutsches Haus only six weeks; the indignities he suffered at the hand of the archbishop were made more unbearable by the welcoming reception he had from the Viennese nobility. In the archbishop's household he dined with the servants, 'below the valets, but above the cooks', but, what was worse, he was unable to accept valuable invitations to give concerts. During the six weeks he gave two concerts (for the archbishop), one with three new works; one of these, a violin sonata he composed between eleven o'clock and midnight the night before the concert, and 'so as to get it finished I only wrote out the violin part, and kept my own part in my head'. At the beginning of May, Mozart moved to new lodgings near St Peter's Church, having decided to leave the archbishop's service, and stay on in Vienna.

Brahms lived in an apartment in the Deutsches Haus in 1863-5, also the first years he settled in Vienna.

92 ANDROMEDA FOUNTAIN BY G.R.DONNER IN THE COURTYARD OF THE OLD TOWN HALL
The town council of Vienna, who had been so delighted with Donner's fountain for the Neuer Markt (cf. plate 82) commissioned the sculptor to carry out a fountain for the interior court of the old Town Hall. This was to be his last completed work – he died at the age of 47, probably from lead-poisoning, in February 1741, shortly after completing the Andromeda relief. Like so many of the greatest artists of Vienna he died penniless, although his work enjoyed great success. His funeral expenses were paid by friends, and by his widow selling three old dresses (for 42 florins). The Emperor graciously paid his widow 250 florins, which covered the artist's outstanding debts. The inventory of all his possessions (6 fine shirts at 1 fl. 30 kr ... 6 armchairs covered with green cloth at 51 kr ... 2 portraits of the deceased and his wife, of no value ... 1 teapot and 2 ordinary cups ... etc.) and the materials and tools in his workshop amounted to 533 fl. 17 kr. The sculptor possessed 4 books (at 1 florin): Pozzi's *Architectura*, a dictionary of mythology, a Latin dictionary, and Ovid's *Metamorphoses* (in which the story of Perseus and Andromeda is graphically described).

Donner's sculpture is an extraordinary tour-de-force. The figure of Andromeda is sculpted almost in the round, and the dragon's head bursts out from the relief menacing the girl with greedy jaws. All the rest of the work is in more or less shallow relief, employing ordinary illusionist perspective to give an effect of depth and of distance. As in the Neuer Markt fountain Donner made use of the affinity of water and lead.

The surrounding balcony dates from the early eighteenth century and came originally from a house in the Wollzeile; the cast iron grilles are by Simon Vogl, 1725.

93 COURTYARD OF THE SAVOYSCHES DAMENSTIFT
The Convent for noble ladies in the Johannesgasse was originally the palace of the Duchess of Savoy-Carignano, built in 1688 in the spate of palace building after the second Turkish Siege. The fountain in the courtyard is by F.X. Messerschmidt (cf. plate 14) and J.M. Fischer (1741-1820), the group of the Widow of Sarepta probably by Fischer, the lions crouching at the sides certainly by Messerschmidt. The fresco above the fountain depicts Wisdom mirroring the rays of Divine Knowledge and probably dates from the same period as the fountain (c. 1766-70).

94 CAMESINA HOUSE, DOMGASSE 5
Mozart lived in this seventeenth-century house (in the best apartment) from 1784-7, and it was here that he wrote *The Marriage of Figaro*. It was here too that he was visited by Haydn, who played quartets with him and his friends, and that his celebrated meeting with Beethoven took place in the spring of 1787. Mozart's work-room has been preserved as a museum. The photograph shows the façade of the house at the end of the street.

95 GARDEN HOUSE IN THE COURT OF THE EIGHTEENTH-CENTURY HOUSE, ULRICHSPLATZ 2
The photograph shows the garden house with fragments of sculpture at the end of the house near the church of St Ulrich (cf. plate 54). Several of Vienna's most famous musicians lived in this district, which, until the nineteenth century, had many similar houses. In the church opposite the house Gluck was married, and Lanner and the younger Johann Strauss were baptised.

96 CHURCH OF ST CHARLES BORROMEO
The church of St Charles was built in fulfilment of a vow made by Emperor Charles VI for the ending of the plague of 1713. The architect was chosen by competition, and J.B. Fischer von Erlach won a victory over Hildebrandt and the Emperor's theatre designer Ferdinando Galli-Bibbiena. It is an interesting variant on the typically Austrian baroque pattern, the combination of dome with two west towers (cf. note 43). Here the towers have been made into a double feature, the columns lending height (they are over one hundred feet high), and the side pavilions supplying the mass, although both elements are clearly subordinate to the majestic dome, which reaches to a height of 235 feet. The columns themselves have a double function, being clearly based on the idea of the triumphal Trajan's column in Rome, and at the same time representing the pillars of Hercules, the device of Emperor Charles V which was combined with his motto 'Plus Ultra'. The overseas of Empire of Charles V had now passed to the Spanish line of the Habsburgs, and there is no doubt that Austria's imperial pretensions are symbolised by this church.

The church was not finished in Fischer's lifetime, and was completed by his son. The reliefs on the columns are in the main the work of Johann Christoph Mader (1697-1761), and much of the decorative sculpture on the dome, on top of the

columns, etc., is by Lorenzo Mattielli, one of the finest Italian sculptors who contributed to the new Vienna that arose after 1683; he came to Vienna in 1712, but his talents were lost to the court of Dresden after he was defeated by Donner in the competition for the fountain for the Neuer Markt (plate 82).

Brahms lived for many years near the Karlskirche, and it was in a house behind the church that Moritz von Schwind lived, and where many *Schubertiaden* took place.

97 HOUSE SIGN FROM THE OLD 'RED HEDGEHOG', AND OTTO BÖHLER'S SILHOUETTE OF BRAHMS ON HIS WAY TO THE INN. HISTORICAL MUSEUM
The 'Red Hedgehog' is an eighteenth-century wooden house sign (cf. plate 19), which dates from a time before there was an inn in the house. This was first founded in 1838 as a very smart wine-house; later, until the house was pulled down in 1885, it was for many years Brahms' regular 'local'. In 1825 the Society of the Friends of Music bought a room in the house, and it was here that Schuppanzigh's quartet first performed some of Beethoven's last quartets (cf. note 76).

98 JOHANN STRAUSS MONUMENT IN THE STADTPARK
Bronze statue and marble relief (symbolic of the Danube), erected 1923, are by Edmund Hellmer, a sculptor who contributed to the adornment of many Ringstrasse buildings.

99 KURSALON IN THE STADTPARK
The competition held in 1863 for the design of a Kursalon in the Stadtpark was won by Otto Wagner, but his project was not carried out. It was built in the Italian Renaissance style in 1865-7 according to the plans of Johann Garben, and opened on 8 May 1867 with a Promenade Concert given by Eduard Strauss, younger brother of Joseph and Johann. Eduard Strauss continued his promenade concerts into the twentieth century, and they helped keep alive the tradition, now revived under Willi Boskovsky.

100 THE AMERICAN, FROM THE PRATER MECHANICAL ORCHESTRA. FOLKLORE MUSEUM
See note on plate 87.

101 TOMB OF GEORG SLATKONIA, BISHOP OF VIENNA, IN ST STEPHEN'S CATHEDRAL
The success of Emperor Maximilian I's foundation of the Court Orchestra depended on the musicians at his court who were responsible for its administration. His first court composer was Heinrich Isaac (c. 1450-1517), the greatest German composer of his age, and the director of the orchestra was Georg Slatkonia, (1456-1522) a brilliant organiser and teacher, who had studied music at Vienna University. In the famous engraved Triumph of Emperor Maximilian Slatkonia is depicted as director of the Hofburgkapelle, an appointment he had received in 1498. In 1513 he was created bishop of Vienna, 'a feeble prince of the church, but a great musician'. The tomb, one of the finest Renaissance tombs in Austria, was commissioned by the bishop before his death in 1522. The inscription round his effigy reads 'Beatus Populus qui scit Jubilationem' (Blessed is the People that knows Rejoicing).

102 CUSTODIAN'S LODGE, UPPER BELVEDERE
Anton Bruckner (1824-96) lived in this small custodian's lodge behind the Upper Belvedere. He had come to Vienna in the autumn of his life, he lectured at the University, where he was the first musician to be given an honorary doctorate, and he was court organist. When he retired Emperor Franz Joseph I gave him the apartment in the Belvedere. He died there on 11 October 1896.

103 SCHWEIZER TOR IN THE HOFBURG
The Schweizer Tor (Swiss Gate) leads from the large Palace square into the Schweizerhof (cf. plate 8). Originally there was a drawbridge over the moat, removed at the time of Empress Maria Theresia. The gate, one of the most note-worthy Renaissance monuments in the city, was built by Ferdinand I in 1552. Through the arch to the right are the steps which lead to the Court chapel, where the Vienna Boys Choir performs each Sunday and Feast day, carrying on an unbroken tradition of music in the Palace from the times of Maximilian I and even earlier.

104 STADTHALLE (CIVIC HALL)
The Stadthalle, Vienna's proud new sports and cultural centre was built in 1958 by Roland Rainer, the architect responsible for the master plan for Vienna's future extension and development. The sculpture in the foreground is by Wanda Bertoni.

105 KASPERL AND DEATH FROM A VIENNESE PUPPET THEATRE. FOLKLORE MUSEUM
These two puppets were used by a Viennese travelling puppetmaster at the beginning of the twentieth century, but in style the puppets with their painted wooden heads date from a century earlier. Kasperl (cf. plate 107) is dressed as Harlequin and Death appears as a grinning skeleton. They typify the combination, to be seen throughout the history of Viennese theatre, of comedy, grotesque and melancholy.

106 'INTERIOR OF THE OLD BURGTHEATER', PAINTING BY GUSTAV KLIMT (DETAIL). NATIONAL LIBRARY
The old Burgtheater closed its doors for the last time on 13 October 1888, and the new theatre on the Ring opened the following night. Gustav Klimt (1862-1918) executed part of the ceiling painting over the staircases of the new theatre (cf. plate 37), and in this painting shows the interior of the old theatre in the 1880s.

107 ACTORS IN THE VIENNESE COMIC TRADITION: JOHANN LAROCHE AS KASPERL – RAIMUND AS WADERLMACHER – NESTROY AS THE NORTH-GERMAN STUDENT – GIRARDI AS THE COURT JESTER. NATIONAL LIBRARY
Marinelli's theatre in the Leopoldstadt, founded in 1781, became a must for every important visitor who came to Vienna around 1800 and later, and they would mingle in the audience with the washerwomen and tradesmen having a night out. This fame derived mainly from the performances of Johann Laroche (1745-1806) as Kasperl (seen here in an almanack picture of 1804), a comic character with a long tradition in popular Austrian theatre. Nelson went to see Kasperl practically every day during his stay in Vienna; he was described as 'quite Shakespearean' by Friedrich Schlegel, the translator of Shakespeare; and he won praise from every visiting German intellectual (who had studied his Viennese dialect before attending the performance).
    This was the tradition that lived on in the work of Raimund, Nestroy and Girardi.

108 STAIRCASE IN THE OLD STERNHOF, SCHULTERGASSE
In 1803 Dr Johannes Nestroy, father of the playwright, moved into the house on the site of the old Sternhof with his family. It was here that the playwright Johann Nestroy lived during his youth. The old house 'The Black Star', which had been rebuilt in 1782, had long theatrical connections, since it was here that Josef Stranitzky, the great Viennese Hanswurst, lived in the early eighteenth century. It was here too that the architect Johann Bernhard Fischer von Erlach lived and died. Grillparzer also lived for a short time in the Nestroy house.

109 OLD VIENNESE HATMAKER'S SHOP. TECHNICAL MUSEUM
The hatmaker's shop formerly stood on the Bauernmarkt, behind the Cathedral. The wax figure in the window is from another shop near the Cathedral, 'The Pretty Viennese Girl', a couturier run by Frau Schoberlechner, mother of Schubert's friend Franz von Schober (cf. plate 2). In 1804 she acquired a life-size wax figure for her window always dressed according to the latest Paris fashion, which aroused much admiration. The snobberies of fashion, as well as the life of the draper's apprentices, were often satirised by Nestroy, and this milieu provided the setting for one of his most outspoken political satires (1849) *Lady und Schneider* (Lady and Tailor).

110 CAR MADE BY GRÄF UND STIFT FOR THE DUKE OF CUMBERLAND, 1911. TECHNICAL MUSEUM
The Duke of Cumberland, claimant to the throne of Hanover, had settled in Vienna after quarrelling with the Prussian royal family. The motor-car made for him in 1911 by Gräf und Stift (still a leading engineering firm in Austria, and builders of Vienna's buses) took into consideration a special requirement of the Duke's – a roof high enough to accomodate his extra high *Zylinder* (top hat).

111 HOFMANNSTHAL'S HOUSE IN RODAUN
Hofmannsthal described his house: it 'was built at the time of Empress Maria Theresia by a Prince Trautson, who was supposed to practice black magic, for his mistress. The garden, full of old fruit trees goes steeply up the hill; at the top you go through a little garden gate out to a little paved open square, and there stands a tiny little church.' The church was built in 1746 and the villa is generally said to have been built by Maria Theresia herself for her governess Countess Fuchs. Hofmannsthal lived for many years in the house, and died there on 15 July 1929.

112 FAÇADE OF THE ARSENAL FROM THE INNER COURTYARD
The Arsenal forms part of a chain of massive fortified buildings surrounding Vienna, built following the 1848 revolution. The government, having seen what the Viennese people were capable of, wanted to take no risks, and the fortifications were meant as protection against the citizens, not against outsiders. The Arsenal was built 1849-56 using competition projects by a number of architects, including Van der Null and Siccardsburg (builders of the Opera), Hansen (who built the Parliament) and others. In the Hall of Fame the painter Karl von Blaas depicted 'the whole of Austria's military history in forty-five frescoes'. The building now houses the Museum of Military History. It was quite a short cycle ride for Schnitzler and Hofmannsthal, since the building is only a little beyond the Belvedere.

113 WILHELM GAUSE, 'WASHERGIRLS' BALL' (DETAIL). HISTORICAL MUSEUM
The washergirl became, in Viennese folkore, a symbol for the attractive and vivacious girl who, however, strictly preserved the limits of modesty. In reality she had a hard life, collecting laundry in huge baskets slung across her back, and doing the washing in large laundries. The Washergirls' Ball was one of the heights of the carnival season, and was much patronised by the young aristocracy. For years the queen of the ball was the 'Fiakermilli', a popular singer and Venus of Viennese night-life, immortalised by Hofmannsthal and Richard Strauss in their opera *Arabella*.
    Wilhelm Gause (1853-1916) was a Rhinelander who came to Vienna in his twenties and earned fame as an illustrator of Viennese popular life.

114 PARK IN THE WERTHEIMSTEIN VILLA, DÖBLING
The villa and park in Döbling were built and laid out by the liberal industrialist and art-patron Rudolf von Arthaber in the 1830s. In 1867 it was bought by Leopold von Wertheimstein, and his wife Josephine and daughter Franziska held a salon there which attracted the most important literary and musical figures for over twenty-five years. In the early days it offered a refuge to the writers Bauernfeld and Saar, later Hugo von Hofmannsthal, like the Wertheimsteins of Jewish origin, was their brightest light, and the young genius would go there to read his poems. Josephine died in 1894, Franziska only thirteen years later, and she left the garden to the Döbling community as a public park, and the house as a popular library. It now also houses a museum.

115 INTERIOR DESIGNED BY ADOLF LOOS. HISTORICAL MUSEUM
This room, which exemplifies the combination of functionalism and decorative elements in Adolf Loos's work, was designed for his own flat in Bösendorferstrasse, built in 1903.

116 EGON SCHIELE, SELF-PORTRAIT, 1911. HISTORICAL MUSEUM
The paintings of Egon Schiele (1890-1918) foreshadow the despair of Austrian intellectuals between the wars. His style closely follows that of Klimt, but where Klimt's broken surfaces create a rich decorative effect, Schiele, whether painting the starving children of the suburbs, the houses they lived in, the Vienna prostitutes, or in his self-portraits, reveals his subjects with an agonising intensity. Both painters died in 1918.

117 VIENNESE BAKER'S SIGN. HISTORICAL MUSEUM
A very decorative shop sign from the Josefstadt, dated 1785. It illustrates the variety of biscuits and sweetmeats for sale.

118 'GIRL WITH A COFFEE GRINDER'. HISTORICAL MUSEUM
This eighteenth-century painting is attributed to Johann Christian Brand (1722-95), famous for his paintings of the 'Cries of Vienna' *(Kaufruf)*.

119 REFLECTION IN THE WINDOW OF A RESTAURANT ON FRANZISKANERPLATZ
The old convent of the Franciscans, its wall decorated with incised circles, and the statue of Moses by J.M.Fischer are reflected in a restaurant window on Franziskanerplatz (cf. plate 29). On the left, part of an old painted inn sign can be seen.

120 'INTERIOR OF CAFÉ GRIENSTEIDL' (DETAIL); FROM A WATERCOLOUR BY R. VÖLKEL. NATIONAL LIBRARY
The Café Griensteidl was founded in 1844 by Heinrich Griensteidl, originally a chemist. In 1848 in the enthusiasm of revolution it was called Nationalcafé for a short time. Later, when it had become the chief 'Literatencafé' it was also known as Café Grössenwahn (Megalomania). It closed in January 1897. Hermann Bahr, with his impressive beard, is seated on the left of the picture, with Arthur Schnitzler sitting to his left.

121 OLD HOUSE IN THE BÄCKERSTRASSE, NO. 7

In der Bäcker-Strasse, da backt man Weisheit und Kipfel
Beide schluckt der Student hungrig und gierig hinein.
(In the Bakers' Street they bake wisdom and pastries
The student swallows both, hungrily and eagerly.)

There were bakers in the Bäckerstrasse before the beginning of the fourteenth century, and the university was founded there in 1365; from that time until the nineteenth century, they flourished side by side (only in 1848 did the students get the upper hand, when they renamed the street Studentengasse).

The house no. 7 is famous for its sixteenth-century arcaded courtyard, a rare survival of Renaissance architecture in a middle-class house.

122 SHOP SIGNS OF THE CONFECTIONER WOLFBAUER, JOHANNESGASSE
Traditional shop signs, with decorative lettering and designs painted behind glass, are still to be seen in Vienna today.

123 PORTRAITS OF VIENNA BAKERS. BAKERS' ARCHIVE
The Bakers' archive has an interesting collection of portraits of master bakers, going back to the seventeenth century. Illustrated here are Jakob Schwab (1634), legs entwined in a pretzel, and another master baker of the same period.

124 SILVER COFFEE-MACHINE. MUSEUM OF DECORATIVE ARTS
A Biedermeier coffee-machine made in Vienna in 1825.

125 OLD BAKERY IN THE LANGEGASSE
An enterprising coffee-house has restored this old Vienna bakery, with the ovens and equipment that had been in use for centuries.

126 WINE-PRODUCER'S HOUSE IN GUMPOLDSKIRCHEN
Gumpoldskirchen, just south of Vienna, is the largest local wine centre, and produces some of the finest wines in Austria.

127 OLD HEURIGER IN SIEVERING

128 BIEDERMEIER GLASS WITH VIEW OF THE KOHLMARKT. MUSEUM OF DECORATIVE ARTS
Glasses enamelled with views of Vienna were made in large quantities during the nineteenth century. In this view of the Kohlmarkt the Great Michael's House (cf. plate 84) is the first house on the right, the site of Demel's a little further down on the left.

129 INTERIOR OF THE AUERSPERG PALAIS (NOW A RESTAURANT)
The Auersperg Palais originally belonged to the Roffrano family, on whom some of the characters in Strauss/Hofmannsthal's *Rosenkavalier* are based. It was built around 1706, probably to plans of Lucas von Hildebrandt, but has been much altered since. It was restored and rebuilt in 1953-4, to house a restaurant.

130 HOLY-WATER STOUP (MEMENTO MORI) ON NORTH SIDE OF ST STEPHEN'S CATHEDRAL
On the side of the Cathedral, near the entrance to the catacombs and the old gravedigger's house is a stoup for holy water in the shape of winged skull, a macabre baroque memento mori.

131 DISPENSARY IN THE CONVENT OF THE MERCIFUL BRETHREN
The Merciful Brethren came to Vienna in 1614 at the request of Emperor Matthias, and from 1655 had a hospital attached to their convent, which later grew into a major metropolitan hospital. Ordinances of 1564 and 1602 restricted the number of city chemists to ten, all within the city walls, which was hard on those living in the suburbs. In 1625 the Merciful Brethren bought an existing chemist's shop, and until 1782 this provided the only facility in the Leopoldstadt. The old dispensary with its painted imitation stucco ceiling dates from around 1722.

132 PLAQUE IN THE JUDENPLATZ CELEBRATING THE EXPULSION OF THE JEWS FROM VIENNA IN 1421
The plaque is on an old house 'The Great Jordan' and shows the Baptism of Christ. The inscription reads:

In the waters of Jordan bodies are washed clean of the
taint of sin
When all hidden sins retreat
So the raging flame rising up through the whole city (1421)
Purges clean the crimes of the Jewish dogs
The whole world was purged by the great Flood
Now again it pays the penalty with raging fire.

On 12 March 1421 two hundred and ten Jews were burnt outside the city.

133 PLAQUE IN THE JEWISH DISTRICT, NEAR ST RUPRECHT'S CHURCH
This plaque commemorates the Jews of Vienna during the Nazi occupation. The inscription reads: 'Before 1942 Place of Refuge: on 28 May 1942 Place of Deliverance: until 1945 Place of Defiance in the service of the Resistance for Austria'.

134 GUSTAV KLIMT, SKETCHES FOR 'MEDICINE' PUBLISHED IN 'VER SACRUM'
These sketches were made in preparation for Klimt's great Medicine fresco, now destroyed, intended for the Medical Faculty of the University. The larger figure is a sketch for the central figure of the painting, an allegory of Medicine. From *Ver Sacrum*, 1901 (cf. plate 68).

135 NARRENTURM IN THE GENERAL HOSPITAL
The General Hospital was opened in 1784, under Emperor Joseph II. The Narrenturm (Fools' Tower) dates from this period, and was originally intended to house lunatics, in twenty-eight cells on each of five storeys. In more enlightened times it was used for an archive and for housing the nurses.

136 VIEW FROM THE WINDOW OF A GRINZING HEURIGER

TEXT ILLUSTRATIONS

Acknowledgements

The author, photographer and publishers wish to thank all those who by their assistance and cooperation made possible the photography for this book:

the Chapter of St Stephen's Cathedral, the Rev. Provincial of the Society of Jesus, the Rev. parish priest of the Dominican Church of Sta. Maria Rotunda, the priests in charge of the Capuchin church and the church of the Barmherzige Brüder, Count Harrach, Countess Karoline Schönburg, the Director of the Institut Français de Vienne, the Secretary of the Österreichische Akademie der Wissenschaften, the Secretariat of the Österreichische Bischofskonferenz, the Niederösterreichische Landesregierung, the Bundesgebäudeverwaltung, the Bundestheaterverwaltung, the Landesinnung der Wiener Bäcker, the Direction of the Palais Auersperg, and the directors and authorities of the following museums and galleries (short titles are as referred to in notes on illustrations): Diözesan Museum (Diocesan Museum), Historisches Museum der Stadt Wien (Historical Museum), Kunsthistorisches Museum, Österreichische Galerie – Österreichisches Barockmuseum (Baroque Museum), Österreichische Galerie – Schloss Belvedere, Österreichisches Museum für angewandte Kunst (Museum of Decorative Arts), Österreichisches Museum für Volkskunde (Folklore Museum), Technisches Museum für Industrie und Gewerbe (Technical Museum), Villa Wertheimstein.

The drawings by Oskar Kokoschka are reproduced by kind permission of the artist.

Thanks are also due to Hofrat Dr Hans Pauer, Director of the Bildarchiv der Österreichischen Nationalbibliothek, for invaluable help in searching out many illustrations, and providing photographs of all items from the Austrian National Library as well as many from the Historical Museum of the City of Vienna, to Fräulein Liesbeth Harrer, to Dr Richard Sickinger, and the Director, Librarian and staff of the Austrian Institute, London.

Index

References in italics are to plates